All Creatures Safe
and Sound

Sarah E. DeYoung and
Ashley K. Farmer

All Creatures
Safe and Sound

The Social Landscape of Pets in Disasters

WITH A FOREWORD BY LESLIE IRVINE

TEMPLE UNIVERSITY PRESS
Philadelphia • *Rome* • *Tokyo*

The cat pictured on the back cover of this book is the same as that pictured on the front cover, after being rescued, cleaned, and cared for. Named Keke, he was rescued by Shannon Jay with his non-blood brothers, Earl and Bubba, and mother, Mama Cat, from the Camp Fire of 2018. Shannon rescued all four cats and fostered them for months until Keke, Bubba, and Earl went home together. Jay adopted Mama Cat.

We extend a special thank you to Katharine Parsons, producer and director of *The Fire Cats*, for putting us in touch with Douglas Thron, who provided Keke's "before" photo. We also thank Shannon for his ongoing work to find missing fire cats and for sharing the "after" photo of Keke.

TEMPLE UNIVERSITY PRESS
Philadelphia, Pennsylvania 19122
tupress.temple.edu

Library of Congress Cataloging-in-Publication Data

Names: DeYoung, Sarah E. (Sarah Elizabeth), 1983– author. | Farmer, Ashley K.,
  author. | Irvine, Leslie J., 1958–, writer of foreword.
Title: All creatures safe and sound : the social landscape of pets in disasters /
  Sarah E. DeYoung and Ashley K. Farmer ; with a foreword by Leslie Irvine.
Description: Philadelphia : Temple University Press, 2021. | Includes bibliographical
  references and index.
Identifiers: LCCN 2020045465 (print) | LCCN 2020045466 (ebook) |
  ISBN 9781439919767 (pdf) | ISBN 9781439919743 (cloth) | ISBN 9781439919750
  (paperback) | ISBN 9781439919743 (cloth) | ISBN 9781439919750 (paperback) |
  ISBN 9781439919767 (pdf)
Subjects: LCSH: Animal welfare—United States. | Emergency management—
  United States. | Evacuation of civilians—United States. | Pets—Social aspects—
  United States.
Classification: LCC HV4708 (ebook) | LCC HV4708 .D478 2021 (print) |
  DDC 636.08/321—dc23
LC record available at https://lccn.loc.gov/2020045465

Printed in the United States of America

9 8 7 6 5 4 3 2 1

Contents

Foreword

LESLIE IRVINE

The aftermath of Hurricane Katrina was a turning point for the welfare of pets in disasters. To understand what has changed since then, Sarah DeYoung and Ashley Farmer conducted fieldwork at seven disaster sites in six states. They interviewed several dozen program coordinators who managed the animal rescue and sheltering efforts. They surveyed and interviewed more than three hundred evacuees. Their meticulous research and careful analysis reveal what has changed since 2005. Importantly, their analysis also addresses what remains to be done.

When Hurricane Andrew devastated South Florida in 1992, it brought public attention to the plight of pets in disasters. According to estimates by those involved in the makeshift animal hospital and shelter, approximately two thousand injured dogs and cats were euthanized for lack of places to house and care for them. The event was the catalyst for the first animal disaster response organizations. Yet over a decade passed before the issue gained political traction. Hurricane Katrina struck coastal Louisiana just after six o'clock on the morning of Monday, August 29, 2005. Two days earlier, a press release from the Louisiana Society for the Protection of Cruelty to Animals had advised New Orleans residents who planned to evacuate the city to take their pets with them. However, many residents who left New Orleans left their companion animals behind. Some residents decided to wait out the storm with their animals, and countless others simply had no way to leave and nowhere to go. When residents who did not evacuate were later rescued, many were forced to leave without their dogs and cats.

Responders in boats, helicopters, and emergency vehicles would take only people, not their animals. CNN's Anderson Cooper reported on a blind woman who did not evacuate because she was told that her service dog could not accompany her. She had stayed in her home with her dog for ten days. Once CNN's cameras arrived, the police agreed to allow her dog to leave with her. The most famous story describes a little white dog named Snowball being torn from a boy's arms as he boarded the bus to leave the Superdome. As the late Mary Foster of the Associated Press reported, "Pets were not allowed on the bus, and when a police officer confiscated a little boy's dog, the child cried until he vomited. 'Snowball, Snowball,' he cried" (Foster 2005).

A massive animal rescue and sheltering effort began, eventually costing millions of dollars and involving innumerable hours of work on the part of veterinarians, animal welfare and rights organizations, and countless volunteers. On September 28, 2005, organizations that had often been at odds came together to form the National Emergency Animal Rescue and Sheltering Coalition. In an open letter to the 109th Congress, coalition members called for action. They pointed out that failing to evacuate pets in disasters threatened human and animal safety. They requested federal assistance in the existing rescue effort. They also called for changes to existing legislation to mitigate future animal catastrophes. They asked for immediate access to emergency areas to rescue animals, financial assistance for animal rescue and the replacement of animal control systems, the establishment of a "Red Cross Model" for animal rescue, and implementation of clear guidelines for pet evacuations.

When the late congressman Tom Lantos saw the picture of Snowball being separated from the boy, he was deeply moved. Together with Christopher Shays, also in the House of Representatives, and Ted Stevens and Frank Lautenberg in the Senate, they introduced the Pets Evacuation and Transportation Standards Act (PETS Act) in the U.S. Congress. Intended to enhance animal and human safety in disasters, the act specified that state and local response plans should "take into account the needs of individuals with household pets and service animals prior to, during, and following a major disaster or emergency."[1] The Humane Society of the United States ran full-page ads in the *New York Times* and *Washington Post*, featuring pictures of abandoned dogs and cats. Captioned "No Pet Left Behind," the ads aimed to generate support for the PETS Act. The public flooded Congress with letters asking the members to do something. On October 6, 2006, President George W. Bush signed the act into law. Along with requiring state and local emergency management agencies to include companion and service animals in their disaster response plans, it also makes funding from the Federal Emergency Management Administration contingent on compliance.

The PETS Act came too late for the dogs and cats of New Orleans. The number of pets who died or were left homeless in Katrina's wake is estimated in the hundreds of thousands. In subsequent disasters, as Sarah and Ashley show, the PETS Act has improved evacuation compliance and reduced barriers for human-animal evacuation. They also show that many misconceptions about the PETS Act circulate among members of the public. Some pet owners mistakenly believe that the PETS Act requires hotels to accommodate their pets. Rumors about what the PETS Act is and is not required to do circulated widely on social media. Even the best-intentioned policies do not please everyone, and a mix of outcomes can result even when policies have wide support. The PETS Act does not address how the law would apply in cities and municipalities with breed-specific legislation, which prohibits residents from owning certain types of dogs, such as pit bulls. The act also does not address the needs of stray or feral pets. These gaps in the policy suggest potential amendments to the PETS Act in the future.

Over 60 percent of American households now include pets, exceeding the percentage of households that include children. In many of these households, pets are considered family members. The human-animal bond has a powerful presence in individual lives. During disasters, the bond can be a source of support or of stress, anxiety, and depression. Sarah and Ashley's astute and insightful book makes a significant contribution to the literature on animal welfare in natural disasters. It brings hidden issues to light through well-organized chapters and jargon-free prose. Its pages offer hope for compassionate and humane disaster policies that can keep *all* creatures safe and sound.

Acknowledgments

Sarah DeYoung

I am thankful for all the animal companions in my life over the years. They helped form my passion for studying animals in disasters—especially Wallace and Fonzie, who both crossed the rainbow bridge several years ago. I still love them today. They were the cats who were my best friends through my first apartment, graduate school, the birth of my daughter, and living in three different states. I thank the students who deployed with us for research fieldwork and helped us gather the data for this book: Javona Brown, Zoe Callaro, Donovan Harris, Shelby Naar, Katherine Nichols, Ashley Reed, and Chloe Wise. I am thankful for my academic support network at the Disaster Research Center at the University of Delaware, particularly Caroline Wellington, Tricia Wachtendorf, and fellow cat lover James Kendra. I also thank my daughter, Marina, for understanding when I traveled for fieldwork. My thanks go to Manoj Suji, who after the Nepal earthquake taught me the importance of observing and documenting details during disaster fieldwork—a skill that undoubtedly enhanced the quality of the research for this book. Finally, I am thankful for the valuable friendship that Ashley Farmer and I formed throughout the course of the research for this book—from writing the grant, to enduring all the late-night and early-morning flights, the long drives (which sometimes involved Ashley tolerating my bad driving), flight connections, delays, and city traffic, to the final stages of writing and revising the book.

Ashley Farmer

My love for all creatures began when I was young, so I must first thank my grandmother Clarice Holland for allowing me to read and scribble in all her encyclopedias and wildlife books. I also thank the rest of my family, who constantly had to deal with me picking up snakes and other animals, including that time I brought home a newborn foster kitten (sorry, Mom). I am grateful to all the companion animals I have loved who have reminded me constantly of why I do the work I do—especially my cat, Rocky; my dog, Emma; and my chinchilla, Brisby. I thank the Illinois State University students who helped with our interview transcriptions: Amaria Beechum, Cassidy Belpedio, Randy Fuller, Dylan Keaty, Madalyn Lane, and Tyler Marcheschi. I am particularly grateful for the Disaster Research Center and the projects I worked on there with Tricia Wachtendorf. It was one of those projects that spearheaded our work on animals in disasters. Many thanks and love go to my husband, Dave, for his support and advice while I was working on this book. And, of course, thanks go to Sarah for being a dependable friend, always humoring me, and being such a strong support system during the research for this book and beyond.

The National Science Foundation (NSF) funded the fieldwork for this book (award number 1760447). Our thanks go to Bob O'Connor at NSF for his guidance during our work. We are both thankful for Ryan Mulligan, our editor at Temple University Press, for his guidance and support. We thank the anonymous reviewers for their feedback on the early iterations of this book and Rebecca Logan and other editorial experts who took the time to review and improve our manuscript. We are also thankful to all the respondents who participated in this research and shared their powerful stories with us, particularly those who lost companion animals in a disaster.

All Creatures Safe
and Sound

Introduction

E vacuees of disaster-affected areas often express frustration, concern, and exasperation over the difficulties associated with evacuating with pets.[1] People with companion animals generally *want* what is best for their pets, including safety and security. However, some of the most striking news stories during Hurricanes Harvey and Irma in 2017 included images of dogs leashed to trees or posts as the hurricane made landfall and cats swimming through murky floodwaters. As Leslie Irvine points out in her foundational book on pets in disasters, *Filling the Ark* (2009), animals are part of the human landscape, so their vulnerability is linked with human vulnerability. Families who are struggling to afford housing and other amenities do not love their animals any less than families who can afford a top-notch doggie daycare and spas for their pet, yet these class differences are also associated with important factors that determine animal well-being in disasters, such as education about and access to spay and neuter surgeries, access to transportation for evacuation, and access to the social networks that make evacuation more feasible. Because it does not account for these differences in resources, the Pets Evacuation and Transportation Standards Act (PETS Act) is not a comprehensive solution for the problem of managing pets in disaster evacuations.

Not only are evacuees aware of these inequalities, but so are organizations and leaders tasked with evacuating people and their pets. Although there is evidence that the issue of evacuating pets in disasters has gained more attention in recent hurricanes, wildfires, and even lava flows, there are still many failures throughout the system of managing pets and animals in disasters. When Hurricane Katrina brought the failings of planning for pets into the national spotlight, lawmakers passed the 2006 PETS Act, which is an amendment to the Robert T. Stafford Act, the legislation for governing assistance and recovery after disasters in the United States.[2] The amendment indicates that states should anticipate that people will have animals and that animals should be included in hazard and disaster planning. The legislation also stipulates that local and state emergency management agencies can request reimbursement of funds to use for movement, relocation, or sheltering of pets in emergencies. As Leslie Irvine explains in *Filling the Ark*, this legislation was a major step forward for disaster management, both in planning and in a symbolic homage to the connection that humans have with their pets. We discuss this connection, also known as bonding and attachment, in Chapter 2.

The rest of the book covers many other developments in the management of pets in emergency situations since Hurricane Katrina, including chapters on social media, animal cruelty, organizational coordination, privilege and power, decision-making, and household preparedness. Although our book is in some ways a continuation of the important conversation Irvine started concerning issues related to cruelty and preparedness, it provides new information and insights on how social media, group mobilization, and sociological and psychological phenomena, such as victim blaming, are all embedded in the landscape of pets and disasters. While Irvine's book begins by asking, "When a disaster strikes, who should enter the ark?" (2009, 1), our book begins with the assumption that animals do belong on the ark and asks, "How do people manage the ark?" The ways in which people manage animals in disasters provides nuanced insights about the social landscape of human communities. A vivid example, which we discuss in Chapter 5, is how the amount of time and resources that a high-income community member has for carrying out pet-reunification efforts can be vastly different from that in communities with less financial resources and privilege. Adding complexity is the fact that in high- and low-income communities, there are animals that are perceived as community or stray animals.

However, even in the case of stray animals, one or two people with access to organizational or social networks can funnel resources and attention to postdisaster communities for the benefit of the animals. Such was the case during the 2018 Hawaii lava flows in which a small group of women on Facebook managed a group of ad hoc volunteers, the Hawaii Lava Flow Animal Rescue Network, to coordinate delivery of supplies for evacuees and their animals. Their actions put a spotlight of national and international attention on animals affected by the lava flows. Other disaster events demonstrated this effect. As one volunteer animal rescuer told us, "Street dogs after Hurricane Harvey became very lucky, and their lives were totally different after the storm." The dogs who had lived on the street before Hurricane Harvey were placed into adoption after the storm, only to be adopted by owners who deemed it glamorous to tell their friends that they had a "Harvey dog." Such outcomes stand in stark relief to the 1.5 million animals euthanized each year in public shelters (ASPCA, n.d.).

The high rate of dog and cat euthanasia is associated with pet overpopulation, which we discuss later in the book. Pet adopters' interest in a "Harvey dog" or "Hurricane Florence cat" was evident in almost every disaster throughout our data collection and fieldwork. While social-psychological principles such as impression management can help us understand the desire to adopt a "hurricane pet,"[3] cultural forces such as social media drive many of the behaviors we observe. Therefore, emergency managers and community leaders must understand the social aspects of people's relationship with their animals if they hope to anticipate how to keep animals safe in natural disasters.

Although Chapter 4 is dedicated to the ways in which the world of social media transforms animal rescue and reunification, we also describe social media's impact on communication, framing, and logistics throughout the book. To illustrate our findings, we also include specific examples from social media and photographs from our fieldwork. These photographs provide additional information for the reader about the ways in which communities deal with and recover from disasters.

Terminology and Scope

This book is intended to be useful and interesting to a broad audience that includes people who have companion animals, volunteer for animal rescue, are emergency managers, volunteer as first responders, or have an interest in animals in disasters. The term "animals" in this book refers to cats, dogs, and in some cases horses, pigs, and other animals that people might keep as companion animals. We acknowledge that in sociological research it is less appropriate to refer to companion animals as "pets" because this denies their social complexity and agency and implies that ownership by a human defines the animal. Companion animals are integrated with human social systems and communities (Bulsara et al. 2007); therefore, "companion animal" is a more respectful and accurate term than "pets." However, the people whom we interviewed for our research frequently use the word "pet" or "pets" as it is commonly used in the United States to refer to animals that live with people and are technically owned and cared for by humans. Sometimes the categories that animals fall into may not be neat and obvious. For example, some people may breed and sell livestock for meat but also have an emotional attachment to those animals. In most cases, livestock for food or other production are not viewed as companion animals. However, cows and pigs are in many instances companion animals and not reared for food or sale. "Owners" of animals can also be a complicated term because there are instances in which people foster cats or dogs, or people may feed and spay/ neuter a group of feral animals (in the animal rescue community, there are "caretakers" of feral cat "colonies"). We include these people among our research because we are interested in how the social dimensions of animal caretaking affect the landscape of disasters.

In regard to disaster-specific terminology, "gray areas" of uncertainty exist concerning the categories into which people fall for tasks and roles for disaster management. "Officials" and "managers" in this book are emergency managers at the local, state, or federal level. Governments employ them to keep people safe in disasters. Other people are also official "responders" but work in the fields of law enforcement, fire, and emergency medical services. People unaffiliated with government groups but who work with responders in disasters are known as "unaffiliated volunteers," though they may go on to form official groups later. We use the term "program manager" to refer to someone who is making key organizational decisions or leading an animal rescue group, including in some cases a nonprofit organization, an informal group, or a government-run shelter service. Many people we interviewed served multiple roles—for example, in official law enforcement and as an animal rescue volunteer. Many were also positioned by their volunteer networks or through official capacities in their jobs at the local level during the hurricanes, fires, and lava flow. However, we also interviewed people who made decisions at the state and national levels to gain an understanding of how those perspectives varied at different levels.

In Chapter 1 we discuss the structure of disaster management in the United States and the way that response is supposed to unfold according to the National Response Framework. It is important to know that there is a saying in emergency management that "disasters begin and end locally," which means that they are supposed to be managed first by local responders, community agencies, and local nonprofit organizations. Contrary to what some people might believe, shelters that open during a mandatory hurricane evacuation are not required to accept pets. The decision of accepting pets is up to the agency in charge of the local shelter. This might be the city, and in many cases, the city partners with national nonprofits such as the Red Cross and Salvation Army. While we discuss this further in Chapter 1, it is important to understand how shelter conditions may vary. For example, during Hurricane Harvey, the city of Dallas enacted colocation of evacuated people with their pets at the Kay Bailey Hutchison Convention

Center. Pets who evacuated with their humans (many were Coast Guard evacuations from Beaumont and Port Arthur, Texas) were kept in kennels in a parking garage adjacent to the convention center in which the evacuees slept, ate meals, and had showers. Some shelters accepted pets into the shelters alongside humans, and some shelters did not accept any pets at all. In sum, we have found that the pet policy at local shelters varies across states and across disasters.

Method of Overall Research

The findings from this book are the result of data we collected over more than two years from people affected by Hurricane Harvey (2017), Hurricane Irma (2017), the Tubbs Fire (2017), the Carr Fire (2018), the Camp Fire (2018), the Hawaii lava flows (2018), and Hurricane Florence (2018). During and following these events, we gathered data from more than three hundred evacuees and thirty-eight program coordinators who worked to manage pets, people and pets, or stray and/or foster animals. Program coordinators include individuals who were in leadership of key volunteer roles in organizations that managed pets.

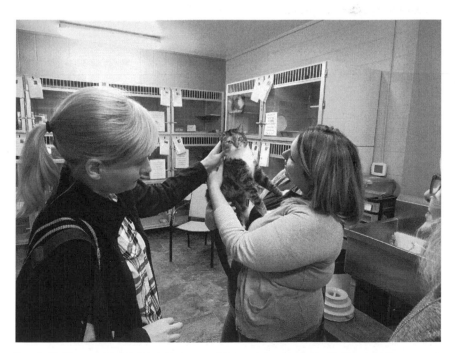

Sarah DeYoung and Ashley Farmer with a cat surrendered in Texas after Hurricane Harvey.

We collected data from the program coordinators primarily in person through semistructured interviews. We gathered data from evacuees through web surveys as well as face-to-face interviews when they were available to meet with us in person. We interviewed program coordinators from large national animal rescue or sheltering organizations, as well as from smaller or more informal nonprofits. We traveled to Texas, Florida, California, Hawaii, North Carolina, and South Carolina, recording and then transcribing the in-person interviews with program coordinators so that we could recall and highlight key themes throughout the data. We used an open-coding approach for both the text from the audio data and images from fieldwork and social media. The themes that make up this book emerged from the initial round of coding: we separated the themes and issues that our subjects discussed into overarching categories, followed by subcategories. For example, in the chapter on animal cruelty, we coded additional subthemes such as neglect, pet overpopulation, and weather exposure. Both of us read and coded the data. It is important to note that we use pseudonyms for people and animals throughout this book to protect their identities. The University of Georgia and Illinois State University granted Institutional Review Board (IRB) approval for this research. In instances in which we name groups or individuals, we do so because they and their involvement in animal rescue work are well-known through news, social media, or other publicly available data.

For purposes of reflexivity and data interpretation, we should note that Dr. Sarah DeYoung has an academic background in community psychology, disaster research, public health, and policy studies. Dr. Ashley Farmer has an academic background in criminal justice studies, sociology, and disaster research. Both scholars have a personal interest in animals—DeYoung has experience in fostering animals, in the trap-neuter-return of feral cats, and in general rescue advocacy; and Farmer and DeYoung each have multiple pets (including a chinchilla and tarantulas). We both grew up in the rural piedmont areas of Appalachia (western North Carolina and eastern Kentucky), which also shapes our cultural perception and experiences with human-animal relationships (for example, sport hunting, pet overpopulation, and agricultural farming are common in these areas). This research focuses on the context of the United States, although some of the issues we present and discuss may be relevant in other settings in which pets are managed in disasters.

Raining Cats and Dogs

Rumor Control and the PETS Act

*I wish it were easier for more people to evacuate with their
pets—more hotels that allow pets, shelters for people and pets.*
—Hurricane Irma evacuee from Homestead, Florida (2017)

"Well, things are better now because of the PETS Act, right?"
When we tell people that we are investigating the social landscape of animals and disasters, some people knowledgeable
about the issue (this includes emergency managers, journalists, and academic peers) often ask a variation of this question. While awareness about
pets in disasters and issues for animals in disaster have certainly entered the
mainstream of news media, disaster research, and even emergency management, there are still significant challenges in implementing various aspects
of the PETS Act, which was passed in 2006. Contrary to popular belief, the
PETS Act does not require hotels and other private entities to allow people
to bring pets during a disaster or mandatory evacuation. Additionally, local
public shelters are *not* required to accept pets. Under provisions of the Stafford Act, local jurisdictions decide how sheltering operations will run. In
some cases, the city or township oversees sheltering, and in other cases, a
nonprofit such as the Red Cross has the power to manage shelter rules. In
many cases, city-run shelters partner with the Red Cross for sheltering during evacuations. Even as we are writing this book, the Red Cross website
states that it cannot accept pets. In an emergency, this may mean that pets
must be colocated with their owners or that evacuees must find other arrangements for their animals. The provisions of the PETS Act do stipulate
that planning *should* account for the fact that people will attempt to evacuate with their animals and that funds can be requested to use supplies and
space for purposes of managing pets of evacuees in disasters. This allocation

means that local officials can make a judgment about the pet population in their area and the need to consider and accommodate pets in sheltering. Additionally, local officials can decide if they will request support of state, federal, and outside agencies to assist with pet-sheltering activities.

This chapter introduces the context behind the PETS Act; how federal, state, and local emergency managers have implemented it since its inception; and how the care of animals in disasters was managed prior to the act. Hurricane Katrina and its well-publicized impact on pets in the affected areas significantly influenced the development of the PETS Act. Nearly 45 percent of the people surveyed about evacuation decision-making during Katrina indicated that their pets were a major factor in deciding whether to evacuate (Fritz Institute 2006). Additionally, many pets left behind were never reunited with owners. To understand the social landscape of pets, it is also important to understand the policy landscape that shapes how and why systems operate the way they do in the United States. We present the ways in which the PETS Act is a marker in the postdisaster policy landscape as explained through Thomas Birkland's (1997) focusing events theory. The chapter also describes how states, local governments, and nonprofits have evolved in the ways they deal with pets and disasters from 2006 to 2018.

People may be hesitant to stay in a shelter because of their beliefs about the likelihood of crime (Farmer et al. 2017) or because of the stigma of using public sheltering facilities. Potential evacuees weigh these options against the risks of staying at home. To enforce evacuation orders, laws vary by state. However, it is rare for people to be arrested or fined for refusal to evacuate. For people to feel that they can evacuate, they must be able to identify information and gather resources that make it feasible. People with pets need to have a carrier or leash for transporting a cat or dog, the pet's medical records, and food for the pet. They must also be able to identify a feasible destination for evacuation—that is, a hotel or friend's house that is within a few hours' driving distance. However, during the most recent major hurricanes, a drive that should have taken a few hours took ten to thirteen hours because of traffic caused by other people evacuating and because of hotels near the evacuation zone being at capacity.

During Hurricanes Harvey and Irma, people shared information across social media that the PETS Act mandated shelters and hotels to accept pets, which was inaccurate. These misunderstandings had consequences. Pet owners might choose an evacuation destination based on false or assumed information, which could add minutes or hours to the overall evacuation process. Similarly, local governments might be hesitant to allow practices such as co-sheltering if they were unaware of the potential for federal reimbursements outlined by provisions of the PETS Act. We saw evidence of decision-making driven by false or vague information throughout multiple disasters. For instance, evacuees said they continued driving in Hurricanes Matthew, Irma, and Florence because they did not know where pet-friendly shelters were located. When a mandatory evacuation order is issued, people often go to hotels or other lodging or family and friends' houses. But what do they do if these options cannot accommodate pets? Public sheltering is a last resort for many, and most people who stay at public shelters have lower income on average. After the hurricane, people condemned others for failing to evacuate because they believed that evacuating with pets should be an easy decision and task (Reed, DeYoung, and Farmer 2020), but in fact an excess of information and resources complicated the necessary decisions for families with animals.

Beyond misunderstandings, there are also limitations of the PETS Act that prevent certain people and animals from seeking safe shelter. For example, sheltering for families with multiple animals may be difficult because of space and logistics. The act does not include provisions that protect ad hoc sheltering, that address any long-term sheltering and relocation needs of humans with pets, or that accommodate for larger animals such as pigs and goats as pets in sheltering. The PETS Act also does not provide specific guidance for management of unowned animals. The population of animals affected by disasters includes stray and feral animals, as well as foster and shelter animals, wildlife, and livestock. Additionally, the PETS Act centers on mitigating problems that arise during the response phase of the disasters. Throughout this book, we argue that there are broader issues in managing animals in disasters that require attention before and after disasters (for example, spaying and neutering as disaster preparedness).[1] This chapter focuses on the issues driving the passage of the PETS Act, as well as its features and limitations.

How Sheltering and Evacuation of Animals Works

Here is a common scenario that unfolds during hurricane season in the United States. When a hurricane is looming in the Atlantic, emergency managers in the southeastern United States work with state meteorologists and the National Hurricane Center to understand probabilities for location of landfall. As the system approaches land, certainty increases about the location and severity of impact. Unfortunately, the closer the system gets, the less time that state and local officials have to set up emergency shelters. Amid all the decisions about evacuation and issuing evacuation orders, they decide what kinds of resources to mobilize to assist with the evacuation. During this time, the governor declares a state of emergency that frees up funds to mobilize the resources needed to assist in evacuation, sheltering, and staging responders for the emergency. The PETS Act stipulates that any supplies used to assist with evacuating companion animals can be reimbursed with federal funds. This means that a convention center in Raleigh, North Carolina, for example, can rapidly purchase dog kennels for displaced dogs or dogs sheltering with owners because the cost will be offset by emergency funds. This process, however, does not eliminate all complications that go along with animals in emergencies. If the shelter is in Raleigh but residents live in Carteret County, they still need to drive three hours to get to the convention center. The gridlocked traffic caused by the evacuation turns into a seven-hour drive. But first, the family must also fit the dogs into the vehicle and make sure to have leashes, crates, and water for the dogs. The drive is hot, and the family may not have a working air conditioner in their car because suggested repairs were too expensive for the household. On the drive from Carteret County to Raleigh, the evacuees might be searching social media to find out information about whether they can bring their pets to the shelter. They are relieved to see pet-friendly sheltering at the convention center. However, one of the dogs is a pit bull mix. There is some conflicting information online and confusion about the policies at convention centers about breed restrictions. The family decides to bring the dogs with them to a hotel, which charges a fee for the dogs. The family uses the last of their funds to secure lodging for one night.

Another scenario is that other families have already experienced this nightmare and decide to try to "weather the storm," but the water rises so quickly around their home that they must evacuate in the middle of the night. The people and dogs wade through waist-deep water. A neighbor with a boat helps the family and dogs out of the floodwaters. As they seek shelter, dogs, cats, horses, and many animals drift through the water. Some owned, some unowned, the animals are searching for dry land. Some do not make it.

Origin of the PETS Act

Disasters that raise the profile of ongoing or potential harm to the point at which legislators prioritize preventing these harms are known as focusing events (Birkland 1997, 2006; Birkland and DeYoung 2011). The failure to manage pets in Hurricane Katrina and the resulting public attention drawn to the issue of pets and disasters during and after Katrina served as focusing events for the PETS Act. While focusing events do not always result in policy change, they have the *potential* to cause policy change based on the lessons learned from the disaster. However, not all events that might theoretically motivate policy qualify as focusing events. They must achieve three criteria: issue salience, group mobilization, and implementation. Hurricane Katrina motivated all three, leading to the eventual passage of the PETS Act.

Issue salience is arguably the driving force behind the way pets are prioritized in emergency planning and has motivated the changes in systems related to pets in disasters in the past fifteen years. Issue salience describes the ways in which problems are presented and at which level they remain important: "The nature of the actors and the nature of the problems interact with each other to promote or impede issue expansion" (Birkland 1997, 10). As Leslie Irvine describes in *Filling the Ark* (2009), mass execution of companion animals by first responders, refusal to evacuate, and forced separation from family pets during Hurricane Katrina all made the issue of pets in evacuation a salient public issue. Although media depictions of the emotional trauma associated with pets at risk and pets separated from families proliferate during hurricanes, they are also common in other hazard events, such as wildfires, earthquakes, and lava flows. For example, during the 2018 Kilauea lava flows, when more than two thousand people evacuated from their homes (Hughes 2018), Hawaii news media focused on "lava dogs," goats, cats, and other animals affected by the evacuation. Debra Stone's (2002) description of how narrative and emotional appeal influence policy was evident during news coverage of the Kilauea disaster. The stories focused on emotions such as worry, despair, anger, and longing. News stories about pets dominate the news cycle during evacuations because they are highly emotional, relatable, and thus engaging to the audience. This was also evident in the bushfires in Australia during 2020 in which thousands of people donated money and other supplies to support injured wildlife. Even though koalas and other Australian wildlife are not companion animals, the increased attention to animals more broadly can also shift focus onto pets in disasters. In an interview with us after Hurricane Harvey, one national program coordinator explained the differences that the PETS Act brought before and after Hurricane Katrina:

> The emergency management didn't know what to do either with animals. They were all varying as to what to do. They weren't including them in rescues—it was chaos, really, with Hurricane Katrina. So after that, the PETS Act helped. The PETS Act provided funding—would only provide federal funding—if these states had plans for the animals, so that helped tremendously, because all of a sudden, states were required to plan for animals [if they wanted federal funding]. So that was huge. . . . And I also think that because of the amount of media exposure and the amount of kind of consistent disasters over the years, people are a little bit more aware of the need to bring their animals with them. I think seeing a few scary stories of dogs left on roofs and being rescued by helicopters, I think that's enough to kind of—has done a lot to put that in people's minds.

However, issue salience alone is not enough to compel state or federal actors to engage in policy making. *Group mobilization* is also an important part of the policy process. As Thomas A. Birkland indicates, "Theories of group mobilization and issue expansion thus explain how ideas, problems, and policies start with a rather small number of people but, for various reasons related to the nature of problems and the political skill of groups, become much more important throughout society" (1997, 10). Animal rights groups, veterinarians, and concerned community members were angry, shocked, and saddened by events that occurred during Hurricane Katrina, such as the separation of children from their pets, law enforcement officers shooting dogs, and news images of drowned cats and dogs. Social scientists gathered data in which it became clear that animals were a major factor in difficulties and refusal to evacuate. These groups circulated petitions, created documentaries about pets in Katrina, and urged their senators and congressional representatives to pass legislation to protect pets in disasters.

However, as important as groups are in pushing an issue agenda, in *Lessons of Disaster,* Birkland also points out that those with policy-making power will probably inherently pay more attention to key issues after major focusing events because of media coverage and increased exposure to the ideas that there are potential policy solutions: "Rather, a focusing event itself, without the intervention of interest groups, causes the same actors that dominated policymaking before the event to consider ideas more intensively than they did before" (2006, 165). Hurricane Katrina crystallized the issue of pets in disasters. We view the PETS Act as a product of the realization of failings in managing pets in Katrina. However, its issue salience has reappeared in each major disaster evacuation. News reporters still focus stories on pets in disasters despite the policy progress at the federal level. This reflects that the PETS Act has not solved the issue of supporting pets in disasters.

Concerns about the management of animals in disasters are not new. Sebastian Heath (1999) wrote about animal management in disasters and emergency management plans in earlier disasters long before passage of the PETS Act. Emergency management programs did not concern themselves with animal welfare, aspiring only to promote self-sufficiency of animal owners, because owners were (and notably still are) individually responsible for their pets, leaving the care of all other animals to animal disaster relief agencies. Emergency management officials considered the care of animals only as it related to public health, largely because animals were—and are—technically considered property. Notably, animals do significantly affect public health first through their owners who refuse evacuation but also through those who leave and later attempt to come back and rescue pets.

Research has demonstrated that pet ownership can impede evacuation, with one study noting that the more pets a household owns, the higher the risk of evacuation failure (Heath et al. 2001). That study also mentioned further impediments to pet evacuation, including potential evacuees owning outdoor dogs and not having a cat carrier.

Animal care in disasters had been a concern for veterinarian associations for some time, although it was not until the 1990s that much of the animal care community became exposed to issues surrounding animals in disasters (Heath 1999). In the 1980s–1990s national and local veterinary associations developed ad hoc groups, called Emergency Animal Rescue Programs (EARPs), through which members would search for animals to rescue and put up for adoption after disasters. Veterinary associations also recognized the need to integrate with emergency management agencies at the local level (Heath 1999).

Research on pets in disasters prior to Hurricane Katrina noted that animal deaths seemed to be uncommon, and injuries were primarily associated with trauma. For example, after Hurricane Fran in 1996, foot abrasions and heat stress were common (Heath 1999). In the preparation for Hurricane Fran, one animal shelter reportedly boarded 153 pets brought in by owners, a surge mostly the result of public-service announcements. After Hurricane Andrew in 1992, approximately two thousand pets were treated for various injuries and ailments.

One key issue prior to the PETS Act was the lack of coordination among the agencies involved with animal-related issues after a disaster. As Heath noted, "Lack of acceptance of existing emergency management structure and lack of training of animal care personnel by professional emergency management have been major holdups" (1999, 145). Furthermore, when emergency management officials would advise the public about animal management in disasters, the only option they could recommend was that pet owners take animals with them and seek pet-friendly destinations. Simultaneously, many emergency managers suggested that shelters for owned pets were mostly unnecessary unless large human populations were displaced (Heath 1999). With the passage of the PETS Act, these recommendations have shifted. Pet owners are still responsible for their animals, but now more emergency managers recognize that, regardless of the number of displaced persons, pets can be an issue that impedes evacuation. Sheltering options for and with pets became more common.

What is most interesting about animal management prior to the PETS Act is that many of the hurdles and issues identified then remain salient issues today. For instance, human evacuation failures because of pets and reentry to rescue pets remain problems. Owners are still individually responsible for disaster plans for pets, and local emergency management officials still bear most responsibility for developing plans for public awareness and effective intervention after disasters.

The PETS Act

The PETS Act of 2006 was an amendment to the Robert T. Stafford Disaster Act, which was itself a revision of the 1974 Disaster Relief Act (DRA). The U.S. Congress designed the DRA and subsequent Stafford Act to ensure that states and tribal governments have plans in place to respond to and recover from disasters. The core provisions of the PETS Act ensure that local and state governments include domestic animals in evacuation planning. For example, the act holds that animals should be included in county and state hazard-mitigation planning documents, including a requirement that emergency plans must specify that all pet owners are responsible for the care of their pets during disasters. Furthermore, townships and entities in charge of sheltering can request reimbursement from the Federal Emergency Management Agency (FEMA) after a disaster if resources are used for sheltering evacuees and their pets. This legislation was an important step forward in planning for animals in evacuation, but it has limitations. Individuals, households, and animal shelters must all still do their part to plan for animals in evacuation and engage in preparedness activities.

From our research, there are two overarching findings regarding the PETS Act. First, the PETS Act has improved evacuation compliance and reduced barriers for evacuation over time, especially in hurricanes. Comparing Hurricanes Katrina, Andrew, and Ike to the more recent hurricanes of 2016, 2017, and 2018 (Matthew, Harvey, Irma, Maria, Florence, and Michael), we find that people who work in animal rescue agree that people with pets now receive more support in disasters than before the PETS Act. Second, the failure of the act's implementation, limited community capacity, and lack of household-level resources all remain challenges for predicting and carrying out successful animal evacuations. Consider the following news excerpt:

> Many pet owners unable to completely evacuate an area are faced with a difficult decision when a storm is bearing down on them: save their own lives but leave their pets behind, or risk death by staying with their pets? Most of us know that our animals are family members and we would NEVER leave them, no matter the consequence to ourselves, but thankfully fewer people had to make that choice because of shelters who were taking people and their pets. (Melanie 2016)

This media account captures the spectrum of the possibilities post–PETS Act: people's care for their companion animals driving them to include pets in their evacuation when possible or to risk harm at home with pets when adequate provisions remain unavailable. Practices such as colocation of evacuees and pets can improve evacuation compliance and reduce loss, trauma, and suffering.

The PETS Act made resources available for sheltering pets and encouraged planning but left implementation to localities, so results varied. During Hurricane Harvey approximately nineteen hundred human evacuees were sheltered in the Kay Bailey Hutchison Convention Center in Dallas, Texas, in an example of co-sheltering; adjacent to the convention center, a parking garage provided an ad hoc staging area to shelter pets that evacuated with the humans in the convention center. Many of those people were rescued from floodwaters because of delayed and failed warnings in Southeast Texas. Residents there were rescued by the U.S. Coast Guard or other rescue organizations. As families and individuals climbed onto C-130 transport planes, they brought their pets with them to Dallas. The distance from Beaumont and Port Arthur to Dallas is a four-and-a-half-hour drive. This means that residents could not have easily driven there in a short amount of time. Additionally, our observations of the co-sheltering, of course, do not account for the pets that did *not* make it out of Southeast Texas floodwaters. This supports our theory that many rural areas do not have extensive sheltering operations that accommodate pets. Consider the scenario in Dallas during Hurricane Harvey in 2017 with that in coastal Virginia during Hurricane Florence in 2018:

> "One of the top calls that came into the EOC (Emergency Operations Center) when we were open (during the recent hurricane state of emergency) was about pets—specifically, could they bring their pets to any of the shelters that we had that folks are located in," said Michael Mason, Accomack County Administrator. The answer to that question was no, Mason said. (Vaughn 2018)

The experience of this EOC demonstrates how the readiness of local emergency planners, sheltering coordinators, and community liaisons often determines whether residents will be able to evacuate safely with their animals. Because many families do consider pets members of their family, they express reluctance to evacuate when they encounter barriers that make it harder to bring their pets with them in disaster scenarios. Emergency managers and other officials sometimes view animal and pet rescue as separate from preventing human loss of life. This often means rescuing people first

and foremost, with animals given secondary attention. This reasoning especially holds in a rescue where space is limited and there is a short time frame
in which to get people evacuated. When emergency managers decide to include pets in shelters during a disaster, their level of knowledge about the
PETS Act (that they can request reimbursement for funds used to shelter
animals during the disaster), their perception of the bond between people
and their pets (accounting for the idea that people will refuse evacuation
because of their pets), and the local culture surrounding treatment of animals all play a role in their decision-making. For example, in Hawaii during
the lava flows in the summer of 2018, some evacuees perceived that government officials did not make reasonable attempts to support rescuing animals trapped near the lava flows. The many free-roaming cats, pigs, and
other animals in Hawaii prior to the disaster might possibly reflect how
people manage animals in that community.[2]

How the PETS Act Improved Animal Welfare in Disasters

The PETS Act does not specify the way in which states will allocate funding
to the county and city levels for setting up shelters prior to and during disasters. This allows local emergency managers to adapt to the needs of the
situation. Despite the variety of outcomes possible depending on the preparedness of local officials, the PETS Act represents a formal attempt at reducing loss of life in disasters. Implementation and interpretation of the act
are influenced by the ways in which people who manage animals ascribe
value to animals in their homes and community. If resources for animals
are not a priority for local leaders and organizational managers before a
disaster, they are unlikely to be included in decision-making during a disaster, as many of our respondents indicated throughout our fieldwork, including this animal rescue program coordinator:

> In my years of doing disasters, I've come to believe more and more
> and more and more and more that if there is not already on-the-
> ground good animal welfare infrastructure and human infrastruc-
> ture—meaning decent, competent, not gold standard but decent,
> competent animal control agencies, sheltering capacities, rescue
> groups—then it's going to be a complete disaster when a disaster
> strikes. There are going to be more animals and people dead than
> would otherwise be. You can't go in after the [event], so the local
> agencies own the disaster. If there is not animal control; if there's a
> shitty relationship between animal control and sheltering; if there is

no money for spay and neuter so that you have animal overpopulation; if you don't have that network and those agencies on the ground, then it's just going to be an absolute—there is going to be way more human and animal suffering than otherwise would be because it can't be created. It's night and day. We see it night and day going into an area that doesn't have animal control. I can't put into words how awful it is.

The frustration expressed by this program coordinator suggests another shortcoming of the PETS Act: it focuses solely on the response and evacuation phases of the disaster. Planning for the well-being of pets before the disaster would also reduce problems during the disaster. Emergency managers know that preparedness and mitigation are important parts of disaster planning, yet there are few predisaster efforts to prepare for animal issues beyond delegating households to have "pet kits." A more comprehensive and effective solution for reducing poor management of pets in disasters includes minimizing animal issues before the disaster. In Paradise, California, pet overpopulation was associated with many households having multiple pets and many families losing their pets in the Camp Fire of 2018. Policy solutions for enhancing the PETS Act would include provisions that promote comprehensive animal wellness programs in disaster-prone communities.

How Local Implementation Affected Outcomes

Broad misconceptions about the PETS Act, lack of knowledge about the funds available, and personal beliefs about pets as nonessential members of the family led to lower implementation of mechanisms available through the PETS Act. Despite the misconception that the American Red Cross runs every disaster shelter, the entity in charge of sheltering varies greatly across each disaster and is largely dependent on local planning for sheltering operations. For example, although the Red Cross had a presence in the convention center in Dallas during Hurricane Harvey, it was not the lead organization in charge of the sheltering facility. At that time the shelter was run by the city of Dallas. This distinction is important because it determines not only participation of volunteer organizations but also the incident command structure and other core operations and rules of the shelter. The incident command structure is the outline for how communication should unfold between organizations engaged in response, mass care, and other essential operations during a disaster. For example, the medical first responders staged at the convention center had daily meetings with the emergency management officials to discuss unmet needs (such as supplies for incoming evacuees and reports of illnesses) so that approval for additional supplies could be granted rapidly. For the management of pets at the convention center, Red Rover (a national animal welfare nonprofit) staffed the care of pets in coordination with the Dallas Society for the Prevention of Cruelty to Animals (SPCA). Coordination and cooperation between groups ensure that there is no duplication of efforts and the response is efficient.

Not only do states vary in their interpretation and implementation of the PETS Act; states also vary in terms of policies related to reunification of pets, which may lead to confusion and conflict among evacuees and people managing shelters for humans in the disaster. For example, states vary in the number of days for which an animal should be kept in a shelter before it can be adopted or euthanized (Wisch and Dillingham 2017), and these standards might change during the disaster. Holding time for impoundment ranges from three to ten days. The holding times caused conflict among volunteers and pet owners after Hurricane Irma and the Camp Fire. After Hurricane Irma, we interviewed volunteers who shared a case in which an owner and a new adopter were both fighting for "custody" of a dog that was left unattended during the hurricane. In the Camp Fire, volunteers issued an outcry on social media when cats were moved outside Paradise and Chico (to Marysville), making it more difficult for evacuees to find their missing animals. There were also cases in which a cat was adopted out across state lines after the Camp Fire and the original owner saw that the cat was adopted on social media. Therefore, a standard holding period during a disaster scenario would make it easier for owners to reunite with their missing animals. However, this is a challenge when shelters have limited space and supplies. Creative decision-making can make a difference in managing pets.

Variation is driven in part by differences in implementation, which describes the degree to which a policy has been carried out across multiple levels, including local, state, and federal. For example, there are many obstacles to achieving the levels of earthquake mitigation and residential building retrofitting that experts recommend. Despite states' rigorous construction standards, if buildings were constructed before new regulations were enacted, it is not likely that all the buildings in, for example, California will be updated to adhere to the new standard for several reasons: funding capacity, risk perception, and limited understanding of the potential consequences for failing to retrofit a building to earthquake-resistant standards. Contractors in residential neighborhoods can choose to build to bare-minimum requirements of building construction. These standards are based on preventing building collapse that would cause loss of life, not necessarily preventing costly damage or salvaging the livability of the home. Similarly, in tornado-prone areas, residents may choose to use public tax funds for a community storm shelter, but only if there is enough community buy-in, a feasible location for the shelter, and often a private corporation to match some portion of the funds for construction of the shelter. The PETS Act faces similar obstacles to implementation across levels. States have undertaken various levels of planning and preparedness regarding pets and evacuation because of varying interpretations of the PETS Act, variations in the perceived risks associated with having or not having pets in emergency planning, and funding capacities. A state veterinarian responder in a hurricane-prone state explained that many responders, shelter coordinators, and volunteers working at the local level were not aware that they would be eligible to apply for federal money to offset costs of managing pets.

The program coordinator believes that the animal shelter may not have been inundated with lost and surrendered pets because humans could bring their pets to public sheltering places. The coordinator's experience also supports the theory of a possible increase in general evacuation compliance because of the PETS Act.

Coordination among Shelters: Challenges, Risks, and Advancements

Lack of communication across organizations can cause tensions between the community of evacuees and the local government. Tension can also occur between nongovernmental groups that have different approaches in managing animals. Many local animal shelters transport stray animals from a shelter in the disaster area to an area outside the disaster, even across state lines, usually in preparation for an influx of "disaster" animals. Thus, animals that are adopted after disasters are not actually "hurricane" animals that were potentially separated from their owners. However, it is important to note that organizational practices do vary and no streamlined protocols exist for disaster holding times. Another issue is that rescued pets after disasters were allegedly euthanized by animal control because they were found to be FIV (feline immunodeficiency virus) positive (even though such cats can and do live long and healthy lives) or deemed to be unadoptable. Lack of coordination also means that there is not a central location for information on lost and found pets. Residents looking for lost animals then have to contact or search social-media pages for multiple shelters.

The PETS Act's Narrow Focus

The PETS Act is designed to protect a very specific group of pets: cats and dogs. While the issue of selectivity regarding which pets qualify has been discussed in the context of breeds such as pit bulls and other large dogs

(Cattafi 2008; Glassey 2018), the PETS Act also does not provide support for stray or feral animals. A program coordinator expressed her concern for the gap between the accommodations provided for owned animals and strays. It is not always easy to identify whether an animal is owned because not every owned animal has a microchip, collar, or other form of identification. Many adoptable but unowned animals are displaced in disasters, she explained:

> One thing that always makes me a little nervous is that there have been great strides made in sheltering and evacuation plans for owned animals but nothing for unowned animals. So it's always scary. We had some of our animals in the shelter here, and, believe me, it was scary to think that our building may flood with animals in it. And there's no place to take them to. Now during Hurricane Ike there were—they were simple—[I'll just] call them pop-up shelters that opened. Texas A&M opened one. Just a pop-up at their rodeo grounds, and they were able to shelter animals from—homeless animals there.

While shelters may want to keep animals close to where they are found to increase their chances of being reunited, there are consequences for keeping too many animals in a shelter in harm's way. The risk was apparent in 2019 during Hurricane Dorian in the Bahamas, in which shelter animals perished:

> Employees were still trying to save the animals when the water reached their chests. They scrambled to stack crates and put dogs up on tables. But the water that had come rushing in far faster than they anticipated was threatening to sweep them away, staff say. As Hurricane Dorian battered the Bahamas last week, they took refuge in the ceiling crawl space of the Humane Society of Grand Bahama's office, listening as their dogs howled—and then the cries stopped. Most of the 85 cats were able to get up high on perches, they learned later. But about half of the 190 dogs died. (Knowles 2019)

Although that disaster took place in the Bahamas, the United States also lacks federal policies that designate specific protections for shelter animals and other stray animals. If an animal shelter evacuates, depending on the type of organization (nonprofit or county shelter), it relies on funds and planning from its own donors or local government. Many times, organizations rely on a memorandum of understanding (MOU), an agreement between two organizations with partner organizations; foster networks; or transport of animals out of state.

While the purpose of the PETS Act is to reduce evacuation refusal by people who own companion animals, we found evidence of people refusing evacuation because of their feral cat colonies. Feral cats are extremely difficult to trap and transport, yet their caretakers remain dedicated to the feeding, veterinary care, and sheltering of the cats. The PETS Act also fails to account for families with multiple animals. While sheltering one or two dogs or cats is feasible, the process becomes difficult for families with multiple pets. The PETS Act also does not create provisions for pets that may be considered large or agricultural animals, such as pigs, horses, goats, cows, chickens, and llamas. Some of the animal sanctuaries we visited during fieldwork, in addition to the livestock that formed most of their clientele, took in pets of families who had nowhere to board the animals while the families were displaced from home during disasters.

For larger animals, costs make evacuation difficult. As a coordinator and evacuee told us, "By far, the biggest reason most people won't try to move their horses [is] they can't afford to." A program coordinator in Miami, Florida, described some of the difficulties of multiple pet ownership encountered during Hurricane Irma:

> Not enough places to go, that's for sure. I was only aware of one place, and you could only bring one animal. What if I have six or I have birds? People were driving ten to twelve hours to Orlando, which normally takes you three hours. But the storm is still in Orlando, and then where do you go when you have fourteen animals? They're not going to get you anywhere. Some hotels are accepting animals—not fourteen of them.

If emergency coordinators expand their plans to account for large animals, unowned animals, families with many animals, and other varieties of animals that humans care for, more families will be able to evacuate in emergencies.

Timing of Planning the Evacuation

Another limitation of the PETS Act is that the law assumes that evacuees will have adequate time between the identification of a threat and evacuation to deliberate and plan for bringing their animals with them. In these situations, public officials have greater cause to entrust planning for animals to individual families. The PETS Act was designed with a "Katrina-like" event in mind or, more specifically, hurricanes as a hazard. While disaster managers still face uncertainties about time lines when planning for a hurricane, the storm's slower onset makes evacuation planning more feasible. Compare the multiday notice of evacuation orders in hurricanes with the rapid onset of the firestorm that destroyed Paradise, California, in November 2018, and there are stark differences in what pet owners can feasibly do for evacuation planning. In fact, many of the evacuees we encountered during our fieldwork were separated from their pet because they had to evacuate very quickly, and their cat or dog was hiding somewhere in the house or got scared and ran away and the evacuees did not have time to look for it. The limits of what can be accomplished in the short time frame of some disasters have long-term implications for pet owners. One evacuee of the Camp Fire described her devastation in searching for her cat:

> As for my sweet cat, Lily, I looked for her from day one at every single shelter and Facebook or website that appeared. When I was allowed into the fire zone with an escort, I had fifteen minutes to look for her. I didn't care about looking for one material thing. Just my cat.

The complexities that evacuees face in fast-onset disasters is another reason that the PETS Act should incorporate additional measures that assist people with animals, including incentivizing pet-friendly accommodations for the displaced evacuees, financially assisting and working with organizations that specialize in matching (matching lists of lost animals with animals that are found), and recruiting experts who specialize in finding lost animals after disasters. Shannon Jay is an expert cat finder who spent thousands of hours in burn zones after the 2017 Tubbs Fire in Sonoma County and 2018 Camp Fire in Butte County to locate lost cats. He brought the lessons learned from the Tubbs Fire (such as effective trapping of displaced cats) to the town of Paradise after the Camp Fire.

Shannon does his own fund-raising. However, since his services and expertise are essential, it would be advantageous for the PETS Act to incorporate funds for local training and expertise for people like Shannon before disasters and to prevent unnecessary bureaucratic barriers from keeping them from doing their work. As in the case of the Butte County and Sonoma County wildfires, reuniting pets with owners is usually the most time-consuming part of postdisaster efforts for groups involved in animal rescue. Volunteers conduct many of the reunification efforts. Additionally, smaller nonprofit organizations and individual owners usually fund feeding and medical care for displaced pets. The displacement, care, and loss of pets can be a core aspect of recovery for a family and a community. Therefore, amending the PETS Act to broaden the scope of postdisaster funds to cover

A man and his dog reunited after the Butte County Fire, California. (Source: North Valley Animal Disaster Group)

longer searches, more care, and training of experts for tracking and reuniting can directly contribute to long-term community resilience. We offer more solutions later, including incorporating technology, using social capital, and centering harm reduction as a primary outcome.

Lack of Long-Term Planning

The PETS Act is designed to meet short-term needs during the acute phase of the emergency and does not account for the long-term needs of individuals and families who need space, supplies, and shelter to continue to care for their pets in the wake of a disaster. A shelter official who took in animals temporarily and agreed to foster them for a time so families could evacuate brings up the range of time lines faced by families trying to return home or take back their animals after evacuation:

> People have flooded completely out of their homes, and they were in hotels and living with relatives; they had those issues. But it was a temporary thing. So we agreed to take their animals and hold them for thirty days to give them time to get into a stable living

relationship. Unfortunately, that worked for a lot of people, but we still have some of those animals way past the thirty days.

Animal owners had difficulty reestablishing their resources to allow them to take back the animals they had sheltered before evacuation, not only in the major hurricanes of 2017 and 2018 but also during the Kilauea lava flow, where many people could not afford rent outside their original home because housing is so expensive on the island. If their own homes were damaged or destroyed, they could not return or house their animals. The Hawaii Lava Flow Animal Rescue Network on Facebook was filled with posts searching for foster families for animals that had been surrendered by families who needed to leave Hawaii to find more affordable housing.

The high cost of staying in the area evacuated after the disaster was also a problem during the Sonoma County wildfires. Many families evacuated to rental properties that charged approximately three thousand dollars a month or more and did not allow pets because the properties were also vacation rentals in a tourist-driven area. Thus, families were not in a position to return to reclaim their pets, and the shelters were forced to house them long term. Similarly, officials began making announcements in the weeks after the Butte County wildfires about long-term planning for displaced pets. On Twitter, Butte County posted an announcement at the end of November 2018 after the Camp Fire: "In order to try and ensure sheltered animals are as healthy as possible, the County requests that residents begin planning for long-term care options for their animals." People needed to retrieve their animals. However, this was difficult for the evacuees who were still living in temporary housing after the disaster. At that time, 1,601 displaced animals were located at four shelters. While the county acknowledged that it was healthier for animals to be placed in homes, there were limited options for many displaced evacuees for long-term housing. Additionally, many people were still unable to locate their missing pets or confirm if their pets had perished in the fire. The problems call for many potential policy solutions: To ease the burden on displaced evacuees and their pets, temporary pet-friendly housing for families should be available so that people can return to reclaim and reunite with their pets. To make this happen, a new provision to the PETS Act could offer incentives (tax breaks) to owners of rental properties who adjust pet policies for disaster-displaced families.

Geographic Limitations

Despite the example of colocation in Dallas during Hurricane Harvey, local shelters can decide not to accept pets, which may cause evacuees to either refuse evacuation or drive a great distance to find pet-friendly accommodations. When there are not shelters accepting pets, evacuees face a burden in finding alternative solutions for sheltering. As one evacuee from Hurricane Irma indicated, finding alternative arrangements for pets during an evacuation can be stressful, time-consuming, and difficult in terms of logistics: "Taking my pets to a relative's house they'd never been to, under the stress we were under, was one of the hardest things. They inconvenienced my grandmother greatly. But no shelter was available in Monroe County.

Great distance poses problems for residents in rural areas and those who are displaced far from their community, such as residents of Beaumont and Port Arthur during Hurricane Harvey, who were flown to Dallas by the U.S. Coast Guard. Similarly, residents from the 2016 Fort McMurray wildfire relocated to Calgary and Edmonton, Canada, cities that were several hours away from their community. Nearly every person in the town evacuated, except for essential personnel. There were no people left to check on pets and feed them and provide water. Additionally, after the Camp Fire, many people left Paradise permanently, so volunteer groups had to coordinate feeding of animals left behind. Being so far away from pets that were accidentally left behind can also cause anxiety and uncertainty because families worry about who will feed and provide water for the animals while they are away.

Ad Hoc Care

The PETS Act's intention to increase evacuation compliance among families with pets limits its effectiveness as a protection of animal welfare. It misses several opportunities to offer necessary protections, coordination, and best practices for governmental and nongovernmental organizations necessary to aid animal evacuation and protection in disasters. The PETS Act does not provide guidelines or provisions for ad hoc groups carrying out rescues. During our data collection, we interviewed volunteers who pointed out the benefits and shortcomings of untrained animal rescue volunteers. For example, while these groups have the potential to supplement official rescue operations, many of their members lack technical expertise. Groups such as the "Cajun Navy" emerged as citizen responders during Hurricane Katrina and have redeployed for Hurricanes Harvey, Florence, and Maria and numerous other disasters. Multiple groups identify as the Cajun Navy, but they all have similar operating structures of deploying citizen rescuers. While these groups serve an important role in human and animal rescue, group members may not have specific training related to handling, transporting, and managing large animals. A specific example of this is equine rescue. Some of the equine groups we interviewed were concerned that ad hoc volunteers lacked the technical training and materials needed to carry out the successful rescue of horses without causing injury or death to the horses.

The PETS Act does not protect those who participate in ad hoc sheltering and animal rescue, even given the extraordinary circumstances a disaster situation creates and the constraints on official resources. As Hurricane Florence made landfall, Tammie Hedges of North Carolina was taking in animals found in the floodwaters or surrendered by owners (Brown 2018). She was caring for twenty-seven cats and dogs when Wayne County Animal Control forced her to give them up to the county. Hedges was arrested on twelve counts of practicing medicine without a veterinary license, including dispensing and administering pain medications to the animals. A volunteer was quoted in the news as saying, "It was all over-the-counter stuff you could literally find at the Dollar Tree," and the charges were "bogus" because vet offices were closed during the hurricane (Brown 2018). One of the drugs she was allegedly using was Tramadol, which is a narcotic and available only by prescription. Shortly after her arrest, petitions circulated online demanding she be released and the charges dropped. The volunteer makes a valid point. Not only were vet offices closed, but shelters were inundated during this time and traveling during the hurricane would have been dangerous. However, citizens without veterinary training who operate without credentials and training can also put animals in danger. There should be a balance between supporting people who carry out ad hoc sheltering in extreme circumstances and protecting animals from fraudulent and unsafe veterinary care.

Effect of Rumors and Fraud on Evacuation and Recovery Efforts

In disasters, rumors abound and can influence decision-making for evacuation and sheltering. During Hurricane Harvey, FEMA listed information about the PETS Act on a web-based rumor-control list in response to public confusion surrounding terms and provisions set forth by the legislation. This was the main rumor that FEMA was seeking to dispel during Hurricanes Harvey, Irma, and Maria. Social-media posts by less informed parties falsely claimed that evacuees with pets had to be accepted at hotels and other lodging facilities. The PETS Act does not mandate private companies, such as hotels and lodging industries, to alter their policies during evacuations. The risk posed by misinformation is significant; false rumors could lead to mass abandonment of pets if evacuees' plans did not work out. Social media seems to be one of the key sources of rumors or confusion surrounding provisions of the PETS Act.

The impact of the confusion about the act was evident throughout the data we gathered, both from evacuees and program coordinators. One commonly shared post during Hurricane Irma read, "JUST A REMINDER: If you're evacuating to a hotel/motel & they DON'T accept pets, don't be angry, calmly tell them that's against the law & after Hurricane Katrina Congress created the Pets Evacuation and Transportation Standards Act (PETS) to require states seeking Federal Emergency Management Agency (FEMA) assistance to accommodate pets and service animals in their plans for evacuating residents facing disasters. Please share by COPYING and PASTING."[3] While some of the information in this post is correct, the information about hotels being required to accept pets is false, regardless of the state in which they operate. Of course, as private organizations, hotels may decide to waive the pet fees, accept pets, or adapt their policies to accommodate people with pets, but they are not required to do so by the PETS Act.

The emotional stakes of pets in distress leads scammers to organize fraudulent fund-raisers for pet rescue. Some of the volunteers we interviewed after Hurricane Florence reported that multiple groups claimed that they were carrying out equine rescue and providing warehousing space for hay for large animals affected by disasters. Some of the fraudulent groups posted social-media videos from inside actual warehouses that stored supplies for horse evacuation, falsely claiming those warehouses as their own. One interviewee described a fund-raising video for a fraudulent group that showed a warehouse she recognized as belonging to a legitimate organization. It is unclear how the scammers obtained access to those spaces or what role they played in the actual relief efforts. Instances such as these may lead potential donors to rethink donating resources or money to animal rescue groups, even if they are legitimate. The mere existence of so many groups using animals for emotional appeals during disasters also demonstrates that people are highly motivated by their concern for disaster animals. It also demonstrates that people are aware that there are many organizations working in animal disaster issues. Indeed, many small ad hoc groups form specifically to meet the needs of pets in disasters.

Rumors about what the PETS Act can and cannot do in providing resources for government groups and other actors can ultimately affect evacuees and their animals. Communication about shelters that are pet-friendly and transparency about co-sheltering can prevent some level of confusion and decrease the amount of time that people spend deliberating about their evacuation.

Conclusion

The PETS Act reacted to the increasingly salient public problem of pet evacuation with an explicit goal to increase evacuation compliance. This limit in focus and unclear perceptions about decision-making related to pets also limited its effectiveness for helping families evacuate with confidence that their animals were being adequately planned for and for protecting animal welfare in disasters more generally.

The PETS Act can be viewed through the focusing event framework because it reflects that failures of managing pets in Hurricane Katrina led to major policy change. The PETS Act has limitations because of varying levels of state- and local-level implementation and local resources. Rumors created confusion about provisions of the PETS Act. The act also has limitations because it is designed to meet the short-term needs of families evacuating with animals, of specific breeds and species, and of single-animal families. Further limiting the act's effectiveness, the provisions assume that disasters will be slower in onset rather than fast events such as wildfires and earthquakes, that evacuee decision-making will be deliberate, and that residents will not only have made plans that include their pets but also have adequate resources and time to decide how they will evacuate with their pets. We challenge these assumptions in exploring the true social landscape of animals in disasters.

2

Our Cats Are Our Keiki

Animal-Human Bonds during Disasters

Sarah had just finished interviewing volunteers at a transfer station for "fire cats" in Paradise, California, in the spring of 2019 when her cell phone rang. It was one of her students, Zoe, waiting for Sarah and the other students to pick her up from the one remaining coffee shop in Paradise. "Dr. DeYoung, please don't be mad, but I have a dog," explained Zoe, who was spending the afternoon at the coffee shop while the others finished interviews because it was spring break at the University of Georgia and she wanted to finish her midterm papers before proceeding to the next round of interviews. Thirty minutes later at the coffee shop, Sarah and the students found a small trembling dog, a Chihuahua mix, on Zoe's lap. The employees of the coffee shop were taking photos of the dog with their phones and posting on social media about it. Zoe explained, "He was just darting through traffic with no owner in sight, so I ran over there to get him!" She motioned to the four lanes of traffic outside the coffee shop. Half-joking, Sarah said, "Zoe, when I said animals-in-disasters fieldwork, I didn't mean you're supposed to actually rescue animals." The dog had on a pink sweater and a crystal-studded collar with a phone number. When they called the number, a confused elderly woman answered the phone and said she did not have a dog. They took the dog to Paradise animal control. The officer there scanned the dog for a microchip and tracked it to a veterinarian's office and left a message with the staff there.

The group hesitantly walked away while large dogs barked, their echoes filling the shelter. The tiny dog shivered. They wondered if they had made the right decision. Luckily, that night at dinner, Zoe got a text message. The dog's owner explained that her mother-in-law, who had answered the phone call about the dog, had dementia. Overjoyed, the owner went to animal control to pick up her dog, thankful that they had been reunited.

This ordeal was taxing for the research team and the woman who lost her dog, yet it was a fraction of the emotional ordeal that evacuees face when they are separated from their companion animals or the ordeals that volunteers face when managing animals lost during a hazard event. However, because of her commitment to animals, Zoe took responsibility for the tiny dog—running across several lanes of busy traffic to make sure that it was safe. Taking responsibility for an animal is linked with emotion, bonding, and attachment. The people who become involved in an animal's life often view the animal's well-being as a reflection of their own integrity.

The entire ordeal of evacuating—losing a home, being displaced, all the while experiencing trauma and stress—can be amplified by grief associated with losing a pet. If the social ties of the person were intertwined with a companion animal, the loss can be even more severe. In this chapter we discuss ways in which attachment, bonding, and family roles influence evacuation decisions, care maintenance, and the ways in which humans carry out various roles and tasks of responsibility (surrender, fostering, and dedication to transient animals).

In Hawaii, where the Kilauea lava flow forced animal evacuations, residents refer to their pets as "keiki," meaning "child" or "little one." One post on social media showing an evacuee's lost cats was captioned, "Please help, our cats are our keiki!" This is one way that people demonstrate their attachment to their pets. During Hurricane Harvey, some animal shelters agreed to temporarily board pets until after the disaster. Unfortunately, because some families lost their homes and faced challenges in finding affordable pet-friendly rentals, establishing a safe place for companion animals is often difficult or impossible.

Psychological attachment theories and family bonding theories can explain the feelings people have toward their pets. This chapter also includes our findings demonstrating that pets experience trauma and undergo an adjustment period after the disaster in which they need appropriate space and support for recovery. The trauma that the pet and the owner experience is often long-lasting for both people and animals, as indicated by this evacuee/respondent:

> Evacuation is not the most difficult part of the experience for our pets. Being in another home, being around other pets (our friends' pets), [and] now being back in the upstairs of our house and con-

fined to particular rooms while construction takes place is the hard part for our pets.

In this chapter we also discuss the ways in which the sociozoological scale affects (1) which pets get left behind; (2) bonding that strengthens education campaigns, such as in the case of sanctuaries; and (3) which animals typically get media attention during disasters, such as in viral videos of a rabbit being rescued during the 2017 California wildfires.

Sociozoological Scale and Attachment

As Leslie Irvine (2009) explains, sociozoology is a concept that focuses on understanding the ways in which humans designate value, importance, and emotional attachment to certain animals and species. Basic ideas surrounding sociozoology include inquiries such as: Why do we consume some animals for meat but not others? Why are certain animals used in medical research or factory farming? Although these are useful examples, a more subjective question to describe sociozoology is the following: Why is it that humans hunt or farm some animals for food but deem other animals as vital members of the family? As Irvine describes, we define an animal's worth based on its place in human society and the household. However, some people care for animals that are not physically located within their households. For example, people take care of feral cat colonies and have refused evacuation because they remained dedicated to these cats. And some people have deep attachment to horses, but the horses may reside at another farm or outdoor location, most certainly not inside the home.

While most people share viral posts of cats and dogs after hurricanes, some are focused on creatures that are less visible and less likely to garner widespread emotional support. In her discussion of policy narratives, Debra Stone (2002) explains that groups who used images of oiled sea otters were more likely to garner funds for oil spill recovery, and Leslie Irvine (2009) notes that animals deemed "cute" are more likely to garner attention and public outcry. This is important because such emotional appeals can be a key catalyst for group mobilization, especially in animal advocacy. We found a similar theme emerge in our observations that was specifically evident in viral videos and other news stories associated with dramatic disaster evacuations. During the Sonoma County fires two viral popular stories involved "cute" animals. The first was a video of a man rescuing a rabbit on the side of the road, which even caused ecologists to chime in, saying that these human actions interrupt the natural ecosystem. The second popular story was of a college student who put her large dog in a duffle bag and rode her bicycle to safety because traffic was severely congested as flames approached her apartment. Others posted social-media messages after the 2018 California wildfires, encouraging people to create space and resources for wildlife.

Species-specific attachment also emerged when we visited several animal sanctuaries. One of the most illustrative examples is from a rural pig sanctuary that sheltered several animals during Hurricane Florence. As we toured the sanctuary, it became clear that owners Oscar and Johanna view their pigs as family members. Johnnie the pig, for example, has free range of their house and comes and goes as he pleases. Many of the other pigs run around the farm as well. Furthermore, the owners explained that each group of pigs had a specific social structure, mode of communicating, and environmental preferences. They also explained that the popular "teacup" pig leads to overpopulation of pet pigs. People purchase these pigs at flea markets and other venues, not expecting that the pig will become much larger. When the pig grows to an unmanageable size, the family is likely to surrender it to animal control. However, most county and city animal-control facilities are designed to temporarily shelter dogs and cats, not pigs, chickens, goats, and other animals.

During disasters, surrender of farm animals also becomes a problem because there is not a central location or boarding facility for these larger animals. Owners becoming displaced in a location without a yard or space to contain their animals also leads to surrenders after the hazard. However, because pigs and other farm animals are not included in the PETS Act, it is difficult to find boarding facilities for them during a disaster. It was clear that it takes a tremendous amount of work and resources to maintain a sanctuary for farm animals, such as pigs. This also is linked with the socio-zoology scale because in the words of one of the sanctuary founders, "It takes a certain kind of person to care about pigs."

Evacuee Attachment

In 2017 Sarah deployed to Dallas, Texas, to gather reconnaissance data at a large public shelter on Labor Day weekend. Hurricane Harvey had made landfall a week before. During interviews with evacuees, an elderly man recounted the pain of losing his cat, his last living family member. He said that by the time he realized he needed to find the cat carrier, the first floor of his Port Arthur home was already underwater—the carrier was lost. In a desperate effort to care for his cat, he scattered cat food on the roof of the car where the cat was stranded. The evacuee was rescued by boat, but the cat stayed on the roof of the car. Tears welled in his eyes as he shared the story.

It was not clear why the cat was not brought onto the boat. Another elder evacuee mentioned he left his Dachshund dog on the roof of his house when he was rescued by boat. Again, it was not clear why the animal was not taken onto the rescue boat. The man said he was relieved that the dog was not microchipped because he was almost certain that his pet would not survive, and he did not want to find out what happened to the dog. Perhaps by not knowing, the evacuee could even imagine a possible pleasant ending for the dog in which a rescue boat found it and then it was subsequently adopted by a family. Many people who have lost an animal have engaged in these phases of grief, including imagining an alternative ending for the animal, albeit unlikely or improbable.

While some preferred not to know the fate of their animals after disasters, many people we interviewed or surveyed found it particularly distressing not to have closure over the fate of their pet. For example, people who evacuated from the Hawaii lava flows and the Sonoma County wildfires in California expressed heartache at not knowing what happened to their animals. From our observations, the timing of evacuation may be linked with this form of distress over being separated from the family pet. Specifically, fast-onset disasters were more likely to result in pets left behind unintentionally, causing the family distress during and after the disaster.

Not surprisingly, the speed of the evacuation makes it difficult to gather the pet and the supplies needed for evacuating with the pet. Cats are skittish and often hide when stressed. This makes it hard to quickly capture the cat or dog on the way out during a hasty evacuation. We learned in our discussions with evacuees that it is possible that the rapid nature of the evacuation causes long-term distress, anxiety, and guilt in humans who were unable to bring their pets with them. In addition to guilt and feelings of regret, being forced to evacuate without pets may have caused a heightened sense of losing control of the environment and outcomes. In psychology research, lack of perceived control is associated with extreme stress and depression. In addition, many people feel that their companion animals are directly tied to their social support and well-being (Schaffer 2011).

Stress and anxiety can also be present even among pet owners who were able to bring their pets with them. When housing options were not abundant for the evacuee and when family stress overlapped with pet stress, there were instances of triple stress—stress about housing, family members or friends, and pets. Often evacuees expressed discomfort at inconveniencing other people because of their pets, and some evacuees even said that they would rather sleep on the street or become homeless than be separated from their pets. Consider the following statement from a Hurricane Harvey evacuee from Houston:

It was incredibly difficult to be gone for so long. It was hard to have three dogs at a friend's house. My friend also had a large dog and a cat, and after a week of staying there, we had conflict because it was very stressful. No matter what, I would've always taken my animals with me. They are part of my family.

An evacuee we interviewed in Clearwater, Texas, also shared her story of having to move in with her son and daughter-in-law after Hurricane Harvey because her house had been flooded and destroyed by the storm. She had two small dogs and was prepared to move to a hotel because she felt that she was imposing on her son and daughter-in-law as "newlyweds with a nice new house," especially because the two small dogs, as a result of stress from Hurricane Harvey, were urinating in the house (likely a trauma-related symptom). The evacuee described this stress as particularly difficult and said she would choose her living situation based on where she could bring her dogs. This family conflict is linked with the issues related to short-term versus long-term recovery. Both instances demonstrate the need for disaster assistance programs that include provisions for housing that is pet-friendly in the weeks, months, and years following the hazard event. Disasters may push many families into further economic peril, and prohibition of pets and exorbitant pet fees are more likely to lead to owner surrenders.

Throughout the data for our project there was a theme of people viewing pets as family members.[1] Viewing pets as members of the family is a key variable in evacuation decision-making research (Heath and Linnabary 2015). In a household study conducted after Hurricane Ike, Sandra Brackenridge and her colleagues (2012) found that reasons for evacuating and not evacuating were both associated with pet ownership. The study on Hurricane Ike also showed that commitment to pets was significantly related to lower odds of evacuating but that attachment had no effect. Here it is important to emphasize the difference between attachment and commitment. Caroline Schaffer (2011) explains that commitment involves how much investment and resources owners are willing to provide and sacrifice for their pet, whereas attachment involves viewing the pet as central to one's social and emotional well-being. Schaffer also explains that a specific form of attachment in which a pet becomes a "self-object" occurs when the pet becomes an extension of a person's identity and purpose. According to Schaffer, when a self-object pet dies, the person linked with the pet becomes emotionally distraught and severely distressed, and the separation between the person and self-object is "completely devastating to a person" (2011, 3). This is critical in understanding the landscape of pets in disasters—the variety of decisions and behaviors involved—because even though not every pet is a self-object, the perceived social support that an animal provides for an individual and a family is crucial to recovery in the weeks and months following the disaster.

Pet attachment can also unfold as a shared experience with others on social media, particularly during loss or reunification. The elements of shared misery over pet loss or shared celebration over reunification were particularly evident during the Camp Fire in November 2018. Many of the reunification photos and stories received hundreds of "likes," reactions, and comments. Interestingly, many of these reunification stories went viral beyond the groups that focused on pet rescue and reunification, demonstrating a considerable amount of interest from the general public and consumers of media about the topic of animals in disasters. We posit that this is also partially driven by the fascination and likability associated with feel-good stories. Research findings suggest that these positive stories can attract audiences and the consumer base for various news outlets (McIntyre and Gibson 2016).

Unfortunately, the public may not have been fully aware that some of the reunification stories had unhappy endings. For instance, respondents we interviewed in Santa Rosa, California, explained that sometimes reunification stories went viral, but the pet (usually a cat for this organization) did not survive long after the reunification because of extreme lung damage, burns, and other injuries. Thus, the joy of reunification was short-lived. Many evacuees talked about finding their animals as an important symbolic part of mourning and experiencing hope throughout the entire experience with the disaster. An evacuee whose home burned to the ground in Concow, California, talked about the grief of never finding some of her missing animals:

> I think sometimes [we] are reluctant to talk about that part of it, but it's a reality. . . . It's heartbreaking to be worried and not sure . . . if your animals are safe or alive. . . . When we thought we found Max— well, that's not Max, but there were ten thousand views of that video. People wanted to believe that we found him. . . . But you just have to hope. There is this saying in Spanish that I tell my patients, "Esperanza muerta ultimo"—"Hope dies last"—so you hope until you find their body and you know they're gone. And then you grieve. But it's really hard to give up on hope.

Viewing animals as family members was also associated with stories of persistent searches and somewhat dramatic rescue and reunification. For example, the owners of a pig sanctuary in North Carolina, Johanna and Oscar, shared a story that demonstrates the emotional bond and commitment to reunification. During Hurricane Florence, they sent emails to all the adoptees' families who might be in the path of the storm, letting the families know that they could bring the pigs back to the sanctuary for temporary boarding during the storm (which was much farther inland than some of the coastal locations in which the adopted pigs lived). One family who had adopted a pig named Belle from the sanctuary was in an area that was likely to flood from the storm surge. Johanna was following the updates from the family on social media as the storm made landfall, although the family repeatedly indicated that they were fine and not likely to evacuate. Later that day, Johanna saw that the family posted on social media that they did evacuate and left behind all their animals. It was unclear if they were compelled by law enforcement to leave without bringing their animals. However, because of this post, Oscar immediately drove more than two hours to reach the coastal area with a boat and supplies to rescue Belle the pig. Oscar was stopped at a checkpoint and barricade around the flooded neighborhoods. He indicated that he was attempting to rescue animals that were in a specific location, but officials at the barricade said they could not let people go in because of fears about safety and potential looting. Using social networks and maps, he found a route through a national park to get to Belle. When Johanna was recounting these events to our research team, tears welled up in her eyes. She turned to Oscar and asked him to finish the story. Oscar told us that he was able to get to Belle, and along the way he rescued several cats and dogs that were swimming in the water. When Belle arrived back at the sanctuary with Johanna and Oscar, they were steadfast that the sanctuary is her home and that she will stay there indefinitely.

Even owner-surrender situations can reflect bonding and attachment. There were instances in which owners surrendered their pets because their living situation was untenable after the disaster. In many of these instances, their grief over this choice and situation reflected the level of attachment that they had for their pets. One resident in Houston gave up her pit bull after her apartment flooded and she lost everything, including her job. She cried for forty-five minutes before leaving, devastated.

People who left their animals behind still displayed concern for their pets, as shown in this example described by a shelter coordinator during Hurricane Harvey:

> We were lucky that we had a lot of owners concerned about their animals that they did leave [behind]. So we were getting a lot of phone calls saying, "We needed to evacuate, and I left my animal; could you please go check?" You know, that kind of thing.

The attachment and commitment of humans to their animals are likely major reasons for the motivation to engage in early community reentry.

Checking on animals during and after the hazard event often was the source of conflict between residents and officials tasked with preventing early reentry into affected communities. Early reentry also caused conflict within and between volunteer groups working on response and rescue. For example, during the Camp Fire, volunteers and residents posted pleas on social media to be allowed to go past barricades to locate missing animals, to feed and provide water for animals that remained in the communities, and to search for the remains of their pets if they perished in the blaze. Emotional attachment and bonding brought about the conflict. People who lived in Paradise were upset and distraught that they could not return to check on their animals for several weeks after the event. Community members viewed groups that facilitated reentry as "on the side of the people" and groups that set up additional barriers to prevent reentry as unnecessarily authoritarian. We as authors are not advocating for unsafe early reentry. Rather, in nearly every disaster, our observations suggest that people will try to reenter communities to retrieve, feed, or check for remains of pets. There is an ongoing tension between the emergency managers and first responders' need to secure the scene and prevent early reentry and animal welfare advocates' emphasis on the urgency of reentering as quickly as possible for the well-being of animals. There has been little work or research on how to meet the seemingly conflicting needs of emergency management (securing the scene, evacuation) and animal welfare advocates (feeding animals left behind, welfare checks, and pet rescue). Research in this area indicates the emerging consensus that the goal of saving people is linked with saving animals (Glassey 2014; Irvine 2009).

Early reentry, an understudied area of disaster research (Siebeneck and Cova 2012; Siebeneck et al. 2013), can be dangerous, as illustrated by this example of a man in Hawaii who had to be led out of the area by a USGS drone when he became surrounded by lava:

One of the tougher moments I experienced while covering the Kilauea eruption in Hawaii. The man walking away from the river of lava is carrying an animal carrier and has been searching for his cat every day since May 28. On that night, this man had to be rescued by a USGS drone. He was trapped on his property as an outbreak of lava quickly approached his location. Fortunately, a USGS drone was in the air nearby. He was able to use his cellphone flashlight to signal the drone. As USGS pilots flew the drone to him, he was then directed to follow the drone to his escape path. He lost his home and didn't have enough time to get back for his cat. So each day now, he walks around Leilani Estates in hopes of finding his cat. As he walked past me after taking this image, he looked absolutely heartbroken. As an animal lover myself, I cannot even begin to imagine his pain. (Mezeul 2018)

However, we argue that officials and groups should identify new solutions for allowing special teams to reenter areas that may have surviving animals. In Sonoma County, California, in 2017, a community member used his military background to build rapport with the National Guard, who managed barricades so that he could assist an organization working on trapping and identifying cats that survived the fires. This illustrates that there may be instances in which barricades can be "negotiated" and that first responders can work in tandem with animal welfare groups. We acknowledge that this may be a complex task and requires careful planning. However, there also seem to be instances of barriers and barricades being set up because of unfounded fears of looting rather than solely for the protection of human health and safety. It is important to specify the reasons for setting up such barricades and to know how long these will last. If barricades are put in place for a prolonged period in communities that are relatively safe to reenter (with protective gear and by trained volunteers), animal rescue teams should be permitted to search for missing animals or to feed animals left behind. It is also very likely that someone denied access at a barricade will find another way, as Oscar did when rescuing Belle the pig. Residents, journalists, and others will almost always try to engage in illegal reentry. We saw evidence of this especially in the lava flows in Hawaii.

Allowing for a mechanism for official early reentry of select teams would increase reassurance of owners who are experiencing high levels of distress about the well-being of their pets behind the barricades. Feeding and providing water for the animals before the owners can return to the community also assure that the animals will stay in place instead of roaming and that they have a better chance to survive. Feeding operations in disaster-affected communities that have been evacuated increase chances of successful reunification because they keep pets alive and in one place. This is important for the long-term recovery and resilience of the community members since pet loss in disasters is associated with higher levels of post-traumatic stress (Hunt, Al-Awadi, and Johnson 2008; Lowe et al. 2009; Travis 2014).

Volunteer Attachment

Not only do evacuees become attached to animals, but volunteers and staff members may also become attached to the animals they are managing during disasters. During Hurricanes Harvey and Irma and in the Camp Fire, volunteers talked about fears of animals being transported out of the disaster area. The volunteers' main concern was that the owner of the lost animal might still return. In some instances, the volunteers expressed worry about not knowing where the animals were going to end up after the disaster. For example, in this interview with a program coordinator, we learned that volunteers were resistant to animals being sent away:

> It's partly because of the possibility that, however remote, the animals' owners may come back. It's also because we don't want—our volunteers were upset that we would send our animals away. It was unexpected and shocking to me that they were so resistant to us transporting animals out, because they didn't know where they were going [*pauses*] [because of] the attachment.

This suggests that volunteers working with animals during a disaster may become particularly attached to the pets, potentially because of the unusually stressful circumstances of the disaster and evacuation. Some of the volunteers at the shelters or within animal foster groups evacuated from their own homes and therefore were finding ways to cope.

Related to this, some people fostering cats or dogs during the disaster decided to adopt the animals permanently. The term "foster failure" is popularly used in the animal rescue community to describe this situation. The phenomenon of keeping the foster pet after the disaster seems to be important. As one foster-failure parent explained, she had adopted out nearly a hundred dogs after fostering them for a short time, but a bond emerged with the dog with whom she experienced Hurricane Harvey and she chose to adopt it.

This is similar to the concept in psychology known as misattribution of arousal (White, Fishbein, and Rutsein 1981). In this well-known psychological experiment, people crossing a bridge together who experienced biological symptoms associated with arousal because of fear, such as a pounding heart and rapid breathing, reported feeling attracted to the person with whom they had crossed the bridge. Another explanation of bonding through trauma comes from research that suggests shared trauma increases social cohesion (Bastian, Jetten, and Ferris 2014). More recently there has been media focus on the concept of trauma bonding in the contexts of human romantic relationships (Reid et al. 2013). It is possible that trauma bonding occurs between people and animals and that experiencing a hazard together can increase human-animal bonding.

Similarly, after the shelter Saving Grace in North Carolina put out a mass social-media call for emergency fosters during Hurricane Florence (to make room for incoming dogs from coastal counties), more than two hundred people lined up to foster dogs for the duration of the hurricane. Those families adopted approximately thirty of the dogs. Although those dogs were not specifically "Florence dogs," when the families had the opportunity to spend time with the dogs, it likely increased the opportunity for close bonding. During the Hawaii lava flows, volunteers and animal groups used the foster strategy to find space for displaced animals. Fostering can be an effective way to find "forever homes" for the pets while providing a safe temporary location for the animal.

Dogs as Emotional Support in Evacuation Centers

During Hurricane Harvey we saw several instances of dogs in public shelters for therapeutic purposes. While these dogs may be considered working animals in the sheltering scenario, their presence was a striking addition to the scene of dismal fluorescent lights and mass-distributed relief supplies. Children stopped to rub the fluffy bellies of the Golden Retriever–type dogs brought into the shelters by various faith-based and other organizations.

After traumatic events such as disasters, cuddling with "comfort dogs"— crisis response animals trained to work during emergencies—can help ease the stress of the situation.[2] Animals can bring an uplifting and positive presence in helping people cope, providing a much-needed distraction and calming companionship. After mass shootings and other traumatic events, therapy dogs visit the affected communities to help elevate the mood of children and their families. The animals have played a significant role in consoling victims, and comfort dogs have even been shown to lower anxiety and blood pressure (Morrison 2007). Ultimately, having animals around in a postdisaster scenario can benefit survivors, volunteers, and even first responders.

Grief and Regret

During Hurricane Matthew in 2017, evacuees indicated that they regretted leaving their cats behind (Farmer and DeYoung 2019). Some evacuees mentioned that they left a litter box and food for the cat in a location viewed as "higher ground," not realizing that they might not be able to return to the community to check on the cat immediately after the storm. Our findings from Hurricane Matthew also revealed that people who had cats were more likely to leave some animals behind. This suggests that cats may be viewed as independent and resilient, leading to a higher number of them left behind in evacuations. The lasting guilt and regret associated with the evacuations can also come from the outcome of the pet's health after the evacuation. An evacuee in Hurricane Matthew described their oldest dog dying after the evacuation. The evacuee perceived the stress from the evacuation as the primary cause of the dog's death.

Similarly, after Hurricane Harvey, a couple near a bayou in Dickinson, Texas, shared a story about regret of a family member who lived on the other side of the bayou. During the night when the floodwaters were unexpectedly rising after the rains, an elderly couple went to a friend's house to watch the Mayweather versus McGregor boxing match on television. While the couple was gone, the dogs that were in an enclosed kennel in the backyard drowned. The elderly woman was experiencing depression and guilt associated with the death of the dogs.

We heard another story about grief and regret when we were interviewing families affected by the 2017 Santa Rosa fires. A woman told us that her sister-in-law's house had been destroyed by the fire. Afterward, the family searched for weeks for their cat. They found her partially burned collar stuck in a fence, so they began to grieve, thinking she had not survived. Later they found the cat and were relieved that she was okay. However, the cat began urinating on the dog bed in the home where the family was now living. Because this added to the stress of the general situation, the family surrendered the cat to the animal shelter. Meanwhile, the woman with whom we were speaking was volunteering at that same shelter where her sister-in-law had surrendered the cat. Seeing the cat (named Zeus) there isolated and alone made her feel guilty and upset. After two weeks of seeing the cat at the shelter, she decided to adopt it. However, this was "the family secret" because the woman who adopted Zeus had not told the sister-in-law that she had taken in her former feline companion.

Trauma Recovery for Animals

After the woman adopted Zeus, and after two weeks of quiet confinement in a bathroom, Zeus returned to her normal behavior of appropriately using the litter box. This suggests that the trauma associated with the fire and displacement was temporary. Similarly, after Hurricane Harvey we encountered a family with a dog that continued to find ways to escape from his fence after the flood. This was not normal behavior for the dog, and the family suspected it was associated with stress and trauma. Another evacuee indicated that after they escaped to the second floor of a townhome during Hurricane Harvey, the dog had to use the bathtub as a toilet because there was no way to go outside for several days. After the storm, the dog was confused about the appropriate place for relieving itself. This also suggests that the experience of the storm or disaster can traumatize a pet because of disruptions in bathroom routines, general displacement, fear and anxiety, and separation from the owners/family. While many news stories focus on separation and reunification, there is less emphasis on the longer-lasting trauma that the animals themselves experience. There should be more research and emphasis on how to prevent animal surrenders after disasters because of frustration over a pet's changed behavior, which may be a sign of stress and trauma. Many animals are surrendered in the postdisaster time frame not only because of long-term housing and displacement issues but also because of the frustration that pet owners have over the appearance of stress-related symptoms immediately following the disasters, such as litter-box issues in cats and dogs regressing in potty training. If owners learn that these symptoms are temporary and that the animal's trauma symptoms are likely to ease with the passage of time, there may be fewer postdisaster owner surrenders.

Although loss and grief affected many, families and individuals alike used their grief as a springboard to help other people reunite with their animals. This was evident on social media, especially in photographic posts in which people memorialized their animals but expressed simultaneous joy for people who were able to locate their pets. We should note that this was seen more in wildfires than in hurricanes. Similarly, there were fewer instances of online victim blaming in wildfire evacuations in which people were unable to evacuate with animals than in hurricanes (Reed, DeYoung, and Farmer 2020). We suspect that because the onset of the fire evacuation was rapid, people were more empathetic and understanding of those unintentionally leaving their animals behind. In hurricanes, we saw instances of people expressing death wishes for people who left animals behind. Leaving animals behind does not always mean that there was an absence of attachment or commitment, especially in instances when it was unintentional, such as occurs when a cat hides in the house during a rapid-onset evacuation or when a dog runs away from an owner at an evacuation transit point.

Many volunteers who attempted to rescue animals that they had found out about during the disaster still felt lingering despair when they were unable to help rescue the pet. After Hurricane Florence, one volunteer tried to free a horse trapped behind a chain-link fence under floodwaters. She was unable to free him. In recalling finding the horse's body later, she had tears in her eyes. It was clear that she had a sense of frustration about being unable to rescue the horse. Her intense grief reflects her overall commitment to the well-being of the animal, even though it was not her horse.

Animal Bonding as Motivation for Volunteering and Leadership

Viewing animals as important leads humans not only to have animals in their lives as pets but also to take on volunteer tasks or key leadership or organizational roles in groups that focus on animal welfare. Although this

Horse in floodwater during Hurricane Florence, South Carolina. The horse did not survive. (Source: Sandy Clarke)

is not surprising, we see this form of enthusiasm as unique in disasters in general. This is not to say that first responders, emergency managers, and other key personnel are not passionate about their jobs; rather, the social networks, resource mobilization, and emotional atmosphere of animal rescue creates a very specific sense of shared community. Furthermore, animal rescue groups are active when there is not a disaster (for example, responding to cruelty cases, spay and neuter campaigns, or general lost-and-found reunification). This arguably makes the animal rescue community tight-knit. Several times throughout the fieldwork, interviewees talked about their passion for animals and animal welfare as one of the key reasons for becoming involved. Animal attachment seems to be instrumental as a catalyst for people and communities to mobilize and organize during and after disasters for animal rescue, reunification, fostering, and adoption.

When we interviewed key leaders, founders, and organizers, almost all the individuals stated that they had a memorable experience or bond with animals linked with their motivation for their work. The founder of a major foundation that leverages and coordinates resources for disaster-affected pets shared his story of creating the foundation. During Hurricane Katrina, he was trying to help a friend locate her lost Great Dane among the kennels that were sheltering displaced pets. Not only did he spend days searching for the dog, but he also realized that there was a great need to assist with the problem of pets in disasters because there were many smaller, lesser known pet rescue organizations that were not getting enough media attention and therefore not enough resources to assist animals in disasters. Similarly, some of the key coordinators in national-level animal rescue groups mentioned their love of animals as a motivator for getting involved in rescue work.

Shannon Jay, a famous cat trapper in California, lost his cat in Sonoma County during a nondisaster time. The tactics he used to track his cat inspired him to assist in efforts to trap cats after the 2017 Tubbs Fire that swept through Coffey Park and other neighborhoods in Sonoma County. Transferring his widely renowned skills, Shannon deployed to Paradise after the 2018 Camp Fire, which destroyed 90 percent of the structures in Paradise and killed eighty-five people. Shannon worked independently to rescue more than one hundred cats from the Tubbs Fire and the Camp Fire burn zones. When Sarah met Shannon in Paradise in the spring of 2019, he indicated that losing and then finding his cat inspired him to join the efforts after both fires. Using humane cat traps and tactical military gear such as a thermal scope, Shannon has become one of the most successful trappers in the disaster animal rescue community.

A wildfire evacuee we spoke with in Chico, California, who was still searching for her missing cat became involved in efforts to raise awareness about treatment of fire cats in shelters and to organize efforts for feeding. At the time our team interviewed her in March 2019, she said that there were ten volunteers feeding cats with more than one hundred feeding stations in Paradise. As we interviewed her, we noticed that she was wearing a cat collar as a bracelet—a tiny double-looped collar with a shining silver bell. It was clear that she was emotionally bonded with her missing cat and that this bond drove her not only to take action to find her cat but also to care for other cats lost during the fire. Many of the people active in pet disaster work are also people who do day-to-day animal rescue efforts such as fostering, volunteering at physical shelters, recruiting other volunteers, fundraising, and providing veterinary services and other forms of animal care. It is also likely that people who engage in animal rescue work may have specific personality traits that make them more empathetic to animals affected by disasters.

Flyer hanging in coffee shop in Paradise, California, after the Camp Fire.

Research suggests that the identity construction and narratives in which animal rescuers partake is unique, specifically in describing terms of moral guidance and group solidarity (Young and Thompson 2017). It is important to note that there may be various motivations and philosophies for doing rescue work with animals (Greenebaum 2009). It is also important to consider that not all disaster animal groups were active prior to the disaster, but the skill sets specific to animal rescue are transferable in disaster scenarios. These skills include reunification efforts, vaccination and public health education, spay and neuter work with feral and stray animals, animal handling, and grief counseling. In fact, we argue that since animal rescue groups carry out reunification and adoption efforts on a day-to-day basis, they are ready for disasters. The same degree of day-to-day work may not be practiced in the realm of human health and social services, aside from in hospitals and foster systems. While the sheer number of animal rescue groups makes them a powerful resource in disasters, it seems that the passion of these people is a critical part of animal rescue in disasters. It is their attachment to animals that forms the foundation of successful animal work during disasters.

Conclusion

Disasters can be traumatic for residents, first responders, and volunteers who encounter and experience animal loss. It is important for officials managing disasters to acknowledge that because so many people view their cats and dogs as their keiki, they will make evacuation, sheltering, and reentry decisions based on their pets. Like many other lessons from disaster research, one cannot control what people will do, but it is possible to plan, support, and facilitate the resources that people need to keep their animals safe and to become a volunteer or leader in animal rescue work. Volunteers are critical because they fill an important gap when official resources cannot meet the needs of families and animals. Some of the volunteers are the animals themselves, as in the case of therapeutic dogs in relief and sheltering centers. Often, the volunteers even display bonding with their animals, such as the instances of foster failures after disasters.

Our exploration of the complexities of attachment, guilt, and trauma finds that animals themselves may display behavioral signs of trauma after the disaster. It is important to educate owners and support them as they cope with their animals' stress and symptoms. It is especially important to emphasize that the symptoms (such as inappropriate toileting) may be temporary. This knowledge can reduce animal surrenders after disasters because many surrenders are associated with the overall stress of navigating recovery. If families have a plan and guidance for helping their animals alleviate trauma symptoms, they have a better chance of avoiding surrender. In the following chapters we integrate these and other key findings with important lessons learned from recent disasters throughout the United States.

Trunking in South Beach

The Darker Side of Pets and Animal Welfare in Disasters

Animal cruelty occurs in nondisaster times, but it can be brought to light during disasters, as one program coordinator implied when she told us, "You know, there are certain parts of the country that are way more prone, both for cruelty and disasters. The Southeast, we get a lot of response requests there, so it tends to be a lot." Some of these animal rescue groups specialize in assisting with animal sheltering during disasters and other crisis scenarios, such as large-scale puppy mills or other cruelty cases. They work throughout the United States across multiple disasters, and many are members of the National Animal Rescue and Shelter Coalition (NARSC). The coalition outlines best practices for sheltering, evacuation, and response and for coordination with other working groups. Along with National Alliance of State Animal and Agricultural Emergency Programs (NASAAEP), the coalition and teams put together a list of best practices for disasters, including decontamination-exercise guidelines and other planning tools (NASAAEP, n.d.). While these documents are useful for practitioners and responders, they are designed to be used for the acute phase of emergencies and do not include the scope of managing the social aspect of animals in disasters.

Disasters reveal complexities of social landscapes. One afternoon during fieldwork in North Carolina after Hurricane Florence, we visited a cat sanctuary that took in coastal cats during the hurricane. While we were walking through the facility, we saw a white-and-black cat that had faded pink coloring on his back. We asked what happened to him, and the volunteer with us said that some teenagers spray-painted the cat and a good Samaritan had brought the cat to the facility. Another cat at this same location was on a special diet because he was dangerously overweight. Animals that are victims of neglect and abuse arrive at shelters or face death year-round, but in disasters the plights of these animals are often in the spotlight. Animal advocates on social media highlighted many of these instances. This social-media comment (made during Hurricane Florence) exemplifies that animal suffering is a major concern for community members and animal welfare advocates in disasters: "This dog looks like he was in bad shape before the hurricane. He has been neglected! Maybe this is a blessing in disguise for him, and he will get a loving home with people who will care for him properly." This comment was not unusual. In some of the cases we observed or heard about from volunteers and organizations, the state of animals prior to the hazard event was already poor. This is evident at both the household and community levels. In sum, the resources available to a community for managing and caring for pets, including spay and neuter programs, lead to specific conditions or outcomes for animals during and after the hazard event. The social-media post just quoted also reflects the general sentiment that people who leave pets behind do so intentionally and should be punished. Interestingly, we also found that victim blaming and shaming of people who leave pets behind are more frequently displayed in slower-onset events such as hurricanes rather than quick-onset disasters such as wildfires (Reed, DeYoung, and Farmer 2020).

In their book *Animal Management and Welfare in Natural Disasters*, James Sawyer and Gerardo Huertas (2018) describe a system for assessment of animal welfare called the Five Freedoms. Veterinarians and animal advocates in the United Kingdom developed the system in the 1960s for agricultural animals, and groups throughout the world working in animal welfare began to formally adopt it in the 1970s. The Five Freedoms are:

> Freedom from hunger and thirst
> Freedom from discomfort
> Freedom from pain, injury, and disease
> Freedom to behave normally
> Freedom from fear and distress (2018, 44)

As Sawyer and Huertas (2018) point out, these concepts should be guiding principles in disaster management for animals. All these freedoms can be addressed by emergency management officials throughout multiple phases of a hazard event. For example, freedom from hunger and thirst should be addressed by responders and groups who coordinate large-scale feeding-station efforts after a wildfire or other event. After the Camp Fire in

Dog surrendered after Hurricane Harvey in Texas (later adopted).

Paradise, several advocacy and rescue groups organized to set up more than one hundred feeding stations for cats left behind, and the stations were maintained by a cadre of more than thirty volunteers. Freedom from discomfort, pain, injury, and disease requires expertise from veterinarians, experienced humane trappers, and emergency management through efforts to move animals safely out of the hazard area. Freedom to behave normally can be applied to recovery. Animals placed in temporary foster care in a home, pasture, or other comfortable space will experience less stress and trauma than animals housed in crates, carriers, or confined spaces. Fear and distress are some of the more gut-wrenching aspects of animals in disasters: for example, we can imagine the distress that a horse might feel as it is surrounded by floodwaters. Despite efforts by individuals and groups to prevent suffering, animals are vulnerable to disease, injury, and death in disasters. Sometimes animals face harmful outcomes through inadvertent decisions (such as the horse Bandit's owner failing to cut the fences before the flooding in Hurricane Florence).

Sometimes the suffering results from lack of resources for transportation and evacuation, which we discuss further in Chapters 5 (power and privilege) and 6 (evacuation decision-making). Not knowing where to bring a pet during a hurricane or having a cat slip out the door during a wildfire evacuation is not the same as purposefully tethering a dog in an area that is likely to flood. Many instances of suffering are also systematic and tied to the ways in which animal care operated at the community level prior to the disaster. One of the most illustrative examples of this is pet overpopulation. Observations made by civilians, volunteers, and other people bolstered our perception of spay and neuter programs as tied to the entire problem of animals in disasters. For example, a volunteer firefighter shared these thoughts with us after the Carr Fire: "Pet overpopulation is a big problem in Shasta County because many poor people use pet breeding as a form of income. Also, spaying and neutering is very expensive, so many people cannot afford it. Thousands of cats are put down every year at [Organization 1]."

Another key point is that a pet overpopulation problem makes animal management more difficult during a disaster, as described by a program coordinator in Texas after Hurricane Harvey: "I think a little bit—a lot of the national organizations, HSUS [Humane Society of the United States], Best Friends, . . . doing this nationwide advertising and focusing on companion animals, and focusing on adopting and not buying pets, has made a difference." When asked if she thought that general pet overpopulation makes a disaster worse, the coordinator said:

> Obviously in Houston it did. It was horrible. I think that what happened at the Energy Center was the population of animals that was all homeless before the storm. And people were not going to come get them because they didn't have a home to start with. So in a place like Houston—we're lucky; we're smaller. We're one hundred thousand population, but it's not like Houston. The organizations in Houston—I'm not going to say any names, but I'm just going to say animal organizations in Houston have neglected this problem for so long that it's of epic proportions now. So it takes a disaster like this to see how bad it is, but I'm sure we didn't have, that we know of, a lot of animals perish in our area. But I know that Houston had a lot.

Another program coordinator described the connection between spay and neuter programs and disasters:

> Part of it is animal overpopulation in an area is part of a system. There is not that good structure on the ground. You have to have low-cost spay/neuter available. Otherwise, it just won't get done for the people who won't have resources. And those are the people that populate the human shelters. If you've got resources, you are not going to be spending more than a night or two in a mass human shelter. You just won't. You've got the money to get out, and you've

got gas in the tank. You have a car. So if you have less animals, if you don't have the shelter overcrowding, then you don't have so many animals that you've got to evacuate prestorm. Honestly, that's not even counting all of those animals living on the streets that are just drowned and dead.

Massive operations to reunite pets with people coincide with opportunities or pathways for reducing pet overpopulation. After the Tubbs Fire, group coordinators joked with us that there were no new kittens born in Santa Rosa in the spring of 2018 because the mass trapping efforts for lost fire cats resulted in sterilization of so many community cats. Groups, volunteers, and civilians repeatedly emphasized that pet overpopulation was linked with community resources, which coincided with thriving or suffering animals, including the extent of animal suffering during disasters.

Trauma of Hazards on Animals

Freedom from distress and fear is one of the Five Freedoms. We found evidence from our data that animals experience trauma and behavioral issues during and after disasters. It is important to revisit this concept because people can manage animal well-being and suffering by understanding how a hazard affects companion animals. We describe earlier that dogs in Texas were trying to escape their enclosures after Hurricane Harvey, a behavior they did not display prior to the event. Additionally, evacuees after Hurricane Harvey described their dogs becoming calm when they are normally "hyper" or active, dogs barking at water, dogs "crying" more and acting nervous. These behaviors are also associated with housing and relocation issues. Consider this response from an evacuee from Hurricane Irma: "It is hard for them because I lost my house in Irma, and we have moved from place to place until I could find long-term housing. They have been not themselves. They have been more whiny and needy, and they have had more accidents." Another evacuee said about her dogs: "Some of them still show slight signs of stress from the long travel and being in kennels for transportation."

Evacuees also expressed signs of distress in their cats: "The older cats had more anxiety and jumped at the slightest sound." An evacuee from the Camp Fire in Paradise reported, "One cat we found fifty-one days after fire. He stays very close to us now. He doesn't venture out of our motor home."

This shows that animals experience long-term behavioral changes associated with disasters and other traumatic experiences. When disasters happen, animals are confused and scared. Combine these effects of the disaster with possible abuse and neglect by humans, and the animals may have severe trauma symptoms. It is also possible that abuse and neglect may increase after disasters because people view an animal's trauma symptoms as "disobedience" or "being bad," and in turn the humans might engage in physical or other forms of punishment. This is another reason that education and outreach are important after disasters. Such outreach programs could explain that an animal's toilet problems are not deliberate and that physical punishment is not appropriate or effective. Educating people about trauma symptoms in animals can reduce rates of surrender. Also, in this way, enabling people to support and comfort their animals gives them greater control over the future of their animals.

Laws and Law Enforcement

Throughout our fieldwork, we saw evidence that people continue to believe that looting is widespread in disasters despite social-science evidence that criminal activity does not spike in hazard events (Tierney, Bevc, and Kuligowski 2006); however, cases of animal cruelty do occur during disasters. Ironically, this fear of human looting can adversely affect animals because it may cause people to refuse evacuation and "hunker down" through the storm with their animals. After Hurricane Harvey in Dickinson, Texas, a neighborhood displayed plywood spray-painted signs that said, "Looters will be shot." This is important to document because people's fear of crime can influence their sheltering decisions, which affects their companion animals. Consider this response from a woman in Florida who evacuated with her two dogs after Hurricane Irma:

> After Hurricane Katrina and women being raped at the shelters, I would never stay there. Instead, I had to drive to my closest family member all the way in Macon [Georgia]. The reason I evacuated so quickly was because of the storm surge and how dangerous that can be. If storm surge was explained [and] easier for people to understand, they would be more worried and leave sooner because of it.

Fear of crime is also associated with keeping dogs for security. During Hurricane Irma, security dogs in Miami-Dade County may have been seen as more "disposable" by their owners, according to some program coordinators we interviewed. This level of disposability led to a greater risk of abandonment during hurricanes.

However, the perception of certain breeds also made them susceptible to violence by law enforcement in disaster zones (i.e., being shot). One evacuee in Port Arthur, Texas, told us that a family member's dog was shot by law enforcement after Hurricane Harvey. This is eerily similar to instances described by Leslie Irvine (2009) after Hurricane Katrina, when companion animals were killed by first responders. Port Arthur, like the Lower Ninth Ward in New Orleans, is predominantly Black and heavily policed. (In fact, a police officer stopped us while we were walking out of an evacuee's home for an interview in Port Arthur. The officer was curious about what we were doing, and after we briefly explained our research, he left.) Our data suggest that cruelty toward animals has been carried out by a range of people, from law enforcement to civilians, to people at official government shelters.

Another way in which fear of crime affects animal rescue in disasters or the perception of increased criminal activity is that some volunteers may be fearful of carrying out animal rescue. This was the case for a program coordinator we spoke with in South Florida who had rescued a dog from someone's yard after Hurricane Irma:

> People will kill you here. People will shoot you. People will do bad things. So nobody was taking action because everybody's scared. They post on PAWS; then they took it down like, "Don't ever tell who told you about this dog." People were just very scared. So it was kind of unpleasant. I did what I did. I know I did the right thing. We took the dog to a secure place. It was at the veterinary office. And we told the guy, "Listen, we can report you to Miami-Dade right now. You're going to go to jail. You're going to get a fat ticket. Just take care of it."

The belief that looting and theft increase after disasters may also influence decision-making of public officials, first responders, and emergency management. In all the disasters for which we collected data, there were instances of people attempting to reenter disaster zones to rescue animals but being prohibited by the police or the National Guard because of concern about looters.

Finally, lack of accommodation for pets during hazard events causes people to take matters into their own hands and break minor rules to save their animals. However, as many evacuees indicated, the evacuation process is also stressful for animals. Many people in southern states such as Florida lamented that it was not the actual hurricane that was difficult for their animals but the late-summer heat. As one evacuee told us:

> My parents lost power for eleven days, and it was really hard on the animals because it was so hot. My home in Key Largo never lost power, but we were not allowed to go back for a few days. My husband went back because he is law enforcement, but those three days in the heat were horrible for my poor animals.

The most obvious example of suffering of animals in disasters is the influx of stray dogs and cats that stretches the limits of smaller animal rescue facilities. In this chapter we describe the complex scenarios in which these situations unfold and point out that, like many issues in disasters, the villains and victims are not always well-defined. In some cases individuals make decisions to operate outside the legal system because of the perceived benefit to the animals involved, such as the North Carolina woman who operated as an animal rescuer during Hurricane Florence.

State and Local Laws

We observed groups and individuals breaking protocols or making choices that were not necessarily illegal but somewhat covert operations. Many were instances in which organizational or physical barriers prevented groups from carrying out tasks such as managing feeding stations in burn zones, searching for remains of pets, and attempting to identify animals for reunion. An example of a covert operation concerns the man in North Carolina who took a boat through a wildlife preserve area to find an alternative entrance to the neighborhood and rescued not only the "target pig" but several other cats and dogs. Other such examples include a nonprofit group going "undercover" to adopt cats from a shelter. Many people believed that the shelter carried out excessive or unnecessary euthanasia after a wildfire. So groups and individuals may employ rule bending to protect animal well-being.

A recurring theme throughout our data and throughout this book is that reentry was related to high levels of conflict. This happens among volunteers, civilians, public officials, and other actors. The concern for animals suffering was frequently mentioned as a reason for this conflict, as a volunteer stated after the Hawaii lava flows of 2018:

> The local government decided that animals are mere property and should not be rescued. They, civil defense, also actively blocked many of us volunteers from going to rescue and evacuate animals facing certain death by lava, dehydration, or starvation. On top of that, many cruel owners intentionally left animals behind to die and refused to assist in granting access for volunteers to go save them.

Intentional animal abandonment during a hazard event—whether a hurricane, lava flow, or wildfire—arguably violates all the Five Freedoms. During Hurricane Irma, there were reports of people abandoning animals on interstates during evacuation. In one *USA News* story, officials described the extent of the abandonment: "Palm Beach County Animal Care and

Control director Dianne Sauve said the agency recovered roughly 40 dogs in the days before Irma made landfall in Florida. Some were tied up, others were in pens or in enclosed yards, unable to escape" (Rossman 2017). One resident from the Florida Keys who spoke with us described taking care of animals in her neighborhood after Hurricane Irma: "We stayed home and ended up feeding and caring for neighbors' abandoned cats and chickens. It was sad to see that people left any animals behind."

One of the reasons for focus on pets in disasters in news media and disaster coverage is the widespread concern for animal welfare. Stories of animal abandonment during Hurricane Irma caused Florida state legislators to propose HB 1738, which would create financial penalties for tethering dogs during a hurricane. The bill, introduced by Republican senator Joe Gruters, was popular and had bipartisan support. The bill failed to pass, but the proposal itself gained substantial media attention. The attention reflects how vocal animal advocates are and how they use disasters to leverage new legislation.

New images of dogs tethered to posts and fences were the major inspiration for the grant proposal to the National Science Foundation. The striking emotional tone of these images seemed to attract a large audience—at least on social media. While Irvine (2009) and other scholars have studied animals in disasters, we wanted to understand the mistakes and successes that humans encountered in managing pets in disasters. Therefore, we set out to understand the behaviors, decision-making, social settings, and policy landscapes that led to so many instances of animals left behind in dangerous conditions. As one program coordinator described:

So they [dogs] come right here [Miami], and, like, there's just no respect for them. There's no commitment. And since [animal abuse is] so popular, people just don't see anything wrong with it. There's a lot of abuse. There's a lot of illegal breeding. There's a lot of religious things like Santeria and animal sacrifice and stuff like that. So it's a lot of bad things happening. A lot of people dump dogs in a nursery area here—it's called Redland—that's like a popular dumping ground. . . . And during the hurricane, there was just nothing . . . no rules. Like, there's no—you have written contracts, like, you're supposed to keep the dog for a week [at animal shelters]. But nothing else matters; it's just me [the evacuee]. I need to leave. I need to take the dog. The dog is not mine. If you release your own dog in front of the shelter—I mean, I started seeing that. That was unbelievable to me. I'm like, "This is heartbreaking." There were people that were leaving chained dogs during the hurricane. I was going to those calls, rescuing those dogs. They were left behind. It was unbelievable.

I rescued a pit bull that was left for six days with no water and food.
Chained.

While legislation surrounding animal abandonment in hurricanes or
tropical storms is newer to the public agenda, many states do have statutes
and mandates that prevent people from leaving dogs and cats in hot cars.
According to the Animal Legal Defense Fund, thirty-one states have laws
that outline legal protections for companion animals left in extreme heat
or cold in vehicles. Many of these laws focus on protections for good Sa-
maritans who might break a window or intervene in some way to save the
animal.

Neglect and Overcapacity

When fissures erupted on the Big Island of Hawaii, nearly two thousand
people evacuated, so groups and residents had to mobilize to get animals
out of the lava zones. People had to evacuate quickly, and some left pets
behind or struggled to find rental housing that allowed pets. Some sanctuaries and shelters agreed to take in pets temporarily, while other groups facilitated a foster network. When Sarah visited evacuation centers, shelters,
and sanctuaries on the Big Island, there was evidence that some groups were
stretched beyond their capacity, at least during the acute phases of the eruption.

Accepting too many animals into holding facilities led to potentially
unhealthy conditions in some cases. At one facility, there was no official
check-in system or security mechanisms that are common at other facilities.
Multiple species of animals were housed at this location, and some cages
had been labeled "evacuees." There were far too many cats in some of the
catteries. The location could have been particularly overwhelmed because
the lava eruptions were ongoing, even at the time we visited this site, but it
was clear that there was no more space for new animals.

Similarly, another location we visited after Hurricane Florence specialized in dogs but had farm animals in its facility. The farm animals were all
kept in the same enclosure with no green space. The smell was pungent;
other farm-animal facilities we visited there were well-kept spaces with
greenery, areas for roaming, and clean pens. The contrast between the me-
ticulously planned and maintained farm-animal space and the unkempt
space at the other facility was striking. The level of care for the large animals
was reflected in the knowledge level of the volunteers and staff at both organizations. In the well-maintained sanctuary, the coordinators described
how animals such as pigs have social systems, hierarchies in their groups,

and emotional reactions to affection from humans and other animals. In the sanctuary in which farm animals were contained as more of an afterthought, a volunteer joked about the severe obesity of one of the pigs (a condition described as life-threatening at the other sanctuary).

Abandonment

Abandonment is the most commonly reported form of cruelty in disaster news media, but few studies focus on how to mitigate the problem. Many studies focus on personal responsibility for pets in disasters (e.g., K. Thompson 2015). However, there should be multistakeholder responsibility for reducing abandonment. Shelter managers, first responders, and other personnel should not increase the burden of animal evacuation on residents in a hazard zone and should make every effort to facilitate safe and timely evacuation. For example, handing out cat and dog carriers can be a quick, low-cost solution for ensuring that evacuees have a way to transport their animals to the evacuation destination. Furthermore, there are times during the hazard when community services can reduce rates of animal abandonment. Specifically, prior to the onset of the hazard, emergency managers should deliver clear communication through multiple channels about accessible, pet-friendly shelters. Proper planning and coordination are key for reducing harm and suffering. Even if a key decision maker does not view pets as essential to the family structure, families will refuse evacuation based on the well-being of their pets. If an emergency manager's goal is to ensure public safety, then it is important to plan for decision-making of families and communities and what might motivate them to leave or stay behind.

The History of Dogfighting in the United States

Nondisaster-time cruelty laws and ordinances can influence the ways in which disasters unfold for animals. This means that disasters can exacerbate conditions for animal cruelty. In South Florida, one reason for apprehensiveness toward rescuers may be concerns about criminal activity. In Miami, a program coordinator we interviewed mentioned "trunking" as a pastime for some residents who owned dogs, or in some cases, some residents were illegally breeding dogs. Trunking occurs when someone puts two dogs in the trunk of a car to fight. The driver and/or passengers put the music on full blast for fifteen minutes and drive around, so nobody hears the dogs fighting. By the end of the fifteen minutes, whichever dog survives is the "winner." People involved in this practice can place bets on which dog will come out on top.

Trunking shares some similarities to traditional dogfighting. Since the passage of the Animal Fighting Prohibition Act of 2007, dog fighting is a felony in every state.[1] Some view dogfighting as a "sport," and it has been linked to other illegal practices involving gang activity. Dr. Randall Lockwood, senior vice president of ASPCA's Forensic Sciences and Anti-Cruelty Projects, described trunking: "It's nothing that a professional would engage in, because it defeats the purpose of recognizing a well-trained dog and breeding a successful fighter" (Zinda 2017). In the case of South Beach, these well-trained dogs are typically illegally bred pit bulls.

As occurs with many other problems in communities, disasters can exacerbate or highlight issues more clearly. This was the case in Florida after Hurricane Irma, as we learned about the intricacies of dogfighting, trunking, breed-specific legislation (specifically concerning pit bulls), and the way that this can all culminate in affecting disaster evacuation and sheltering. A dogfight involves two dogs placed into a pit by their handlers, then released to fight one another as spectators place bets on which dog will win (Evans and Forsyth 1997). Dogfighting, a baiting sport, has existed for many centuries. Originally, animals such as bulls and bears were used as entertainment by aristocrats and British royalty (Evans and Forsyth 1997; Kalof and Taylor 2007). It was not until 1835 that baiting sports became illegal in England, and dogfighting continued illegally "underground."

Dogfighting emerged in the United States almost immediately when colonization began. New York passed the first U.S. law that outlawed the practice in 1856, but it continued to spread. Throughout the 1900s, animal rights activists continued to put pressure on legislatures to implement legal sanctions for dogfighting, and as a result "dogmen" have continued to operate in secretive matches (Evans and Forsyth 1997). Louisiana and other southern states have become the center of dogfighting: "In Southern Louisiana, it is not uncommon to see a whole yard packed full of dog houses each with a Pit Bull chained to it. Estimates reveal there is a fight somewhere in Texas, Louisiana or Mississippi every weekend" (Evans and Forsyth 1997, 66). Indeed, the pit bull is viewed as the "ultimate gladiator within the dogfighting subculture" (60); fighting dogs were, and still are, used to intimidate and instill fear in others (Kalof and Taylor 2007).

Though dogfighting is a felony in all fifty states, it is still a difficult law to enforce. There is little incentive for police to investigate dogfights (Evans and Forsyth 1997). Some consider dogfighting a "folk crime," in which there is little stigma or moral culpability linked to the offenders. The idea of dogfighting as a folk crime then begs the question of how subcultures, geography, and economic conditions facilitate or are associated with animal cruelty. These contexts become even more dynamic in hazards and disasters.

Pit Bulls, Dogfighting, and Disasters

It is not accidental that there is an abundance of pit bulls in South Beach. One respondent outlined the context and history of dogfighting in the Miami area:

> You're going to go to a Miami shelter today; you're going to probably find around three hundred pit bulls. You're going to find another one hundred black Labs. There's so many of them. . . . We have illegal breeders here in Miami. We have dogfighting existing, unfortunately. There's a lot of illegal breeding. . . . You can go to subareas, right here, in the farms; you see people selling dogs, pit bulls. It's a lot of dogs. . . . They're this organized crime, and they make a lot of money on that. So they're going to protect it with everything they have. That's the only income for them that they do. So that's very serious. I don't know what kind of money we're talking about. But I know that those fighting dogs, they're not small money for them. So they will protect them very much, and the consequences might be very bad. . . . But that's why you go in a shelter and you see, like, "Why all of a sudden they have so many pit bulls?" That's why, because we have breeders, and we have fighters. If you go to a Miami shelter, you will easily find three hundred pit bulls. Same in Broward; same in Miami-Dade. It's a lot of them.

We found that the prevalence of pit bulls in shelters is not an exaggeration. Our visits to area shelters confirmed this. When shelters become overcrowded, there are often special adoption days when the cost to adopt a dog is minimal or there is no charge, as described by one shelter coordinator:

> Unfortunately, because of overpopulation, the shelter does a lot of free dog days. So what happens is that they [those involved in dogfighting] pay homeless people, and homeless people go, adopt the dog for free, and they sell them to fighters for two hundred, one hundred fifty, one hundred dollars five seconds later. . . . There is no process in place. You call the shelter; you can adopt up to four dogs. Nobody checks anything. Nobody checks any records. You can have a criminal background for abusing animals, and nobody would know.

During disasters, the abundance of street dogs at shelters makes it easier to adopt dogs for fighting.

Despite the rapid adoptions for dogfighting, there were also accounts of abandonment before or during hurricanes. People surrender pit bulls in specific "dump zones" in the Miami area. One interviewee indicated that she has seen many dogs let loose in this area to fend for themselves, which is something that happens during disasters as well:

> For some reason, people think that dogs can survive in there by themselves. They can't. And they perish so quickly. There is no food in there. They're nurseries. They cannot eat avocados or climb the trees for fruit. There's nothing in there. There's no food. There's no water. So during summer it's brutal. That's the dog we found that was twenty pounds because he couldn't find any food. And people were scared. Nobody's going to pick up a pit bull from the street. Nobody. Nobody. So they perish if they don't eat roadkill or something. Then, that's it.

In this way, pit bulls are extremely vulnerable to neglect, abandonment, and abuse. In disaster research, this is known as differential impacts (e.g., Neumayer and Plümper 2007). Based on our observations and interviews, pit bulls experience injury, neglect, and abuse at significantly higher rates than other breeds in South Florida. Literature on tracking crimes against specific breeds is scarce. However, tracking crimes against animals can be useful in tracing other types of criminal behavior (Geldenhuys 2018).

Breed-Specific Legislation and Disaster Sheltering

It is difficult to estimate just how many cities ban or place restrictions on certain breeds of dogs. For example, in Louisiana, six cities have banned pit bulls altogether, while others have labeled pit bulls as "dangerous" or placed limitations on ownership. Breed-specific legislation refers to laws that regulate or prohibit certain dog breeds or types of dogs to decrease dog attacks. In most cases, those dog breeds are labeled vicious or dangerous. In Miami-Dade County, pit bulls are a banned dog breed. Unless the owner had a pit bull prior to the implementation of the legislation (at which time the owner had to follow very specific registration guidelines), pit bulls are not allowed to be sold, purchased, or otherwise obtained and brought into Miami-Dade County (Sec. 5-17.6). This leads to issues concerning companion animals and hurricane evacuation and sheltering.

Current legislation pertaining to disasters does not consider breed-specific laws passed in various cities and how those states and municipalities manage emergency preparedness with these bans in place (Cattafi 2008).

Approximately thirty states have some type of restriction or ban in place based on dog breed. Alternatively, roughly twenty states have some sort of anti-breed-specific legislation in which they are prohibited to pass regulations on dogs based on breed (Wisch 2020). The controversy surrounding this type of legislation is ongoing.

Breed-specific regulations gained traction in the 1990s. Various battles emerged in courts across the country, where citizens challenged regulations regarding pit bulls and lost, most notably in *State v. Peters* and *American Dog Owners Association v. City of Yakima*. Both cases concluded that city bans on pit bulls were acceptable. More recently, legislation about breed restrictions has had pushback, as animal activists point out that allegedly aggressive animals or "vicious breeds," such as pit bulls, cannot necessarily be determined by breed but rather are related to human negligence and abuse (Cattafi 2008).

More important, the statutes banning breeds and types of dogs such as pit bulls do not provide care provisions during disasters. As Amy Cattafi writes, "A failure to address BSL [breed-specific legislation] in emergency preparedness provisions for animals creates an inevitable gap in the enforcement of the laws. Such a gap will most likely be addressed only at the most unfortunate time: during a disaster" (2008, 369).

While Miami-Dade County prohibits ownership of pit bulls, there are many pit bulls in the communities that regularly experience hurricane evacuations. Then the question arises of what these people do when threatened with disaster and how emergency managers can plan for this. As evidenced in Miami after Hurricane Irma, this likely resulted in higher abandonment of animals or people not seeking emergency shelter or not evacuating because they knew their pit bulls were in violation of the local ordinance.

Cattafi (2008) offers the suggestion that lawmakers should amend the PETS Act to include a clause banning breed discrimination during emergencies. This could temporarily suspend any breed-specific regulations or bans on certain types of dogs so that owners could seek public shelter or foster their dog when needed. While it is not really possible to know how many declined evacuating or seeking public shelter because of owning a banned breed during Hurricane Irma or any other disaster, our respondents witnessed dogs being abandoned outside shelters (for various reasons, including lack of vaccination records). Realistically, the breed-specific legislation, in this case in Miami-Dade County during Hurricane Irma, likely contributed to and/or exacerbated current problems the municipality has with pit bull ownership and overcrowded animal shelters.

Fraudulent Animal Rescue Groups

During disasters, prosocial behaviors emerge in communities. People check on and help their neighbors (including pets), and donations from outside affected communities pour in as a show of support (Quarantelli 1994; Rodriguez, Trainor, and Quarantelli 2006). This is the prevailing outlook from disaster research. There still are, however, those willing to take advantage of others to receive donation money or supplies or even to get credit for something they did not do. The emotional appeal of animals in disasters seems to make an ideal target for con artists. After Hurricane Florence in the Carolinas, horse owners working with rescue organizations faced a conundrum: How can you tell when you are dealing with a legitimate group rather than a fraudulent organization? One horse owner, who helped with rescues in the past, described her frustrations with fraudulent groups online:

> The networking abilities are great, [but] the fraudulent aspects are unbelievable for hooking folks up with the wrong people. . . . The major issue that I see is, say, I'm a new horse owner, and I've got three or four horses. I've never done disaster evacuation before, and when it happens, maybe I don't own a trailer; for whatever reason I can't go, and I'm looking for help. You go online; there is no definable way, no single registry anywhere, that I know of, that I can point people to to say, "Pick your evacuation help off this list; they can actually help you—probably without getting you or your horse killed. They're probably not going to defraud you for your money; they're probably not going to take your horse and disappear to the meat market."

Her frustrations come from recent observations of various groups and ad hoc volunteer organizations posing online as animal rescue groups. She became skeptical of their requests and noticed that while some groups seemed legitimate, others were "taking credit" for operations and tasks that were actually carried out by different groups. It was also via social media that she witnessed various discrepancies:

> I am in possession of a video right now that I haven't decided what I'm going to do with that was put up on a self-deployment website as "Here, look at our warehouse, look at everything we're doing, look at all this stuff, [and] send us money!" That's not their warehouse. How do I know this? I've been sending stuff up there. There's a lady who tried to call BS on that situation and got kicked out of their group. And is now getting threats from them as far as, if you don't

shut your mouth up, we can have three thousand people on your doorstep to show you how this really works. She has a great deal of actual state-approved livestock-response protocol, and she was trying to help this warehouse get set up for rescue. And she got a whiff of this video and . . . the group who she was helping, an actual 501(c)(3), is so scared of this other group they kicked her out. . . . How in the world can you shoot this video and send it out to thousands of people saying it's your facility? It's not even your facility.

In this instance, she recognized that this group did not own this warehouse. Another volunteer we interviewed indicated that she takes precautions and is wary of fraudulent and dangerous scenarios, approaching situations with those she does not know with great caution. She also attempts to connect others to groups she knows are genuine. She indicated that she would like to see a more streamlined process for validating groups in future evacuation and sheltering incidents, especially in online venues:

There needs to be some way to indicate the certified disaster response teams that have actual FEMA training, and there is not. . . . I mean, there's got to be a way that people can validate these groups; I don't pretend to have that answer. So, as frustrating as Facebook or whatever is, I'm sorry, it's here to stay. You've gotta learn to work with it somehow, and there's got to be a way to validate this stuff. And for the actual people who aren't gonna kill your horse or steal your money or resell your hay to identify themselves . . . preferably in one central location, although that's probably a pipe dream, but [it] could [be done] at least county by county. Spit it out, folks. Say who you're working with. Who is it okay to trust, or who's your official liaison? Where is your official distribution hub? They need to say.

The interviewee later went on to say that some groups were inappropriately on ELO (emergency liaison officer) channels representing themselves as authorized first responders in the county when they were not. This happened again on social media after she had helped send a truck full of supplies to the group. As she described:

That same day, I saw this other group inside the warehouse where we sent all that stuff, walking around saying this is [a specific] animal support network. I picked up my phone and videotaped it right off my computer screen. . . . They got challenged on it, and they yanked it off.

The identities of those involved were unknown, but it does highlight issues with how social media can influence or bolster fraudulent claims. It is also likely that the group claiming the warehouse as their own was using the name of an organization with which they were not affiliated, because it has become a well-known ad hoc volunteer group and might garner more support from those likely to donate.

Fraudulent representation is not the only issue. A respondent also described a scenario during past hurricanes in 2004–2005 in which her neighbors had a boarding facility and agreed to take in six horses for someone else. The person who left the horses never returned, so the boarders were responsible for the huge vet bills for the animals. They had been unprepared for that situation. It also made the respondent wary of helping anyone she did not know without having some protocols in place, such as consent forms.

During Hurricane Florence, one volunteer described acquiring more than a hundred bales of hay that she was unable to send to anyone who needed it because the last trucking company she used had all the hay stolen from the truck. The group spent a great deal of money to haul hay, and it "disappeared out the back door to somebody who turned around and resold it."

The problem with fraudulent groups posing as legitimate animal rescue organizations is difficult to measure, as many of these groups likely operate only on social media and then disappear. As one respondent emphasized, "You better be darn careful who you contribute to, or it might just be filling somebody's pocket. We don't have any way to verify that stuff."

It is difficult to determine to what extent these issues are true representations of frequent instances of fraudulent groups rather than how much of this perception is linked with general skepticism about controlling donations in disasters (Nelan, Penta, and Wachtendorf 2019). However, it seems that the general concern as well as enthusiasm about supporting animals in disasters may lead to more instances of people taking advantage of this enthusiasm and empathy.

Organized Corruption in Disasters

Hurricane Katrina struck the Gulf Coast in 2005, bringing catastrophic damage and, later, many allegations of fraud, corruption, and court cases involving the New Orleans Police Department, housing contractors, and various government officials. Many focusing on fraud during Hurricane Katrina point to the thousands prosecuted by the Hurricane Katrina Task Force, later renamed the Disaster Fraud Task Force, for various charity scams, insurance fraud, benefits fraud, identity theft, and contract fraud. By

2010, some 1,360 people had been charged with fraud at the federal level related to Hurricane Katrina (Frailing 2012).

As described previously, some people create groups that claim to need disaster-specific donations. In 2008, eight Houston residents were convicted for such a scam, in which they obtained Social Security numbers and filed for FEMA emergency assistance checks. The perpetrators garnered nearly ninety-three thousand dollars (Alpert 2015). False websites posed as charity organizations, and in some cases, individuals were also falsely applying for aid. These were not the only types of corruption. Federal contractors and politicians also engaged in fraud after Hurricane Katrina, Super Storm Sandy, and other disasters by mismanaging disaster funds (Frailing and Harper 2017).

Fraud is most prevalent during the recovery period (Voigt and Thornton 2015). Again, groups may take advantage of all of the media images emerging of animals surrendered or abandoned during the disaster and attempt to ask for donations to support the "disaster animals" when the organization may not exist at all or may be not be tasked with disaster operations. This is *different* from legitimate organizations using funds for discretionary purposes. For example, groups such as the ASPCA may bolster social-media posts and efforts for donations during a disaster. The images associated with calls for donations may include a dog in flooded water. However, if the ASPCA obtains funds beyond the response phase of the disaster, it is up to the organization to spend those funds on other specific tasks, such as spaying and neutering. Spending the donations in this way may contribute to potential donors' general suspicion of making donations.

Corruption, Animal Cruelty, and Lies in Organized Pet Shelters

Corruption is not specific to any one disaster. It did not take long for stories of corrupt animal organizations to emerge after Hurricane Florence hit the Carolinas. Sally is a horse owner who volunteers with a large organization focused on equine rescue and transport during disasters. She did not mince words when discussing the corruption and animal cruelty she has witnessed in shelters surrounding her county. She described a horse named Cosmo whose owner lost him while he attempted to evacuate by boat during Hurricane Matthew:

> And then you've got corruption. I mean, the manager of the shelter when we pulled Cosmo out of the black water, she said, "I want this horse." She said, "I'm gonna make sure I get this horse." I have a video recording of her saying it, of the owner [of the horse] telling us what was said to him. He was a Black man, in his eighties, and

this was a very small town.[2] . . . When he went to get his horse, he was told, "You can pay a one-thousand-dollar fine, you can sign your horse over, or you can go to jail." And animal control was standing there; all he saw was a guy in a uniform, so he signed the horse over. Next day on Facebook, the director of the shelter posted, "Oh, he signed the horse over to me, not the shelter," blah blah blah . . . and we saw where she was trying to sell it on Facebook about a month later.

The boat of the horse's owner, Mr. Mason, had flipped over during evacuation, at which point the horse ran off. The shelter owner claimed that the horse was tethered to a fence, but the owner denied this and described that his horse had a lead rope but was never tied down. His having to sign the horse over was also not legal. As Sally mentioned, that is not how it works. For example, no owners had to pay to get their dogs and cats back unless they were repeat offenders for leaving their pets behind. According to the respondents we interviewed, there were issues with this in the county overall. For example, residents were told they had thirty days to pick up their pets, but ten days after the hurricane struck, the rule was changed to only fifteen days.

In the end though, Sally and others in the community worked to help Mr. Mason get Cosmo back. A month after the hurricane, the shelter owner was asking around to see if anyone wanted to buy the horse. Although the community had to pay four hundred dollars to get the horse back, on Christmas Eve they went to Mr. Mason's house and surprised him by returning his horse. As soon as Cosmo saw Mr. Mason, he ran over to him and put his head on his chest.

This happened in a small town. The shelter owner has a sordid history of corrupt events such as this. Sally mentioned that the job pays very little and there are few others willing to take on the task of managing the animal shelter. The respondents indicated that this is probably the reason why the corruption continued. This involves animal cruelty allegations as well. Sally and another respondent, Kasey, told us about situations with this shelter manager in the past:

She gives [cats] to her friends, whoever she wants. She was giving cats to two of the city officials who said they were taking them as barn cats for their friends. They were taking them out and shooting them. . . . They take them out and let them loose and play target practice with them. A lot of people that have cow barns do it too. They did that where I worked on the dairy farm. I had to leave; I can't do that. . . . We're talking hundreds of cats. [The shelter owner] had to know they were taking them. . . . The numbers were so high there was no way they were taking that many cats for barn cats. I don't even know if they got fired for that; that was in the news a while back.

This example reflects the treatment of feral cats at the shelter as well, particularly during Hurricane Florence. Several witnesses attested that feral cats were not evacuated during the hurricane and remained in a padlocked cage, even though the shelter is prone to flooding. Locking animals up means they are incapable of escaping to safety. Caging feral cats is usually cruel and uncommon by best standards of shelter practice (TNR [trap, neuter, and returning the cat to the community location] is more humane). Sally showed us pictures of the remnants after the hurricane, which included food bowls infested with maggots, syringes lying outside, and the remains of deceased cats still locked away. She said that some of the cats had likely died even before the hurricane hit. Though some volunteers tried to rescue the cats before the flooding, they were threatened with arrest by sheriff's deputies—what Sally called the "good ole boy" mentality there. This shelter was not necessarily committing corrupt or cruel acts because of the hurricane, but the hurricane did make certain acts easier to legitimize or get away with. Shelters that are already corrupt can also use the aftermath of a hurricane to engage in other shady practices, such as stealing donations for themselves. This was also prevalent with this county shelter, according to one volunteer:

A lot of the supplies that were donated disappeared, [like] the good [horse] feed. The vaccines too. All the medical supplies for all the animals disappeared. And me and my friend happened to stop at the old shelter that floods one day just to look around and found all the good feed and medical supplies at the very back of the shelter in one of the rooms, where [the shelter owner] could get it and take it home without anyone seeing. . . . She was feeding her own horses with it. That's why I didn't help this year; I saw a lot of corruption going on.

Fraudulent groups might also operate in this way, receiving donations meant for other people, animals, or organizations. It is apparent that the donations for this shelter were for the shelter itself, though the owner was taking them as her own. Amid all the problems within this shelter, nothing significant has changed. Mr. Mason evacuated for Hurricane Florence as well. By this time, he had sold his horse but did own several goats. He told others as he left that he was putting the goats on his roof to ensure their safety. During Hurricane Florence, one of the first pictures Sally recalls seeing was of the shelter owner post on her social media was of her taking Mr. Mason's goats. It is unknown if Mr. Mason ever got his goats back.

Rumors and Alleged Corruption amid the Camp Fire

Many organizations have been working on finding lost pets after the wild-fires in California. This is a tedious task, especially for the rescue of cats, who are generally skittish. After the Camp Fire, stories emerged on social media about the questionable euthanasia of cats. One animal rescue worker told us:

> They have euthanized, they say, thirteen, when we have information on seventeen cats, based on diagnosis of feline leukemia virus, feline immunodeficiency virus, or feline heartworms. And it's based on really outdated information that those cats—like FIV has a really low transmission rate. And even if it's a cat that's kind of aggressive, it's fine in a one-cat household. . . . I mean, it's something that I think previously was recommended [to euthanize], but it's not anymore because they've got a lot more information. So they did that, which is really upsetting because they also claim that some of these cats were feral when we have information from the people who trapped them [that] they were not. And they are like, "All these pets have been reunified." That's false. [There are] animals that were trans-ferred from [this shelter] to local shelters and stuff and have not been reunified, so it's a lie.

She then discussed how they found out the cats were euthanized. They have people in the community who are "matchers" and work to find the owners of each cat they keep track of that came in during the one of the major wildfires in California. This includes matching cats on social media through various shelters. In one instance, they could not find out any ad-ditional information about a cat at the animal shelter. Records showed the cat being brought into the shelter but never coming out (even though the cat was apparently no longer there). This volunteer, with two others, had a list of twenty cats to match. They went through the shelter and identified eight cats on the list, five of which were still in the shelter, two were adopted, and one had been reunited with its owner. However, this left twelve cats unac-counted for. Shelter officials indicated that those twelve cats were sent to another location to be a part of feral cat barn programs. The volunteer, how-ever, was skeptical, as the organization where the cats were supposedly sent managed the care only of kittens. She told us that they were later able to confirm that cats were going to be euthanized on the advice of veterinarians:

We've got in contact with the vet who they sent [the cat] to and found out that they were advised that the cats that test positive for those things [FIV] are ordered to be euthanized. [The animal shelter] actually put out a statement they posted on their Facebook. They put out a press release, and they made a private email to me that they were euthanized at the advice of the veterinarian. First, they said they were at [another shelter]; then we found out they were—you know, we had concrete information that the cats were euthanized. And so we put pressure on them, and it was all over Facebook and everything that they had no choice but to respond. . . . And the thing is, it's a really awful sucky thing that happened, and it's horrible, and it's based on misleading information, but they could [not] admit their mistake.

She further described that confirmation occurred because she talked to someone in charge of the euthanasia who did not actually want to do it but felt compelled because the person was told this was protocol for cats that were FIV positive or otherwise deemed sick. The organization in question made social-media posts but not to the effect of admitting any wrongdoing. Rather, it was a method of rumor control and was explicitly labeled as such. The initial social-media post from a county organization began:

Rumor Control We have received many calls and emails from concerned people, many who live outside of the county, about cats in our emergency shelters being euthanized. County animal control does not euthanize animals or coordinate with other facilities for this purpose. In regards to cats considered feral, our shelter had approximately 15 feral cats. The plan for these cats, in coordination with the town, is to sterilize the cats and return them to local cat colonies.

A post made approximately three weeks later for clarification included the following: "We continue to hear rumors about feral cats from the . . . fire being euthanized. No cat, feral or otherwise, from the County emergency animal shelters has been euthanized, except if deemed medically necessary by a licensed veterinarian."

As the rescue organization worker mentioned, other conversations took place on social media. Various comments under the posts mentioned the organization's double-speak, noting the exceptions for medically necessary euthanasia taking place. Those unsatisfied with this response continued to post about it on social media. A fund-raising effort was created as well, with a mission statement for all shelters and rescue organizations to work together for transparency and allow shelter access for treatable animals. The explicit goal of the online fund-raiser was to stop the killing of treatable animals at the animal control shelter. At this writing, they had raised $450.

Various community members alleged having evidence of euthanasia taking place in the county shelter, likely because of cats having tested positive for FIV or feline leukemia virus. That evidence came directly from the matchers whose goal was to keep track of cats going in and out of shelters. The county shelter vehemently denied euthanizing treatable cats, feral or otherwise, though they do not elaborate on what basis euthanasia is considered medically necessary. It is not hard to imagine why a community would be outraged about treatable cats being euthanized as an inhumane practice, especially after so many pets were lost and still missing after the wildfire. Ultimately, the lack of transparency in tracking cats and the outcries against euthanasia in this process highlighted a desperate need for better tracking systems overall and better convergence and teamwork between organizations.

Corporate Crime and Wildlife Impacts

Wildlife also experiences suffering in disasters. While natural hazards of this scale may not seem to be directly caused by humans, extreme events are often associated with human choices (Kelman 2020). Often, legal ramifications for companies that contribute to catastrophic events are linked more broadly with environmental damage and loss of human life, such as the Deepwater Horizon oil spill (Schoenbaum 2012) and the Camp Fire caused by Pacific Gas and Electric Company's poorly maintained power lines (Melo 2020). While outraged vocal groups rally for dogs and cats after fires, wildlife gains less attention in news media. After the Australian bushfires of 2020 in which an estimated one billion animals died, climate advocates pointed to collective and urgent action to prevent future loss of wildlife (A. Thompson 2020).

In the United States volunteers found a dead mountain lion known as P-64 after the Woolsey Fire in 2018. While the primary news articles focus more on dramatic photos of dogs tethered to trees during tropical storms or stories about cats reunited with their owners months after a wildfire, there are also groups and individuals who focus on reducing suffering of wildlife during disasters. From this news article, it seems that the large mountain cat succumbed to injuries caused by the fire:

> When the Woolsey Fire broke out on Nov. 8, P-64 was in the Simi Hills, north of Oak Park. GPS data shows he continued to roam the Simi Hills for the next few days. Sikich and fellow researchers later hiked into the area and used a telemetry device to locate P-64. When

they saw he was moving around within the drainage area, they were hopeful he had made a kill and would survive.

The last GPS point sent by P-64's collar was on Nov. 28, but researchers weren't overly alarmed since the collars commonly go multiple days without transmitting.

Then on Dec. 3, Sikich hiked in and found the cougar's remains. All four of his paws were burned, which the biologist suspects happened as he moved through the burn zone.

"He basically had two options," Sikich explained. "He could have entered an urban area, where there's a lot of firefighters and noise and people fleeing and a lot of disturbance there, or choose to enter the burnt landscape—and that's what he did." (Fonseca 2018)

The bushfire koalas and the wildfire mountain lions are victims of extreme events that continue to worsen because of human-induced climate change. Some animal welfare groups, biologists, and veterinarians mobilize to rescue wildlife during and after the events. Another unlikely species to be the focus of rescue efforts after Hurricane Harvey was bats, creatures who nest under bridges and overpasses that were inundated with floodwaters: "Trapped by furious winds and rain, bats have been drowning in their roosts under bridges or displaced from their colonies and forced to settle on nearby buildings, making them vulnerable to weather and predators" (Oelbaum 2017).

The mobilization by groups to coordinate efforts for wildlife unfold differently than for groups that focus on cats and dogs. Technical expertise is required for wildlife rehabilitation, tracking, and monitoring, while cat- and dog-focused rescue groups can be staffed and run by volunteers with less training and expertise. Technical expertise is also more important for groups that manage large animals such as horses and cows. The issues related to wildlife loss and trauma of personnel responding to wildlife rescue are an interesting area of research, particularly in the context of the 2020 Australian wildfires. Again, we emphasize that climate change is associated with increases in severe weather events, longer and more severe fire seasons, and more intense hurricanes. Therefore, we should consider whether corporate entities and other actors who increase greenhouse gases should face accountability for the mass deaths of animals in wildfire and other hazard events (Lynch, Burns, and Stretesky 2010).

Conclusion

In this chapter we describe animal suffering, criminal activity, and animal welfare in the context of disasters. The core issues should be considered in the context of the other chapters in this book because this provides a broader picture of how the social landscape unfolds to contribute to or minimize animal abuse and neglect in disasters. We describe how various individuals and groups can make poor decisions in disasters or intentional decisions that lead to increased suffering or deaths of animals. Historical context is also important, because some of the situations and issues we observe in the United States are unique and may manifest differently in future disasters or in disasters outside the United States. Coordination among local, state, and federal actors can minimize instances of animal neglect, especially with implementation of animal welfare outreach and education before and after disasters. We also discuss the broad range of criminal, illegal, and ethical considerations of who causes harm to animals and the laws that do or should govern the protection of animals. In regard to climate change and extreme events, the wrongdoers are less concrete. However, this does not mean that a plan of reduction and accountability for human-induced climate change is outside the realm of animal welfare. This will likely become a more salient issue for stakeholders in emergency management and animal advocacy alike as disasters continue to cause mass harm and loss of life.

#LostDog

*Using Social Media for Reunification
and Coalition Building*

During Hurricane Florence, a dog sanctuary in eastern North Carolina posted a call on Twitter that requested people to come pick up dogs for the week so that there would be space for the incoming dogs from the coast. The organization, Saving Grace, successfully sent two hundred dogs home with families for that week, and seventy dogs were adopted.

The image on Twitter of people lining up to foster dogs as the hurricane approached went viral. It appeared in national news stories throughout the United States and on multiple social-media forums. The success of animal adoption to make room for animals from coastal shelters is an example of using social media for a clear objective (rapid adoption) during a hurricane. There were, of course, some less-than-heartwarming details that unfolded after Saving Grace's Hurricane Florence fostering success. Some people who showed up to foster or adopt dogs said that they wanted a "Hurricane Florence dog" and were disappointed that the dogs in the sanctuary at the time were not the dogs who were "swimming through flooded waters," as one volunteer at Saving Grace described when we visited the sanctuary. Yet the model of "foster a pup" for the week or weekend worked well because this freed up space at the brick-and-mortar shelter for dogs coming in from the coast. The strategy of moving animals out of a disaster zone is not new; animal adoption groups often transport dogs from southern to northern states after major disasters. What is unique and innovative about Saving Grace's approach is that it combined the foster strategy with the power of social media. By using social media, fosters showed up quickly and in great numbers.

In 2017 and 2018, California experienced some of the deadliest wildfires in state history. "Fire cat" groups emerged at this time, and most of their operations were through social media. One person we interviewed described how she started rescuing animals with her mother and then started helping others look for lost cats. Other people started hearing about them through word of mouth and wanted to help:

> They asked how they could help, and it was very unorganized, and it was we're all self-starters, and we took it and ran. And they were amazing. . . . The entire thing was organized through social media [through Facebook]. . . . Well, . . . there was a group that posted lost-and-found pictures, and they did matching. There was no rescue involved, and it was an online group. When I started doing that, some of those people decided to break off from that group [to do] rescue and reunification, which was both in the matching team and the field team, so that's where that relationship was born.

Social media allows for online coordination of "real life," on-the-ground efforts for saving animals in disasters. For example, this volunteer indicated that she used Zello (a radio communication app) and Twitter:

> I am a volunteer with [a rescue organization]. We were the original remote volunteer organization to help in disasters and organized loosely after Hurricane Harvey. We have a number of emergency professionals on our team, rely primarily on Zello and Twitter during evacuation phase/rescue events, and coordinate with groups and individuals on the ground.

In 2010 when more than 125,000 people died in the Haiti earthquake, some people tweeted their harrowing experiences. Social media facilitated rescues, donation drives, and recovery efforts. While people in disaster research often credit the Haiti earthquake as the beginning of major social-media involvement, the animal rescue network—even outside disaster response—has exploded over the past decade in social media. While there is no official count, nearly every U.S. region, city, and county has a "pets page" on Facebook. Social media has changed the framework of research, scientific communication, marketing, nonprofit management, and emergency management. While research on risk communication and social media is burgeoning (e.g., Sutton et al. 2013), there is a scarcity of research on social media and animals in disasters. Although most of our data is from primary interviews with people in the field and web surveys (evacuees as well as program coordinators), we also saved and archived social-media posts from Hurricane Harvey to Hurricane Dorian. Not only did these posts guide us to important fieldwork locations, but their content also provides important information about sentiments, perspectives, challenges, and tools created in social media.

As we were writing this chapter, Hurricane Dorian (August 31, 2019) was in the Atlantic Ocean and projected to move along the Florida coast as a major-category hurricane and turn toward the Carolinas, as Hurricane Matthew did in 2016. Posts from the American Humane Society and other organizations ran ads for keeping animals safe in disasters. Some of the ads are designed as information campaigns (i.e., what to do to keep your pets safe). Many are strategically timed because as social-media users search and follow #Dorian, they are also linked to the organizations doing animal rescue work—in short, they may be more likely to make a donation. In this way, social media is becoming essential to the sustainability of an organization's programs. After the disaster passes and audience attention fades, organizations need to maintain financial momentum, a volunteer base, and branding. Nonprofits are not the only groups recognizing this, as local emergency managers, researchers, and a broad range of actors use social media throughout all phases of a disaster.

In researching how people make decisions for evacuating their animals and how program coordinators manage their organizations to operate animal rescue in disasters, we made use of the many on-the-ground issues illustrated and introduced through images and narratives available on social media. In fact, most of our major leads for research fieldwork and face-to-face interviews came from Facebook, either through people viewing our research page and reaching out to us or through our advertising our study in relevant groups. For example, Shannon Jay, "the cat trapper," became famous through sharing his videos and efforts of trapping fire cats online—first with the Tubbs Fire in 2017 and then the Camp Fire in 2018. His video featured on the Dodo (a website that shares emotionally compelling animal-related videos and stories) included clips of searching for cats under charred trucks in the scorched landscape of Paradise. The video depicts Shannon painstakingly using a car jack to lift a truck to free a wounded and starving cat meowing underneath. Finally able to reach the cat after the truck was lifted, Shannon artfully grabbed the cat by the scruff and quickly shoved it into a carrier. Volunteers scanned the cat for a microchip, took it for veterinary treatment, and entered it into foster care. After watching this video, Sarah sent a Facebook message to Shannon to learn more about his work. Within moments he responded. He was still trapping fire cats in Paradise in March 2019 when Sarah and her students arrived in Chico and Paradise.

When we talked to Shannon, he explained that even though his fame had grown on social media, his credentials as a law enforcement officer also assisted in his ease of entry into Paradise during the weeks in which residents were not allowed to return to their homes.

The online groups are highly interactive and dynamic. Another volunteer in Paradise with Camp Fire Pets and Reunification indicated that most of the group's work and efforts were coordinated through social media and that most of the core functions of organizing information about pets was conducted by a small group of women who banded together after the Tubbs Fire. Similarly, the Hawaii Lava Flow Animal Rescue Network was based on Facebook and drove donation efforts and logistics from Hilo to Kona for transport of supplies for pets and people evacuated from the lava flows. When Sarah interviewed a volunteer in Hawaii, she learned that a small group of women ran the group. These groups essentially divided tasks and delegated roles so that the Facebook page was a key hub for information during the disaster. During Hurricane Florence, a group that staged pet-supply intake and intake of pets at the North Carolina State Fairground also facilitated most of its requests for donations and volunteers through Facebook. Similarly, during Hurricane Harvey, local groups and national groups alike used social media to direct evacuees to find pet-friendly sheltering, to post photos of lost pets, to share photos of stranded animals, and to post updates and urgent need requests.

Most of the groups formed during disasters that are dedicated to animal response are run by a combination of people with different roles, from information volunteers to experts in animal rescue (including veterinarians, vet techs, and emergency responders). The groups vary in size, scope, and mission. Many of the social-media groups, such as Hurricane Harvey All Lost and Found Pets, focus mainly on reuniting pets with owners. Some groups also focus on sharing messages and information about pet-friendly sheltering during the onset of the disaster. The mission and scope of the group often depend on the forum—that is, groups on Facebook may have a different approach than a Twitter account focused on animal issues in disasters—while some groups have a presence in multiple forums. Many of our examples in this chapter focus on Facebook because numerous groups we interviewed across the seven disasters indicate that Facebook was their most valuable tool for communication and logistics. Of course, negative aspects of social media include rumors, fraudulent solicitation for donation funds, and group "drama." In this chapter, we specifically explain how some group conflict and tension can be amplified on social media.

Qualms, suspicions, and tangible setbacks are created or exacerbated by social media. As one equine program coordinator mentioned after Hurricane Florence:

I don't know that for sure, but there's social media, and then there are the individuals, local drives—like, call Joe Schmo's feed and seed store, give him fifty bucks, and we'll go pick up the feed—and stuff like that. That's the kind of thing, I think it's good, but you better be darn careful who you contribute to, or it might just be filling somebody's pocket. We don't have any way to verify that stuff.

In Chapter 3, we describe some of these suspicions related to fraudulent activities associated with online groups. However, our goal is not to describe social media and animals in disasters through a valence of "good" or "bad" but rather the ways in which social media affects the social landscape of pets in disasters, and vice versa. As practitioners in emergency management know, social media is a tool for organizations. The utility of social media is not without its downside. FEMA has an entire page dedicated to rumor control during disasters. Social media makes it easier to spread misinformation faster and to more people, which can be dangerous because the content that people see on social media can influence actual decision-making about sheltering, spread false information about people or groups, or spread false medical and scientific information. We describe the most interesting examples of using social media in disasters before and during hazards, the ways that groups shift in role and type through their leveraging and use of social media, and the pros and cons of social media. Some of these pros and cons are more specific to groups in disasters in general, and some are more connected with the characteristics of the hazard and its geographic context.

Before the Disaster

During our deployment for Hurricane Harvey in multiple areas of Texas we began to hear about the critical role of social media in coordinating, communicating, and planning for animals in disasters. During our fieldwork, we learned that nearly all information disseminated to and from the community flowed through Facebook during Hurricane Harvey, as indicated in this conversation we had with shelter coordinators:

INTERVIEWER: How did people find out about the fact that they could bring their animals here?

INTERVIEWEE 2: Just mostly we posted it on Facebook. And . . . a lot of people were calling, saying, "I don't know what to do; my house flooded, and I have this dog, and I don't know what to do. Can you help me?" And we said, yeah, we can hold her.

INTERVIEWEE 1: Social media, or the human shelters too; we had a relationship with them. So that was helpful too. They would tell us stories; like when we would drop off stuff, they would give us updates on the animals and what they needed.

While Hurricane Dorian was churning in the Atlantic in late August 2019, public officials used news media to share warnings about consequences for leaving pets behind. While the story was published in a local news outlet, the story circulated through social media regarding mandatory evacuations in Brevard County, Florida: "'If you dump your pet off out on the side of the road, I'm personally going to walk your butt into our jail. So don't do it,' [Sheriff Wayne] Ivey said" (Neale 2019). It is likely that Sherriff Ivey was recalling Hurricane Irma, in which numerous reports circulated of people leaving pets on the side of the road.

The before-the-storm time frame is also associated with social milling on social media (Drabek 2018). This means that people use social media to check to see what others are doing before deciding about evacuating. If friends and peers are posting pictures of preparations for evacuation, this decision may have a contagious effect. While it is unclear if there is an impact from the warnings such as the one from Sherriff Ivey on these decisions, it is clear that the before-the-hazard phase can also be used to encourage people to follow accurate and timely sources that will be likely to communicate options for pet-friendly sheltering.

During the Disaster

Many people used social media to gather information both before and during the event. During the Camp Fire in Paradise, one evacuee indicated that social-media information was confusing as the fires approached her house:

> There's, like, a lot of conflicting stuff on Facebook. . . . They didn't really have a lot of new information either—just that there was a fire near Paradise—so we called. I called the nonemergency line for the police department, and they told me that there [were] only two [zones evacuating].

The zones evacuating did not include hers. However, ash started falling from the sky, so she decided to evacuate. While she started social milling by checking Facebook and then checking with the police department, she ultimately used environmental cues to make the decision. Volunteers can also use social media to find animals that need rescue; for example, the pit bull discussed earlier that was rescued from someone's backyard was discovered through Facebook by a shelter coordinator we interviewed:

There were neighbors taking pictures, on Facebook, and tagging rescues: "Who can come?" Nobody—you know, stuff is flying; there is a hurricane situation. Who's going to leave the house and go rescue a tied-up dog? So I went when I could. I didn't go the same day. I went the next day, when it was a little bit calmed down. Because, luckily, we were brushed; it didn't go right through us right here, but it was still dangerous. So I went the next day, and it took me forever to find her because people didn't want to release the location because, apparently, the people who owned the pit bull were very conflictive, and they didn't—they were scared.

In this way, social media was a way to try to coordinate the rescue of the dog without involving official channels of emergency support. This makes the rescues more complex because it is unclear which protocols should be implemented and to what extent volunteers place themselves at risk trying to carry out the rescue. The use of social media in this way can also be beneficial because it enables unofficial groups to organize, with or without the official permission of government. During the 2018 Camp Fire in California, Butte County Emergency Management selected key groups to liaise for animal evacuation. Because some of the lead groups that were working closely with Butte County were perceived to operate heavily on command and control, several emergent groups formed a coalition with smaller official nonprofits to essentially combat failures related to the communication barriers and tension among response groups in Paradise. A member of one of these emergent groups told us, "It's not just that this particular fire. . . . County doesn't want us here." When we asked, "Why do you think that is?," she said, "I'm not going to speculate [*laughs*]. . . . We are not welcome here. And we're highly successful, and I don't know if it's loss of face. I don't know if it has to do with funding. I don't know if it's a power play."

In this way, social media can be a tool for groups to manage workarounds when other groups are wielding power to maintain control of the disaster zone. In fact, for some groups such as Houston-based CrowdSource Rescue (CSR), social media is the main way that dispatchers communicate with one another to verify posts, tickets, and information. CSR rescues people for its missions but also tracks tickets of pet rescues. Finally, groups also use social media for donation requests during the hazard event. When asked for their sense of how most people who are doing equine rescue manage the donations, one respondent answered that it was mainly through social media.

While the requests continue after the event, the imagery from the response phase is more likely to go viral during donation requests. The images of cats and dogs pulled from floodwaters or an ashy landscape are often captioned with links for "how to help," that is, where to donate. During Hurricane Florence, this program coordinator indicated that horse rescue networks used social media during the hurricane to send and coordinate requests for hay, transport, and other needs. Additionally, during Hurricanes Harvey and Irma, program coordinators indicated that social media was key for tracking and managing animals, as described by a volunteer with a nongovernmental organization:

> We used *every* means we could, and then we had an online spreadsheet, so people knew where *all* the animals were kept from Harvey. This way we could check to see who was in need and who was not. Since I was helping with the entire affected area, I could send volunteers from one shelter in need to another with excess [supplies] to gather what was necessary. We were also able to coordinate supplies and volunteers better using Facebook pages and Twitter to organize.

In Hawaii, local shelters also created spreadsheets that coordinated available fosters with animals and groups that had needs. For example, if a large farm had extra space for goats, sheep, or other animals, it could add its name and contact information to the spreadsheet. Animals as small as hamsters and fish were also part of the request list. Most of these efforts were through coordination with the Hawaii Lava Flow Animal Rescue Network and the Hawaii Humane Society.

After the Disaster

After hurricanes and wildfires, people use social media for reuniting lost pets with their owners, transporting and managing pets for adoption, memorializing pets and grieving, and making sense of the event. Reuniting pets and owners can begin during the event and last for months or even years afterward. After the Camp Fire, some cats were reunited with their owners six, seven, and eight months after the fire. Social groups often form specifically to facilitate reuniting pets with families. For example, in the Camp Fire, volunteers and residents of Paradise and surrounding areas frequently cited social media as key for reuniting lost pets with owners, as one volunteer told us:

> Social media played a huge role in reunifying pets and owners. When I returned to my property two months after the fire, I found a cat. Posted him on Facebook, and the post was shared many, many times. Found his owners and reunified him in twenty-four hours!

Also, I know that updated microchips linked to cell phones played a big role in reuniting pets and owners.

In response to our question, "What in your opinion worked well in this event?," several people commented that social media facilitated success: "All the Facebook updates and pics people have been posting. And how many people are out there messing [setting up food stations] and helping those whose pets were lost."

Efforts for reuniting pets was most striking with the cat matchers after the Paradise Fire. Dogs were also among the missing pets, but because cats were more likely to be already outside or more difficult to catch in the hours and minutes leading up to the evacuation, they were more likely to be missing after the fire. There was also a higher number of cats in Paradise before the fire (partly a result of the lack of spay and neuter infrastructure). The intriguing aspect of cat matchers is that they can operate from anywhere in the country. There were two main database pages: one of lost cats and one of found cats. Cat matchers painstakingly search the images to locate cats for reunification, which can be quite time-consuming. Imagine having a missing tuxedo (black-and-white) cat from the Camp Fire. When a "found" picture is uploaded to the database of a cat brought in by trappers, volunteers need to see if there is a missing cat who has the exact pattern as the found cat. This becomes more difficult when owners have outdated pictures of their lost cat. Additionally, cats from the burn zone in the days and weeks after the fire may have sustained injuries that made them less recognizable.

After fires and hurricanes, timing is important for adoption efforts because there can be conflict about who the owner of the animal is and, if adoptions happen without efforts to locate the original owner, conflict can also arise. In Miami-Dade County, two of the program coordinators we spoke with indicated that in one instance dogs were left in an evacuation zone and then reclaimed by the original owner. Individuals had taken the dogs with the intent to save them because they were left behind and deemed to be abandoned, but then the original owners wanted them back. This is strikingly similar to the conflict we heard about over Belle the pig, adopted by a family living in eastern North Carolina. The sanctuary owners saw that the adoptive family evacuated without the pig from a post on Facebook, which prompted them to rescue her.

Again, adoptions often occur across state lines. Pets flown from Florida, Texas, and the Carolinas were sent for adoption by coordinating agencies in Delaware, New York, New Jersey, Maine, and other states. The rationale seems to be that it makes sense to shift animals from states with pet overpopulation issues. Headlines highlighting these adoptions use the "Hurricane Animals" tagline. Social-media posts of these "hurricane" animals

"Cat matching" computers in Paradise, California, after the Camp Fire.

make their adoption more likely. Sadly, hundreds of animals die in local shelters throughout the country daily, animals without the flashy "disaster" tagline.

Memorials after the Event

Online groups dedicated to mourning pets after disasters serve as collective memorial space for people who lost pets. This happened after the Paradise Camp Fire, and weeks and months after the fire people posted images of and stories or information about their pets. The posts in the mourning group are similar to an obituary: an image of the pet and a description of how the pet lived and died (if there was confirmation of remains). Often images are shown with depictions and illustrations of rainbows, as rainbows have come to be synonymous with heaven or the afterlife for pets. We noticed evidence of volunteer burnout on these pages, as many of those posting memorials were still actively searching for their own cat in addition to other cats—months and even years after the disaster. Some reunion stories were reported in the news, but the contrasting silence of those still searching caused a great deal of pain. The memorial pages also serve as a place where people can connect and share their stories to feel less alone in their experience and a place for building a sense of community and collective solidarity. Many people in these groups share condolences, words of prayer, and other words of concern. We noticed that there was not a strong presence of formal outreach for mental health resources for the people who lost pets, though it may have been carried out in the days and weeks immediately after the disaster through face-to-face support services.

Some of these memorials are larger in scale and symbolic in nature, such as a 2013 cartoon by Gary Varvel of Smokey Bear mourning with wildlife after a fire. The image invokes a sense of patriotism, as Smokey Bear is a well-known symbol of national parks in America. In this way, the production, posting, and sharing of these images serve to validate how people outside the disaster identify with the affected communities. Few topics seem to do this more effectively than pets and animals in disasters. Also, after the 2020 Australia bushfires, there were global efforts to raise money to assist organizations responding to the massive loss of wildlife.

Types of Organizations and Social Media

The online convergence of various animal welfare and rescue groups through social media can become a hindrance or be extremely helpful, depending on whom you ask. Organizations can either maintain or alter various tasks in the aftermath of a disaster, while new organizations emerge. Various new groups have formed in the aftermath of disasters in online spaces only, creating a virtual presence where volunteers, rescue teams, and evacuees can connect and share information. The reasons for the emergence of these online groups align with the organizational typology of disasters.

The Disaster Research Center typology developed by Russell Dynes (1970) conceptualizes how various organizations work and adapt in responding to disasters. The four types of organized behaviors are based on the tasks and structure of those organizations: established groups (Type I), expanding groups (Type II), extending groups (Type III), and emergent groups (Type IV). Established groups exist before the disaster and can incorporate disaster planning and preparedness; therefore, they remain unchanged for the most part in carrying out regular tasks within their existing structure. Expanding groups grow larger and take on new tasks during and after a disaster, which can often happen by bringing in new volunteers. Extending groups also existed before the disaster but did not necessarily plan for all the tasks they become involved with during the disaster, which pertains to structural changes within the group. Emergent groups form on an ad hoc basis during and after an event and often focus on tasks not led by other more-established groups. These new groups have identified a need that has been previously overlooked so take on the task. These groups are more spontaneous and most closely align with the online groups created to deal with specific challenges after a disaster.

After Hurricane Harvey, many pet-specific emergent groups surfaced on social media, particularly Facebook. Their roles after the disaster shifted in some cases but focused on issues such as reunification of pets with owners, including lost and found animals; calls for supplies and donations; and posts for volunteers. One program coordinator explained how social-media groups began to be used:

> The response to this one [Hurricane Harvey] afterwards was so much better. I think social media had a lot to do with it. I think just awareness of animal issues has a lot to do with it. That people weren't—that wasn't a focus before. That was an afterthought; animals were always an afterthought. Oh, and what about the animals too, you know?

Individuals and groups began to realize that pets had been a secondary consideration after disasters. Once identified as an issue that needed attention, either for reuniting animals and owners or garnering resources that were needed within communities, groups emerged on social-media pages to fulfill this need. Facebook was a common social network to place these groups because it allowed for fast access and information sharing. The initial reasons for the creation of the online groups is important too. Many of the groups focused their tasks on pet reunification and became an online space where photos of both lost and found pets could be posted. After the Kilauea lava flows began in 2018, a Facebook page emerged dedicated to reuniting pets and owners and immediately began sharing photos and information. Now this group has a broader focus on animal rescue and is an expanding rather than an emergent group (Matheny, DeYoung, and Farmer 2020).

Emergent online groups with social-media pages dedicated to pets and disasters grow and change frequently. Groups also rebranded after disasters but kept the same core following of people. For instance, the Tubbs Fire in California was the initial focus of a social-media group, but after the Camp Fire, the group changed its name to Camp Fire Pet Rescue and Reunification to shift the focus to locating animals displaced by the more recent disaster. This happened after Hurricane Florence as well, when pets' groups renamed social-media pages from the formerly "Hurricane Matthew Pets" to refocus attention on the most current hazard. The group associated with the Camp Fire was initially started and organized entirely through social media on Facebook. When it began with the 2017 wildfire in California, the group posted pictures of lost and found pets so volunteers could identify pet owners. They did so because official rescue efforts for reunification seemed to be unorganized. The organizational aspects of the group took place entirely online and focused almost exclusively on matching rather than field rescue. Through later wildfires, the mission of the group changed to focus more on rescue (in addition to reunification), and tasks shifted as well. One of the volunteers managing the social-media page told us how this further developed: "And then I have my subteams, my camera teams, my feeding teams, my trapping teams, and my supply teams, and then she's got, like, all her matchers and coordinating, dealing with databases."

Thus, one of the online groups that emerged in the aftermath of the wildfires then shifted focus as more and more people became involved. As she continued to speak about the group's goals and purpose, the founder explained the need for an online presence:

> For owners, they need one place to look online, when you have so many multiple Facebook groups and owners have to go all over the place. Same thing with shelters [*pauses*]. I mean it was horrible. Owners to just be sent from shelter to shelter to shelter, and they're right after the fire. They're already devastated, overwhelmed, and they have no place to live. And yet they're spending hours on all these shelters. That's got to change [*pauses*] and animals were lost. So unifying to find some way to unify the response . . . until the counties change their policies where they take ownership of animal recovery after disasters—and they're really great about working right after the disaster, but as soon as that few weeks is up, back to business as usual. And there are thousands of animals still missing.

Here she identifies that a major challenge was long-term searching for missing pets. Therefore, the online group had this initial challenge in mind. As other wildfires occurred, the group would change the name of the Facebook page to align with the most recent fire. The founder explained that this was necessary so they would have cats just from that fire. For the purposes of aiding reunification, page visitors had to know which fire the photos posted of lost and found cats related to and the location where each cat was found.

Emergent social-media groups expanded by shifting their tasks and even structure after a disaster, either by identifying other disasters where there were challenges or changing focus to animal rescue more broadly. In multiple types of hazards—hurricanes, wildfires, and other events—groups learned lessons from past disasters while often maintaining the same core group of individuals as leaders and volunteers. This strategy is potentially useful not only in animal rescue work but also in other disaster response and recovery efforts. Indeed, there are other social-media group pages dedicated to disaster survivors based in one geographic location or event. However, the animal group typologies are particularly interesting because of their visibility, program sustainability, and project management.

The Pros and Cons of Social Media for Communication after Disasters

The Pros

Attention-grabbing information shared multiple times across social-media platforms can be extremely useful in communicating about pets after disasters. This can go a long way toward gathering donations, resources, and volunteers. For example, after Hurricane Harvey one program coordinator of a fostering and rescue organization mentioned the benefits of social media to share resources:

> During the storm, we had a human distribution center for people who needed bleach and stuff like that. We were able to donate some of that stuff to them to give to people who needed it. And then we had Facebook posts everywhere: "If you need supplies or anything for your animals, don't surrender them. Come get supplies from us."

Facebook posts in online groups were a primary way to share information quickly, especially in this case of sharing donations. Some organizations can become inundated with supplies for pets, including dog and cat food, litter, bedding, treats, toys, and various other gifts. Therefore, this group was able to use social media to share donations with the community. Their message about not surrendering animals is important contextual information too. With various stressors after a disaster, families may not think they can care for their pets if they do not have the necessary supplies and no way to get those supplies. This group made it a point to let families know that they could keep taking care of their pets through these donations.

Sharing information online about supplies and resources was one component used by several groups on social media. For instance, various other organizations were able to use Facebook pages to specify which donations were needed. As another program coordinator told us after Hurricane Florence, they would post on the Facebook page, "Right now, we need fans." Various people brought fans, after which they would post again: "We no longer need this."

Another positive was general awareness of the extent of issues with pets in disasters. The program managers who shared supplies also noted how sharing on social media increased general attention: "I think . . . that social media made a big difference for this one [Hurricane Harvey], in comparison. Seeing pictures and things like that made people—I guess that makes people aware. Instant information." Having this instant access to information, especially as the rescue and recovery are still ongoing after a disaster, does raise awareness in the general population. People share photos on social media after disasters that show cats swimming across flooded roads, wildlife running from forests engulfed in flames, and owners embracing their beloved dogs they thought had perished in floodwaters. A program coordinator compared more recent hurricanes with past disasters, explaining that they were different:

> I also think, again, social media [is important] because you're seeing these sad stories of people not leaving. Before, you just kind of hear rumors. Like with [Hurricane] Katrina you heard rumors of people not leaving, but you never actually saw it. You know, people not leaving because they didn't want to leave their animals. Or stuck in a dome with all these animals and no food and water for them. So I think that made a big difference too.

These images tell us many things about issues with animals in disasters, but they also garner attention and, as a result, get the public talking about how to better address those challenges. The power of social media is that people want to take action when they see images of animals suffering in disasters.

Recruitment through social media is an important factor in being able to manage large operations. After Hurricane Florence, one organization saw around 250 volunteers respond to their relief hub on the first day. Many of those volunteers found out about the organization through the Facebook page. Volunteers came to the staging area where found pets were dropped off and then were given the task of helping oversee animal care throughout the day.

Other times frustration caused people to unite to create a Facebook group, particularly because they wanted to mitigate confusing or incorrect information during the disaster. One respondent told us:

> I was just tired of the misinformation out there. So I just called up a friend and said, "Let's start a Facebook page that everyone can go to and get the correct information" because it was just flying out everywhere, and half of it was wrong. Just like where dogs were, what was

> going on, when they were even arriving, how many, just—yeah, I
> can't remember—where we were gonna be, what staging location. So
> she set it up, and then somebody else came later, which was wonder-
> ful, and we started getting volunteers. It was a full-time job. We
> started to have a volunteer just sitting there answering question after
> question [on social media]. But it was a great way to communicate
> and get people seeing the right information of what was going on,
> what we need at any given time.

As this program coordinator mentioned, their social-media page was designed to set the record straight on where the staging area for pets would
be. While other media sources might eventually share this type of information as well, the benefits of having social-media pages is that information can be shared quickly, in real time, with fast responses to questions
for clarification, and the information stays there for whoever needs to find
it at any time. People who are at the staging areas manage the pages, and
they can provide updated information about urgent needs and the situation. For example, they can see if there is an obvious lack of supplies, such
as kennels or flea medicine. They can also post information about what
they have in abundance to distribute to other groups or members of the
community.

Reunification through social-media groups is also a positive feature of
online sharing. Organizations could quickly and easily share photographs,
noting identifying features and the rescue location. Some of these online
groups worked extremely hard at "matching"—that is, sorting through information on lost pets in an attempt to find the owners of found pets that
had been rescued. As previously mentioned, long-term reunification efforts
remain, although many of the social-media groups that emerged immediately after disasters still exist after the disaster response and recovery, which
enables them to reactivate and remobilize in another disaster. Unfortunately, many areas in the United States prone to wildfires or hurricanes
experience repeated events, so it is useful to have a space online for mobiliz-
ing again.

The Cons

While social-media groups have positive features, there are also downsides.
Many groups were created to help with reunification; however, this meant
an overabundance of various animal groups and the potential for oversatu-
ration or duplication of information. As one program coordinator described:

My major concern was—in the back of my mind, as things were happening—that we wanted to reunite these pets with their owners. Somewhere, there are some people that are going to miss this pet, and we want to—to me, it was making sure that they were properly identified, that we got them their pictures on social media, that there was a central [online site]. . . . We did a Hurricane Harvey website, and that just didn't work because everybody did a Hurricane Harvey website. So we were trying to find a central place to post them all.

The comment that "everyone" did a Hurricane Harvey website was a recurring comment from our respondents. Many groups had the same idea of sharing information on social media. However, this meant that there were numerous online groups, some of them sharing exactly the same information, but people were on their own to sort through that information for what was pertinent.

Another problem is that some people are not on social media. For online groups, there is no way to reach those pet owners, even though the animal likely had an owner actively searching for it and concerned for its well-being. While there are demographic factors that one might expect in how evacuees might consume information, other factors related to the disaster need to be considered. For example, while many senior citizens do not navigate social media, many evacuees might be in a position in which they cannot access anything else for information. One interviewee described this conversation with local emergency management:

She said, well, we're having so much trouble with social media; we're just not using it. We've got ads running on every TV station over here on the coast. I'm sorry, on TV? We're talking about people that don't have power. Where do you think they're going to try to get their help?

This highlights how problematic information sharing can become after a disaster, especially when choosing venues on where to give out information so that it has the widest impact. Online accessibility is a remaining problem, as is sharing information only on television. Another group told us that because of issues with access to social media, they "went old school" and did a bulk mailer with more than twenty-seven thousand items about displaced disaster pets. The mailer included a phone number and information for a website to post photos of lost and found pets.

Some issues with online social-media groups were associated with organizational structure and leadership. For instance, some volunteers said that group leadership lacked clear goals, while other organizations seemed skeptical of forming partnerships, which eroded community trust. This was especially true if there had been negative experiences in the past (in previous disasters) or if the groups in charge of response lacked technical expertise necessary to work in animal rescue. Regarding equine rescue, one person who worked for a rescue organization told us:

> I believe that the self-deployed cavalry situation is out of control. Social media is, again, wonderful and horrible. The networking abilities are great; the fraudulent aspects are unbelievable for hooking folks up with the wrong people. The inexperienced people going out—we're the such-and-such cavalry or whatever and we're gonna come help you, and one or two rounds of, in years past, of trying to let people connect with that. Please don't help me anymore.

Her perceptions were based on past experiences that many volunteers come in after a disaster recruited through social media and then participate in animal rescue that would typically require more technical training and expertise. She went on to describe how this pertains to the use of social media:

> There needs to be some way to indicate the certified disaster response teams that have actual FEMA training and those who do not. And those groups need to somehow identify themselves when they're on social media for proper sharing. They need to put watermarks on their pictures; they need to put banners on their videos, because I can point you to three or four different videos that have been shared thousands of times in the past month. You know the one they call the "porch ponies," and any idea how many different groups took credit for that rescue [on social media]?

The "porch ponies" she described were a group of horses that someone rescued from a porch surrounded by floodwater in Hurricane Florence. The respondent indicated that multiple groups took credit for rescuing the horses in the viral video. Erosion of trust in this instance is based on her experiences with other groups stealing photos and videos on social media from legitimate organizations and taking credit for it. This affected her work and fund-raising as well. She said she would "never touch GoFundMe" as part of the fund-raising process. She would not ask anybody to donate anywhere unless she was able to establish the legitimacy of the 501(c)(3). Instead, she has asked her own friends through social media to help with various efforts and donations. She took her own advice and put watermarks of logos on all the photos that she posted. While forgers could get around this, it would be more difficult for them, especially if a watermark is centered on a photograph. She went on to explain that in many cases, social media may create additional problems, especially by the county emergency management:

> Social media, inappropriate sharing, and all that is a huge problem, but it does somehow have to be managed, not ignored and, yes, even by the county offices. They can't just pretend it's not there, or well, they can; I mean, they are, a lot of them are, but they're not going to solve the problem that way; nor are they going to reach the people they wanna reach. . . . I mean, there's got to be a way that people can validate these groups. I don't pretend to have that answer. Now, at the other end of that equation, if you go back far enough on [a Facebook page], you'll see me posting something like, okay, I just got off the phone with county emergency management. They got so disgusted with this stuff, they refused to post anything more on social media, so where are they going?

Realistically, even with these hurdles to overcome, she continues, "As frustrating as Facebook or whatever is, I'm sorry, it's here to stay. You've gotta learn to work with it somehow, and there's got to be a way to validate this stuff."

Additional issues identified by people we spoke with about social-media groups are accessibility and concerns about where to share information when there are numerous groups with the same purpose. Another issue was concern with lack of organizational goals and lack of trust with various organizations pilfering photos from other groups, which leads to broader issues of trust among animal rescue organizations. Better coordination of online groups and having a central point of information sharing could build better networks for communication in pet and animal rescue after disasters. Furthermore, formal organizations could become more flexible in learning about critical information from the ad hoc online groups. Even though these groups are not perfect, people who are geographically close or directly affected by the hazard are running the ad hoc online groups. Therefore, their level of situational awareness is critical to larger formal groups arriving from outside the disaster area to assist with response. Informal and improvised efforts can lead to the rescue of thousands of people (Kendra and Wachtendorf 2016), and this can be true for animal rescue efforts as well.

Conclusion

One of the main reasons we launched this research project is that it was clear that the landscape of pets and animals in disasters has changed since

Leslie Irvine's book was published in 2009, and one of the biggest changes is that social media creates a space for animal welfare advocates, experts, community members, emergency managers, and other actors to communicate, share information, and coordinate during and after disasters. As the last respondent in this chapter mentioned, social media is likely here to stay. It is important to continue engaging in new research that seeks to understand the effect that social media has on group mobilization and communication, and vice versa. Anyone who has a Twitter, Facebook, or Instagram account is aware of the speed at which information can travel online. Viral posts are common in disasters—some with inaccurate or even nefarious intentions. However, based on our data and observations, social media can also be a powerful tool for groups to manage rescue and recovery.

5

A Mile through Waist-Deep Water

Poverty, Privilege, and Pets in Disasters

n February 2017, the Oroville Dam in Oroville, California, had to be evacuated because the dam was at risk of failing. Almost two hundred thousand people evacuated, and many people had no place to bring their animals. One respondent described the situation:

> One thing is that if people have to evacuate—we went to our friend's house initially and stayed there, at a friend's house. And they have two dogs; we have four dogs. There was three of them, three of us. And so, all those dogs. . . . If people have to evacuate to a shelter, they have to be able to have their animals taken care of. . . . And some people can't be separated from their animals; it's too much. And you know the flood that happened here in Oroville? Like Valentine's Day before? Another nurse friend of mine went down to the fairgrounds where people were evacuated, because a lot of our patients that live in lower Oroville were evacuated there, and I found a woman living in her car with her cat, and it was . . . hot, but she said, you know, she couldn't take her cat in, so she just was living in her car with her cat. And, uh, so I was kind of saying, "What can we do for you?" And she said, "I can't go in the shelter," and she doesn't want to.

This respondent was also an evacuee from the Camp Fire in 2018; her home was in Concow and burned to the ground. This example illustrates that people living in Northern California are vulnerable to multiple hazards and that pet ownership makes hazards more complex for the people living there. Lack of stable income and lack of economic resources can add an additional layer of challenges to evacuating with pets and finding a place to stay after disasters. Poverty and privilege also affect the ways in which organizations and outside groups view and shape the disaster narrative. While it seems obvious that poor families have a harder time with evacuation, there is a gap between this understanding and creating policies that bolster support systems for these families. Moreover, low-income residents may even face blame for their plight in regard to the fate of their animals in hazard scenarios (Reed, DeYoung, and Farmer 2020).

When we describe our research on pets in disasters, the response is generally enthusiastic and positive. People nod their heads, recount a story they read about in the news about animals in disasters, and quite often describe their own pets or animals. Nearly everyone has a pet or has had a pet at one time. Many people have an emotional attachment to their animals and view their pets as family members. While we as researchers and as pet owners knew this before our fieldwork, what we did not expect to find was the extent to which the issues surrounding pets in disasters reveal complexities about people and their social landscape.

Enrico Quarantelli (1988, 2005) describes disasters as opportunities to learn more about human behavior and social systems because researchers can observe and gather data on decisions that people make in crisis scenarios. What Quarantelli did not include in his early work was how the human and animal landscapes intersect in unique ways that provide new opportunities for understanding social systems. During disasters, there are unique circumstances under which the animal rescue subculture collides with emergency management, community members, emergent groups, and a myriad of actors. These circumstances highlight differential power held by those respective groups and actors.

A theme throughout all seven of the disasters for which we gathered data was that people who had access to resources had fewer challenges evacuating with their animals and that organizations with sustainable funding were also more successful in managing the complexities of evacuation, reuniting, and adopting companion animals affected by disasters. In this chapter we focus on the social landscape for the evacuees, including people who live in poverty, people who indicated some awareness of their privilege, and some who indicated no awareness or evaluation about the economic spectrum of actors involved in animal rescue. Some respondents shared comments or stories that hinted at prejudices, biases, and racism.

For example, when we asked for advice about key groups to contact in Port Arthur, some people indicated that we should "be careful going there" or "make sure you know someone there first" to stay safe. The population of

Port Arthur is 49 percent White and 39 percent African American, whereas the overall African American population in Texas is 11.9 percent (Census Reporter 2018b). When we visited Port Arthur, we interviewed residents in a community apartment complex in which Hurricane Harvey flooding destroyed all first-floor apartments. Few people mentioned their companion animals and instead talked about other urgent needs, such as the need for employment and transportation. Admittedly, standing in the middle of this community with our clipboards and meager retail gift cards as research incentives, we could not shake a sense of futility. We came to the community to ask people about challenges in evacuating with pets, when many of the people living there were in such dire straits that coming to ask questions about dogs and cats seemed somewhat irrelevant.

That is not to say that the people there do not care for or love their animals, but the most pressing and urgent needs that the families had in that apartment complex were not directly related to pets.[1] For example, one resident in Port Arthur explained that after the flooding from Hurricane Harvey, he walked along the railroad tracks, slightly elevated from the floodwaters, to get to a small grocer for infant formula, bread, and other supplies. During our interviews, we saw several free-roaming dogs, no cats, and many small children. One family explained that they had to consolidate households when people living on the lower floor sought shelter with families on the second and third floors. The U.S. Coast Guard evacuated one of our respondents who described bringing her dog onto the helicopter with her.

Disasters are challenging for everyone affected, but they are especially difficult for people who do not have enough resources for evacuation and recovery. Kirrilly Thompson and colleagues (2014) indicate that supporting vulnerable populations includes supporting people with their pets, especially low-income people, as one volunteer coordinator described after Hurricane Florence. When we asked one respondent if the disaster caused increased animal surrenders after the hurricane, she said, "Yeah. If you're looking at feeding your kids, and you don't have enough money anymore, you're homeless, what do you do with the animals?"

As noted in Chapter 1, one of the major limitations of the PETS Act is the inability of the legislation to enforce or outline specific funds for housing evacuees with pets beyond the acute phase of the disaster. When the fires in California or lava flows in Hawaii forced people from their homes, the only available rental options were vacation-style homes that have strict ordinances prohibiting pets. These direct circumstances make it more difficult for evacuees, but so do indirect circumstances such as job loss because of the disaster, which spirals low-income families into even more precarious situations. We explore these complexities from the household or individual perspective.

It is also important to understand how inequality affects issues, mission, and the overall culture of dealing with animals in disasters. While Leslie Irvine (2009) posed the question, "Do animals belong on the ark?," we begin with the presumption that, yes, they do, but how do people *manage* the ark? In examining the ways in which humans manage this process, we identify ways in which access to resources changed the processes, outcomes, and norms for the management of animals in disasters. One stark example is that while community members of Coffey Park, California, rallied together to create a physical site for information on missing pets and reunited pets, we did not observe similar instances in League City, Port Arthur, Beaumont, Miami, or Houston after Hurricanes Harvey and Maria. This does not mean that communities did not organize and engage in collective efforts for finding disaster pets in Texas and Florida, but the great differences in resources and time dedicated to California "fire cats" and "hurricane pets" is fascinating. We theorize that higher-income individuals in high-income communities had more time and resources to stage a more detailed reunification site.

Differences in access to resources unfolds throughout every phase of a disaster. For example, wealthier people do not use public shelters as their first choice for evacuation during a hurricane, but lower-income residents are more likely to evacuate to a public sheltering location (e.g., Mesa-Arango et al. 2012). For wealthier households, social networks are likely to be vast, their economic options for temporary lodging are broader, and their means for evacuation have fewer barriers. One obvious example is that relying on public transportation means planning carefully for getting to the departing bus with pets and other family members in tow. This also means that during the acute phase of the hazard, when a mandatory evacuation order is issued, lower-income residents are more likely to encounter sheltering barriers associated with their pets. While we have seen optimal examples of shelter colocation (e.g., during Hurricane Harvey), we often wondered about the animals that did not make it to the human colocated shelters. While there were instances of co-sheltering in Hurricane Harvey, there were also multiple media images of pets in flooded neighborhoods. We also noticed that there were considerably fewer cats than dogs in the colocated shelter.

People are commonly forced to leave animals behind during a rescue, which at times puts emergency managers and first responders at odds with animal welfare advocates and evacuees. However, during the acute phase of the disaster, the focus is on saving human lives. There is limited space on boats in flooded hurricane-affected areas. One notable issue is addressing who is responsible for saving pets and animals during disasters and evacuations. Pet owners are generally viewed as the first in line to keep their pets safe, but when they are forced to evacuate without them, the question becomes more complicated. Sebastian Heath and Robert Linnabary (2015) suggest that planning and identifying vulnerable groups through community-based approaches could help, while emergency managers could prompt evacuations by supplying carriers or leashes to people who do not have them. While increasing evacuation compliance could help with these issues, many pet owners will still be reluctant to leave pets behind during a rescue, especially if they lack other resources such as updated veterinary records and transport kennels.

Constructs of Race

The issues that arise regarding pets and disasters are also shaped by cultural perceptions and stereotypes. Social media reflects the sentiment and general assumption that people who carry out animal rescue are predominantly White, middle-class women. White women were more numerous in our data and observations. This led us to consider the various ways in which whiteness and privilege shape perceptions and the social landscape of animal rescue.

One narrative that we observed on social media about animals in disasters is that animals receive more attention in disasters than suffering humans—more specifically, people of color. The juxtaposition of animals and human welfare in disasters appears in instances in which the severely affected people are a minority community. For instance, this tweet, from @Maddie_Jones515, went viral in the spring of 2019: "Do White people know that the dogs in Flint don't have clean water either? Have we tried that approach?" The way that this tweet resonated with so many Twitter users reflects the sense that dogs receive more compassion than Black people living in Flint. Additionally, racism and stereotypes of humans become linked with animals. In this description of rescued pit bulls, Harlan Weaver describes how ideas about animal behavior are linked with ideas of whiteness:

> No longer partnered with "thugs," these hardworking canine citizens have been very publicly removed from their position as victims of abuse. Recoded as "unique individuals" with stories to tell and love to give, these dogs participate in families in ways that connect them to a tacit, normative whiteness. (2013, 698)

Weaver hints that the pit bulls are framed in a way that reproduces the White savior narrative (Maurantonio 2017) because they have been rescued by White people. Additionally, in this description, Weaver's inclusion of "unique individuals" is interesting because the dogs are awarded attributes denied to people of color when White people stereotype them (Roberts and Rizzo 2020).

Nuances of the social landscape of managing animals in disasters are important to understand the intersection of race, animal welfare, and disasters. Disasters disproportionately affect minority communities (Davies et al. 2018). Marginalized populations, in general, face increasingly severe disadvantages in the disaster recovery process (Bolin and Kurtz 2018). Additionally, environmental justice, health disparities, and other critical issues in the disaster landscape cannot be fully understood without considering systematic racism in the United States.

Racism also affects the recovery process through housing discrimination (Hamideh and Rongerude 2018; Peacock and Girard 1997). Recovery is nearly impossible without adequate flood insurance or disaster reimbursement. Adding to that the housing availability problems after disasters (e.g., vacation rentals taking up a majority of the housing stock in some locations), resource access becomes much more difficult for marginalized populations.

People of color in the United States experience racism in every phase of disasters. We emphasize that more research should aim to understand how racism affects the social landscape of animal rescue. In our fieldwork, many of our interactions were with White people, and most of them did not talk openly about privilege or race. We encountered instances of coded racism when people warned us about entering neighborhoods that were predominantly Black or Hispanic. People also described "looters" coming to take trash from flooded neighborhoods in Texas after Hurricane Harvey.

It is also important to examine the lack of inclusive sheltering and mass care in hurricane evacuations. We observed that heavily policed hurricane shelters are not welcoming places for Black people, indigenous people, and people of color, and prohibiting pets provides another barrier to seeking safe shelter. The examination of racial violence and racial justice is often missing from many mainstream conversations in emergency management,[2] which spills into the animal rescue community.

The issue of animal rescue dominated by White advocates and volunteers adds another layer of complexity to designing effective outreach for pet preparedness, evacuation, and recovery. Visibility and expertise of people from underrepresented groups in the animal rescue community are important, and some people are working to highlight diversity in animal rescue. For example, Sterling Davis of the Atlanta metro region is the founder of TrapKing, whose efforts include raising awareness about spaying and neutering of feral cats in Black communities and increasing awareness about animal advocacy among men (TrapKing, n.d.). With hashtags in his social media posts such as "compassion is cool" and "trap like you know," Davis links pop culture with education. During the Black Lives Matter protests in the summer of 2020, some animal rescue groups acknowledged the need to increase the visibility and resources for groups run by Black leaders and other people of color.[3]

This also highlights another example of why diversity is important in emergency management. If pet-preparedness messages from emergency management come from one kind of person (i.e., White emergency managers), then the messages are less likely to resonate with diverse communities. We later explore long-term organizational solutions (and failures), but Sterling Davis offers models of outreach that can be transferred to disaster preparedness and grassroots efforts in animal rescue. However, solutions such as these face additional systemic challenges. The next section describes how animal rescue advocates and volunteers express implicit biases toward low-income residents.

Policing Poverty

Just as we heard coded language about race in Port Arthur, we also heard instances of coded language referring to low-income communities as less educated, backward, and ignorant about animal well-being. One respondent after the Carr Fire indicated, "Pet overpopulation is a big problem in Shasta County because many poor people use pet breeding as a form of income. Also, spaying and neutering is very expensive, so many people cannot afford it."

There also were instances of more affluent people engaging in moral policing of the disaster survivors and their pets. One volunteer shared with us her thoughts about the dogs she worked with after the Camp Fire:

> What happens when the dog comes in—some of these animals were in rough shape to begin with. We love to believe that they were all super well-cared-for, loved animals. We saw some animals in rough shape. It's a poor area there and not a terribly educated county. We saw incredibly skinny animals; we saw animals with cancers, with tumors that should've been taken care of; we saw fleas, bad teeth, super obese animals. We saw a lot of animals with serious health problems that had nothing to do with the fire. This is just not great ownership to begin with. So if you take one of those animals— maybe it's a super adorable, loving dog but obviously not been very well cared for—you put it in a foster home with somebody who is much more affluent, much more educated, has resources, starts dumping resources into this animal, they aren't gonna want to give it back to someone who is going to put it on a chain in their yard in their new home.

These descriptions reflect ideas about struggling with the notion of who should be reunited with animals after a disaster. In some ways, volunteers and other actors view the disaster as an opportunity to intervene and rescue animals from day-to-day neglect. Another respondent described:

> What I began to surmise here for the past three years, reading these pet rescue reports and all the abuse that go with them, [is that] there is a certain amount of people that are more than happy to get rid of their pet during these disasters, and that's their excuse. I hate to say it, but it's true. I don't know why they tie them up as opposed to letting them run free for a chance. The other thing I realize too is, again, it's about survival. These people are probably just in survival mode. We don't know what's going on in their life in addition to that. So why they leave them like that—I don't know what the thinking is, but it's no different than animal—it is animal abuse.

In other words, these respondents expressed the perspective that animals should not go back to the owners in some cases. However, the second respondent also seemed to acknowledge that there was probably a more complex story to some instances of animals arriving at shelters after disasters. This ambivalence is likely due to the awareness of the extreme circumstances of the disaster, while it also expresses a need to protect the animals.

The task of identifying cases of true neglect seemed to cause stress for some of the volunteers. Our interviews with large-scale organizations that specialize in response to disasters and neglect do corroborate that animal neglect and abuse happen. Our perspective as researchers, however, also includes the knowledge that disaster myths are common. Given that people sometimes accept disaster myths and that people sometimes have prejudiced attitudes toward low-income people, it is possible that some of the sense making about neglected animals from low-income communities could, at least in part, represent biases and exaggerations. While it is true that the town of Paradise was poorer and had more elderly and disabled people than the rest of California (Census Reporter 2018a), the evacuees from Paradise also organized monumental efforts to find and reunite companion animals after the 2018 wildfire destroyed almost 90 percent of the town and killed eighty-five people. In other words, the social landscape is complex.

As described earlier, a woman we interviewed in Texas stated that she would rather live in her RV or in her car with her dogs than seek temporary shelter in a place in which she felt unwelcome. Indeed, this woman had brought her two small dogs with her to her son's house after she evacuated from Hurricane Harvey. Her son and daughter-in-law had a new home and were newlyweds. When the traumatized dogs began to urinate in various rooms of the house, conflict arose between the respondent and her son. She felt as though she were a burden to her son and at the same time expressed sadness over the situation because it was not as though the dogs could help their level of trauma over the evacuation into a new location.

There are two issues at play in her scenario: her access to a social network (her family) and her financial resources for temporary housing because she was not able to immediately buy a new home. Data suggest that most Americans cannot afford to purchase a home (Federal Housing Administration 2019). Similarly, in Hawaii when approximately two thousand people evacuated from Lelani Estates during the lava flows in the summer of 2018, affordable rentals were in scarce supply for evacuees, and people with pets had even fewer options because many rentals had restrictions or limitations about pets. Therefore, the issue of pets in evacuation is linked with access to resources as well as privilege. While it might be obvious that financial security leads to a broader array of housing options, there are more specific nuances in the social landscape of pets and disasters that relate to gender, race, age, and differences in the hazard context.

Fire Cats and Wings of Rescue

When we drove through the community of Coffey Park, guided by two animal rescue volunteers who had been working tirelessly for months to reunite missing fire cats with owners, all that was left were mailboxes and the occasional chimney. After sharing a dinner with us, the two women enthusiastically agreed to drive us through Coffey Park so that we could see one of the primary burn zones. Even though the sun was setting and there was an icy breeze in the early spring, we could still smell ashes from the fire that ravaged the community five months earlier. Coffey Park is also where we spotted the tent site that served as a mixture of memorial and information post for people seeking their still-missing pets. Also posted were flyers for reunited pets and owners.

Two volunteers who searched for lost cats met us for dinner at a cozy diner in Santa Rosa. They described how the volunteers searching for fire cats were a tight-knit community, even though multiple groups were working to trap and reunite missing fire cats with their owners. While the success of addressing pet overpopulation through disaster-induced TNR was astonishing, we were also intrigued to hear about the extensive time, technology, and efforts that went into searching for the missing fire cats. For example, trail cams were set up at feeding stations so that volunteers could document the cats visiting the feeding stations.

"Found Pets" sign in Coffey Park, California, after the Tubbs Fire.

Poverty is also associated with treatment of animals, although there are likely stereotypes concerning impoverished and marginalized communities. After Hurricane Irma, a program coordinator shared that people in poor areas may do things such as illegally breed dogs. Additionally, social vulnerability to disasters interacts with some of the other important issues we identify in previous chapters. For example, while social media has been increasingly important in animal rescue in disasters, older adults are less likely to use it. One volunteer who managed large-scale cat tracking after the Camp Fire confirmed this: "I don't know how every disaster should look. But we're dealing with a lot of senior citizens in this area not used to using social media." This shows that there are overlaps among access to resources, poverty, animal care, and to some extent, stigma and isolation.

This also highlights that privilege in the social landscape of pets can also be associated with capacity. Several of the respondents we talked to mentioned that they or their family members were caring for children or elders with cognitive, mobility, and other issues of access and functional needs (AFN). While issues of functional and access needs have been addressed more thoroughly in recent years in disaster planning (McDermott, Martin, and Gardener 2016), little research or planning has been carried out to understand the ways in which AFN intersects with owning companion animals during disasters.

Another area of need often mentioned was identifying mechanisms for managing the systems for feeding cats and dogs after disasters. The volunteer-run feeding stations in communities in which reentry was prohibited (such as Paradise) became essential for pet survival. However, at the same time, the local brick-and-mortar shelters often became inundated with too many donations of pet food. In part to deal with the problem of too many bags of donated food, while also meeting the needs of low-income pet owners in the community, some shelters (including a cat sanctuary in North Carolina) implemented pet food pantries. Because people who cannot afford to feed their pets may be more likely to decide that surrender is the best solution, pet food pantries minimize animal surrenders.

While research suggests that pet ownership among low-income people is not necessarily related to human food insecurity (Rauktis and Lee 2019), the food-pantry option seems to create positive public relations for the animal shelters that we visited. Moreover, this option might be an alternative for dealing with the influx of excessive donations of cat and dog food during disasters. Because research on reasons for animal surrender is scarce (Frommer and Arluke 1999; Lambert 2014; Scarlett et al. 1999), additional research on animal surrender after hurricanes and other disasters is needed. Another preliminary finding from our observations during the COVID-19 pandemic showed that food pantries are helpful, but they do not account for people without vehicles or easy access to public transportation. Therefore, pet food home delivery can be another mechanism for supporting low-income households with pets.

Finally, there were instances in which volunteers and respondents were aware of their privilege and how their access to resources protected their companion animals. For instance, a program coordinator in South Carolina shared her Hurricane Florence experience with us:

And I say that because this was my first experience with a hurricane as well. I had to be on the run, but quite frankly, I never worried. I've always had animals. I never worried about it. I'm one of the rare ones. This is not your average pet owner. Because, I mean, my cat left in style in a Cadillac, I'm embarrassed to say. She had food and water in the back. She went to a four-thousand-square-foot home and had the run of the house with other pets. I mean, she lives the good life. But that's not your average evacuation route or plan. But I—I don't worry because I know I have people and resources to do all that. But the majority of people don't.

Acknowledging how access to resources can facilitate successful evacuations and recoveries is an important step but should be adopted at multiple levels and translated into policy and planning. We offer some solutions and additional caveats for these issues in Chapters 7 and 8.

That evacuation is more difficult for lower-income people might seem intuitive, but the media usually cover instead stories of heroism, sensationalism, and dramatic aspects of disasters. This drama is highlighted in missions carried out by Wings of Rescue, an organization founded in 2012, and other organizations like it. The organization not only flies animals out of disaster zones but delivers food and other supplies to isolated areas. After Hurricane Dorian struck the Bahamas in 2019, Wings of Rescue posted on social media about a dog who "got a First-Class window seat on her flight to Nassau where she was quickly taken to the vet by the wonderful people at BAARK [Bahamas Alliance for Animal Rights and Kindness]!"[4]

Although Wings of Rescue employs some arguably excessive use of resources for animals, one key strategy is to fly animals from "high-kill" to low- or "no-kill" areas. Various nongovernmental organizations throughout the United States use this strategy. However, Wings of Rescue's efforts are captivating, and donors are likely thrilled by the idea of flying in animals from island communities such as the Bahamas or Puerto Rico. Another sociological critique of the group's approach entails how this adds to the narrative that communities in developing regions need "rescue" from outside groups. However, Hurricane Dorian was catastrophic in scale, and outside resources are necessary and useful after catastrophic events.

However, it is interesting that "hurricane pets" can garner public compassion that seemingly outpaces compassion for humans fleeing Dorian. More than one hundred people from the Bahamas seeking refuge were denied entry into the United States. Of course, a person can be both a compassionate humanitarian and compassionate for animals. Unfortunately, findings from our research suggest that people in poverty encounter more barriers to safe evacuation, even if they have pets.

The Working Class and Vulnerability to Disasters

The night before heavy rains flooded her neighborhood during Hurricane Harvey, Stacey got stuck at work. While her boss required her to work her shift as a waitress at a restaurant, her five-year-old chocolate Lab mix was stuck at home by herself. So Stacey had to find a way to get back before evacuating. The rain began one hour before she was off work and started for home. She had her boyfriend's car but could not get too far and eventually pulled it up onto the curb to avoid flooding the engine. Still determined to get back to her house for her dog, she started hiking down the interstate.

Eventually, a city truck pulled up and was able to get her as far as the local police station. She was five miles from home, so she walked through the floods, waist deep in some places, to finally reach her neighborhood. Once she got there, she had about thirty minutes to gather belongings before water started coming into her house underneath the door. When she left, the water was ankle deep. She, her boyfriend, and several others waited more than twenty-four hours at the main road intersection and spent the night in a U-Haul storage building. All this time her dog was at her side, keeping her warm during the night. As they made their way to safety, the current was so strong they had to cut through people's yards while wading through flooded neighborhoods. The dog, however, seemed to enjoy herself, swimming through the water and having a fun new adventure, seemingly unaware of the disaster unfolding around her.

Stacey was in a position in which she could not evacuate any sooner. As a waitress, she had few protections for deciding not to report to work and was not able to leave until after the storm hit and roads were already flooded. Stacey's situation mirrors that of many others affected by disasters who have to base their decision-making on financial factors that can make a significant difference in whether or not they are able to pay rent in the future, afford a hotel if they leave, or even if they can evacuate at all. The issue of social vulnerability grounded in political ecology research has been linked with disaster studies literature for decades (Bolin and Kurtz 2018). Vulnerability is produced by the economic, political, and social processes that put populations at risk and by institutions and governmental entities that fail to provide protection from hazards (Tierney, Lindell, and Perry 2001).

There are root social factors that affect vulnerability to hazards and disasters. The Access Model (Blakie et al. 1994) notes that unsafe conditions arise in relation to economic and political processes in a society that allocates assets, income, and other resources. Vulnerability then affects not only responses to disaster but also preparedness and recovery. Having limited access to resources produces unsafe conditions in the social environment of those most susceptible to risk (Blakie et al. 1994). For example, the roles that women have in their occupations or in daily life may increase their exposure to risk and adverse outcomes during a disaster (Enarson, Fothergill, and Peek 2018), as was the case with Stacey in Hurricane Harvey.

Stacey noted in her conversation with us that she and her boyfriend were "living in the 'hood. Areas that got hit worst are in the 'hood—always." She was working in a job that required her to finish her shift or face the possibility of termination. Stacey was also originally from another state that did not experience hurricanes and had limited experience about when or if to evacuate. Her evacuation through public shelters, FEMA-approved hotels, and the occasional friend's house is typical of those without financial support.

After staying at the public shelter in the convention center for two nights, she moved to a different pet-friendly location. Ultimately, she spent a full month at a hotel that she described as a "hooker hotel . . . in a trashy area." She spent two weeks at another extended-stay hotel, and then she moved to a different location because her old house was no longer inhabitable. She mentioned that she has not taken her dog to the vet in some time, because it will take awhile to recover financially. It is understandably not a high priority given her financial limitations and the need to find somewhere else to live.

This situation of financial instability is a concern after disasters, and it highlights how resources help in the evacuation process with pets. For example, some of the affected areas in the California Tubbs Fire were very affluent neighborhoods. Those residents, including those with pets, were able to leave and pay for hotel rooms or stay with friends. In another area of Northern California, a mobile home community burned to the ground. No one we spoke with was able to tell us with any certainty where the people had evacuated. Up the street just a short distance was a more expensive neighborhood, and some of its residents had second homes and were better able to navigate evacuation. Rentals in the lower-income areas are a minimum fifteen hundred dollars, and those we spoke to suggested these are not ideal locations because they are in high-crime/low-income neighborhoods.

Program coordinators we spoke to in Texas after Hurricane Harvey noted the difficulties with temporarily fostering pets for owners who cannot return home because of flood damage. While some people live in hotels or with relatives, others are living out of their cars. There is no feasible way they can return for their pets, but they are also hesitant to give their pet up for adoption. It was then three months after the hurricane, and the program coordinators had just spoken to someone who was able to get back into her house later that same week. She had been living in a hotel and thus was unable to return for her dog. This highlights how access to housing affects decisions about animal care and surrender. Some people might have the resources needed for evacuation, including a place to go or money for a hotel for an extended time. Others have to consider the costs involved if they leave: money for a hotel, for gas to drive prolonged distances to a friend or family member's house, and for additional costs for pets, as well as the cost of being unable to work.

Others in California also experienced problems with long-term housing and financial issues after the wildfires. As one evacuee described her experience to us, she noted that some people had lost everything and barely had the energy to even look for their lost pets. She lived in a location that never received an official evacuation notice. At the time, she was living in what she described as an awful hotel, because she could not live in her damaged house. She has been hopping between motels and friends' houses. Some motels allowed pets, but she encountered issues:

> One specific motel called us when we went to go make the reservation that pets were allowed, and specifically cats and dogs were allowed; and then when we went there about two weeks after I had made the reservation, they told me that cats were not allowed. Which is very upsetting, but we didn't have anywhere else to go. So we had been planning to give our cat, Mittens, who is kind of a jerk to other cats, to a foster. She's the tiniest little thing, and she's like this little demon [*laughs*]. So we couldn't bring her. I think most of the places we stayed have a kind of pet fee. I think that for the most part they have been fairly reasonable. . . . Where we are at now it's like thirty bucks for the entire stay. One motel had like ten dollars a day per pet, and another motel was like thirty dollars a week. [For the] one that was ten dollars a day per pet, when we first went in there, we had three pets with us because we had the chicken and the cockatiel. We were able to get someone to foster the chicken for us. But we'd only been out for a week, and we were like, "What do we do? We don't know anybody with chickens." But I had posted online about it. It's really weird to have a chicken in a hotel room.

This evacuee's home was unlivable because of smoke damage and various other problems, such as broken windows. She noted that there have been some issues with getting the insurance sorted out to make a recovery plan. At the time we interviewed her, she was exploring options with a volunteer group that was willing to invest in a trailer for her family to put on their property while she made repairs to her home. She was also the only person in her family who could drive and had a son with special needs, so helping her family was essentially a full-time job. She mentioned that many people she knew are unsure if they will be able to move back because they did not have the ability to get their old jobs back and had to find new places to work in the meantime.

As this evacuee noted, there were additional pet fees at the motels where she stayed, some of which initially cost thirty dollars per day because she had three pets. Some evacuees in Texas after Hurricane Harvey had no choice but to surrender pets because they were living in their vehicles. Evacuee Stacey was stuck at work because the manager of her restaurant decided not to close until the last minute and she needed the income. As highlighted by Elaine Enarson, Alice Fothergill, and Lori Peek (2018), evacuees who are economically insecure have less choice and more constraints when affected by disasters. They have less choice about where to evacuate and more financial constraints that prevent them from being able to return home. There are also considerations for work and income, as evacuating from an area for a prolonged period can mean losing a job that is the only source of income for a family. Pets affect these considerations. Evacuees must find pet-friendly locations or pay additional fees. Because Stacey waded through high water for her dog, it is apparent that owning animals affects these decisions too.

Long-Term Housing and Displacement with Pets

Some families are able to return home relatively quickly after a disaster. This is not always possible, however, and working-class families who lose their homes (or whose homes are significantly damaged) have an even more difficult road ahead of them regarding long-term housing solutions.

Typically, renters experience more problems than home owners after a disaster (Lee and Van Zandt 2019). Research after Hurricane Katrina indicated that among the sample of low-income African American mothers, renters in subsidized housing were most vulnerable to housing loss after the hurricane (Fussell and Harris 2014). Findings from another study after Hurricane Andrew in 1992 and Hurricane Ike in 2008 suggested that housing recovery affected populations differently (Peacock et al. 2014). Income was a significant factor in housing recovery in both locations, with lower-income areas experiencing more damage and longer recovery periods. Those who evacuate with their pets may find that seeking out rental properties becomes difficult. Others who left pets behind or boarded pets may be unable to return for them for some time until they find more permanent housing.

The 2017 and 2018 wildfires in California further illuminated housing issues that emerge for pet owners. As one resident noted, those who lost their homes have a problem now because rental homes might average three thousand dollars a month in the Sonoma County area, but these rental properties do not allow pets because the homes themselves are expensive and the owners want to avoid any damage. Evacuating is extremely difficult because moving somewhere locally is almost impossible. For example, Santa Rosa is a tourist town revolving around upscale wineries and vineyards in which many rentals are reserved for vacationers. The owners of some rental properties eventually began allowing residents to bring their pets into rented homes after the Tubbs Fire.

After Hurricane Harvey, some pet owners boarded their pets at a local pet shelter that offered to take them in temporarily. Housing issues arose when owners stopped responding to the shelter's calls about picking up their pets. Many of the pets were surrendered for adoption because the owners were unable to take the animal back after the hurricane. At the time of our visit to one shelter outside Houston, there were still six pets whose owners were unaccounted for and not responding to messages. When we asked why this might be, the interviewee said, "I think they don't want to make the decision. They know at this point they have to make a decision to surrender the pet if they can't bring it back to their home and don't want to make that decision. I think it's just normal human behavior." She mentioned that flooding from the hurricane destroyed these people's homes, so they were living in hotels, with relatives, in campers, or even in their cars. It would be impossible to take back a pet while living out of a vehicle and sleeping in the backseat.

The resident in Chico, California, who had a chicken in her motel room described her arduous experiences after the Camp Fire. They were moving around from city to city until finally getting into a hotel she described as "awful." She was unable to move back into her house because of the damage, and one of her cats ran off during evacuation and was still missing at the time of our interview. When she first evacuated, she and her family stayed with a friend in another town who had six dogs. After the hotel debacle she stayed with her cousin for six weeks and then in other hotels. She could not afford the pet fees at the hotels. While she was able to evacuate her other pets, including birds, she was still searching for her cat, which she had had since he was a kitten. She recalled that he just showed up on her doorstep one day and decided he lived there.

When we asked her about her long-term plans, she said, "Go home." Unfortunately, she was having a lot of issues with home owner's insurance, as the house suffered a lot of smoke damage. She did not feel comfortable where she was. A further complication was that she was working on commission, without steady employment. She is not the only person from her community to have issues with employment after the fire. Most people she knows had to find other jobs because they do not know if they can move back, and when or if they do, they are unsure of their ability to get their old jobs back.

Another evacuee in California affected by the Paradise Camp Fire was in a motel in Sacramento and at the time we talked with her had been there for three months. A resident told us there was man who was expecting a FEMA trailer, but FEMA was slow to respond because of low supply. Evacuees ended up in various places all over the state. Some were staying on private property in tents. In many locations, ordinances prohibited trailers on property until after debris removal. People who had a place to go or a car were able to evacuate. Many in shelters were lower-income individuals and families, particularly the elderly. The evacuee we talked with saw elderly people living in their cars because they did not want to leave their dogs in the shelters. Their pets were all they had.

For other evacuees who had lost homes, more complicated factors arose. As one evacuee mentioned, she lived on a lot that was communally owned land even though she had purchased the house on the land through a cash transaction with no deed. The partnership had paid the property taxes:

> There wasn't something that said, "[This person] can pay taxes on this house," so they [FEMA] ultimately ended up giving me, for my home, twenty-five thousand dollars [and] a two percent loan to replace our belongings. So then they said I did qualify for a loan to replace my dad's house because I have the deed to that to rebuild there. But I need to build a house for us first and not worry about a rental property, you know, for now. It's just weird trying to deal with all of that. And I feel bad for people 'cause we still had a car. Like, two cars burned, but we have an old car 'cause it would hold all the dogs, and just put 'em in there. But people that don't have the wherewithal to get to appointments or—you know, like, it's overwhelming to try to deal with all that. It's just rough, you know. They send you someplace, and it takes hours, days, multiplied. I can't even count the number of times I went to FEMA and SBA [Small Business Administration], you know. Like more than twenty.

Again, these comments reflect that vulnerability is exacerbated after disasters because of economic loss, general stress, and relocation. Adding to that other situations such as caring for an elderly family member or a child with medical needs, and the recovery process becomes overwhelming for the family. These compounding factors may be associated with increased rates of pet surrenders. Therefore, addressing the root causes of vulnerability by reducing burdens after disasters—such as housing availability—would also likely improve the health and well-being of pets. For example, providing affordable pet-friendly housing, mental health services, and other essential services to disaster survivors are all important. Wraparound care is critical for facilitating recovery.[5] Many evacuees we spoke with also had family members with disabilities and ongoing financial crises. When these families faced pet fees at hotels or rental properties, they were pushed further into chronic stress and poverty.

Conclusion

A lack of resources to evacuate with pets put limitations on people living in disaster-prone areas. These limitations might include financial restrictions, such as not having money for gas or a hotel or not being able to get off work in time to evacuate. Time is a resource as well. Often those who evacuate will attempt to do so early, but this also means being able to take the time off work and plan accordingly. From coast to coast, we learned of people living in their cars, swimming out of their houses or into other areas to help with rescue, and making difficult decisions after disasters about whether or not they could afford to keep their pets.

After Hurricane Harvey in Texas, one shelter manager noted that the owner surrenders seemed to be people who had lost their homes and were doing what they thought was best for their pet. He told us about a college-aged girl who had just moved to Houston a week before the hurricane. She had a first-floor apartment, because it was all she could afford. When Hurricane Harvey hit, she lost everything when the apartment flooded. When the company she worked for shut down because of damage from the storm, she lost her job. She was living out of her car and said to him, "I can't go on job interviews knowing my dog is in my car, because it's so hot outside. And this is the best thing for him." She spent forty-five minutes crying outside. He told her they could keep the dog for her until she could return for it, but she made the decision that this was in the pet's best interests. Fortunately, someone adopted the dog later. While she ultimately made a decision, many have difficulties making these decisions, and others do not have to face these sorts of decisions at all.

Disasters highlight and exacerbate inequalities in society. Despite evidence for the need to support vulnerable populations after disasters, there is still difficulty translating research to policy, particularly in reducing the gaps in available resources for families in the long term, including household companion animals. Addressing the intricacies of privilege and power also means acknowledging that what will work in some communities will not work in others. Inequalities are not uniform; rather, they affect people differently in relation to pet ownership and evacuation, rescue, long-term housing and employment, and ultimately animal rescue overall.

The Orange Glow and Rising Waters

Split-Second Pet Evacuation Decisions during Disasters

Our dog's safety and well-being was a factor in our choice to not evacuate by boat during the flood.
—Texas resident during Hurricane Harvey (2017)

Decision-making unfolds at various phases of the hazard cycle. For people with animals, the decisions become complex in regard to preparation, evacuation, potential reentry, and recovery. We spoke with many program coordinators who were managing recovery aspects and long-term placement of pets displaced by disasters, and we examined how respondents made decisions before hurricanes approached their communities. Specifically, we used a web survey to ask evacuees from Hurricane Harvey and Hurricane Irma when they evacuated and how many minutes, hours, or days they spent deliberating evacuation. Some 56 percent of the respondents from Harvey and Irma (n = 173) indicated that they evacuated before the hurricane; 21 percent, during the hurricane; and 5.8 percent, after the hurricane. For those who evacuated during or after the hurricane, the cues associated with the hurricane may not have been substantial enough for the residents to evaluate the threat as severe. Additionally, throughout our face-to-face fieldwork and data collection, we encountered multiple instances in which evacuees did not receive an official evacuation warning but decided to evacuate because of encroaching smoke, water, or other environmental indicators that the hazard was becoming dangerous.

In broader disaster evacuation research, demographic variables are associated with levels of preparedness and likelihood of evacuating. For example, people with children are more likely to take protective action and evacuate before a hurricane (Huang et al. 2012). We can look at the ways in which people consider themselves responsible for taking care of their animals and evaluate attachment and bonding to understand how this might also apply to companion animals. Intuitively, people who have higher attachments to their pets would be more likely to evacuate if they had advanced warning (Heath et al. 2001). Similarly, pet owners who score higher on sense-of-responsibility scales would probably also be more likely to evacuate with their pets (Brackenridge et al. 2012). However, these scenarios assume that the people have advance warning, access to resources to evacuate, and reasonable alternatives if the first destination for evacuation is not available. Access to resources can change the landscape for evacuating with pets; however, even wealthier evacuees whom we interviewed experienced some difficulties in the decision-making process.

As the chapter epigraph illustrates, people may decide to refuse evacuation because of their pets. This is not new information. Many people who refused evacuation during Hurricane Katrina indicated that they made this decision because of their pets (Hunt, Al-Awadi, and Johnson 2008; Zottarelli 2010). If emergency managers, disaster researchers, volunteers, and disaster survivors have known about this problem for more than fifteen years, why does it persist? The PETS Act has limitations, and there may not be a "silver-bullet" policy solution to improving evacuation compliance. Even in the face of challenges, informal systems emerge. Evacuees and residents may find workarounds to getting back to their animals for early reentry, especially if there is a perception that official responders will not work with them to find ways to retrieve and check on animals. Volunteers will defect from groups if they perceive an imbalance in meeting the needs of people and animals in disasters. Leaders make decisions about partner groups with which they will collaborate and communicate, excluding some groups because of tensions or perceived tensions. Individuals or groups may be competing for funding, power, visibility, or even geographic territory to be in charge of managing a disaster response. How these complexities arise are fascinating from a research perspective but also have important policy implications for managing people and their companion animals in disasters.

Throughout this book we share examples of pets being left behind as unintentional or connected with broader social issues. We interviewed the waitress in Houston who made a dangerous decision to go back and get her dog—a decision related to her attachment to the dog, the constraints of her job, her economic mobility, and the context of Hurricane Harvey. This chapter focuses on the key aspects of decision-making that have the potential to change group reputations, experiences for evacuees, and the safety of companion animals in disasters. We discuss how the speed of the hazard onset and psychological factors influence decision-making, as well as organizational decision-making, which for the purposes of this book is different from best practices or cases of organizational failure. We center our discussion around collective and individual decision-making for pets and animals in disasters. The decisions that people and organizations make can lead to best practices or failure. Organizational decision-making includes personnel and logistics and decision-making for long-term planning.

Speed of Hazard Onset

An evacuee from the Camp Fire in Paradise, California, described the trauma of the evacuation:

> Just about a block from my home, I saw people running in the direction I was going. I picked up a young woman and her old, blind dog, and we helped each other stay calm. Traffic was at a standstill throughout the entire evacuation route. I had to literally drive through flames and flying embers at one point, and it was darker than midnight. All I could see were the tail lights of the vehicle in front of me. I called my son and told him I loved him because I didn't think we were going to make it out. Other people in that same line of traffic did not make it out.

From this description, it is apparent that the evacuees faced a fire approaching so rapidly that many thought they would not survive. Many people and animals did perish in this fire. On social media, outpourings of sympathy for the evacuees and messages of solidarity came from across the nation and the world. There was an especially massive effort and support for the animals and lost pets of the Camp Fire.

Contrast this outpouring of support with the reactions to images of dogs left behind during Hurricanes Harvey and Irma in 2017. Some social-media comments even indicated that people who leave pets behind should be "executed," have their children taken away, or publicly shamed. Why are members of the public so angry at hurricane animals left behind but render an outpouring of support for the fire pets? In their recent article, Ashley Reed, Sarah DeYoung, and Ashley Farmer (2020) posit that the discrepancy in reactions has more to do with the different perception of evacuees leaving pets behind through no fault of their own and those intentionally leaving pets behind. The fire approached so quickly that some evacuees did not make it out alive. On the morning of November 8, 2019, this evacuee said that she saw the fire approaching the land near her house:

> We just got out and then went—well, up at the top of Concow, there's like a big pullout space, and I went there initially. I waited for—I've

Destroyed neighborhood in Paradise, California.

got the four dogs; I've got one of our cats, Cinnamon. And I had her in the car 'cause she was inside [the house]. I grabbed her, but I didn't have time to get a carrier or anything. And she was in the car with my grandson. And when I went to get back in, I had to go back into the house to get a suitcase of court papers. And when I opened the door, she went out the window. And so I just—I said, we have to go. And so when I was leaving, [my husband] Harry was going over toward the chicken coop, and I said, "You need to go now." And he goes, "Well, I'm going [to] try and load the goats." I said, "You don't have time; just let them out of their pen." So he let the goats out, but they went back, and we found them later—they, that's their safe place, you know. So they went back in there, and we figured out we probably should have closed the gate behind us so they couldn't get in there and would've had to do something else because the property has—there's three creeks on the property, and there's an orchard across the bridge—and had they gone in the orchard—it got really smoky and stuff, and right around this large pond, the trees right there didn't burn. So they might've made it to someplace safer, but where the house was and everything, it just looks like a bomb went off. But we also had next to the goat pen, there's a duck pen, with a little pond, so when we looked at pictures, we couldn't get the ducks either. We didn't get anything. We just barely made it out. We ended up driving three lanes to—you know, look, we got out on the road, and Harry, he went out after us, about twenty minutes after us, and there were cars engulfed in flames on the way out. People died in those cars.

When a rapid-onset wildfire is at your doorstep, it is easy to imagine that a cat can dart out the door while you are evacuating. Compare this with a hurricane scenario in which a household has days of advance warning. Of course, people can indeed be stuck in situations and be unable to leave. The judgment falls heavier on hurricane evacuees for several reasons (Reed, De-Young, and Farmer 2020). Humans are generally poor, often messy decision makers, and they prefer heuristics, or mental shortcuts (e.g., Gigerenzer and Gaissmaier 2011). This means that it is faster and more efficient to judge the situation of hurricane pets being left behind than to take the cognitive steps to understand the nuances of the disaster or engage in time-consuming empathy. There is also the poverty factor: the Southeast is prone to hurricanes, and this region may unfortunately face the stigma of being "the South"—that is, "those backward people who leave pets behind."[1] While this offers some psychological explanation for the decision-making and judgment of the broader society during disasters, it is also important to understand individual decision-making of the evacuees and how they processed their evacuation.

For example, Linda evacuated from the Tubbs Fire. She woke up at 3:00 A.M. and got text messages on her phone. She then saw a strange orange glow on her wall, which was the fire roaring through her neighborhood. The text messages on her phone were urgent—messages from friends telling her that the fire was close to her neighborhood and she should leave immediately. Linda had an older dog and a cat. She grabbed the dog and could not find the cat, who was likely hiding behind furniture. She thought about leaving the door open so that the cat could run out if the fire approached the house but mentioned her fear of looters or theft. With sadness in her eyes, Linda shared with us that of course she loved her cat, but she had to leave immediately. Her area of the neighborhood was mostly unscathed by the fire. She described concern for her cat because the National Guard barricade prevented her from returning home to feed her cat and check on her well-being until nearly five days later. Another evacuee from the Camp Fire in Paradise described her cat bolting out the door just as she was evacuating with several family members. A different evacuee from the Camp Fire said:

Roads were few; traffic came to a halt. Some could not get out and burned to death in their vehicles. Ridge residents called 2-1-1 and

9-1-1 and were told there was no danger to them, although they could smell smoke. They waited to evacuate. Many died. Those who evacuated took the pets in their arms, which meant more dogs were evacuated immediately. Many cats jumped out of owners' arms.

This statement shows that people did not receive warnings, which contributed to their last-minute evacuation. Similarly, in Houston after Hurricane Harvey, we interviewed by survey an evacuee who lived in the reservoir zone that flooded after the hurricane passed. She was surprised and angry that she and her fiancé received no warning before her townhome flooded. The respondent was surprised by how quickly the water rose:

> I had no idea water could come up from zero to six feet in a matter of hours. I could write a book! Had I not spent Saturday and Sunday packing and preparing, Monday morning would have been a lot worse. Instead, all we had to do was load the truck and go. I have hundreds of photos. We are still waiting for a FEMA appeal, three months later, after we were evicted from the first place for it being uninhabitable and being denied by FEMA, as they say the place is habitable. (It is not; [it is] gutted and being completely rebuilt.) We had to empty savings to get a new car and new apartment, and FEMA has been difficult. We did, however, receive the $400 grant from Red Cross.

They went back to their townhome in a canoe to retrieve their belongings as the waters continued rising. At the time of Hurricane Harvey, they had two dogs and a foster kitten.

The family of the cat Zeus, who was surrendered after the Tubbs Fire, lost another cat in that fire, and when we interviewed them, they were still searching for the other cat. The woman toured the burn zone near her neighborhood with us. Contiguous to a winery and cozy California cottages, the burn zone also mirrored the misery of Coffey Park—it was clear that the fire had "jumped around." Where in some areas houses burned row after row, some houses stood untouched. In the decimated areas, pools and mailboxes were the only remaining sign that a fire had ravaged the valley several months earlier. The woman telling us her story and who showed us the missing cat signs drove a luxury SUV. Despite her economic situation, she also mentioned that so many of her family and friends had no place to go with their pets after the fire because vacation homes with strict no-pet rules dominated the landscape. What was even clearer was that the decision to adopt Zeus after the fire weighed heavily on her mind because her sister-in-law had surrendered the cat after losing her home in the fire; yet the decision also seemed to bring her a sense of peace because she viewed it as an homage to all the other lost pets of the Tubbs Fire. What also seems to be a common theme of people who evacuated from fires, hurricanes, and lava flows was that some degree of emotional regret was associated with decision-making or the reevaluation of decision-making.

In some cases, even having an evacuation plan seems futile in the event of a rapid-onset fire. The evacuee from Concow told us:

> This was kind of worse because it was just so fast, so even though we actually had an evacuation plan—we had where all of our, you know, carriers and everything were. Harry has a dump truck, with sides and a top to go over it, so we could load the goats—we have pet goats—and load them and then put the other carriers behind them. . . . And there was just no time; I got the dogs in the car.

Decision-making sometimes, from the evacuee's perspective, was related to being in the right place at the right time during the acute or rescue phase of the hazard. One volunteer described the Camp Fire:

> Yeah, and that's how we found out which road was which, like these little dirt roads to walk down to go see if we could find the horses. It's a good thing we did that because they were down there, and you couldn't see them from the road. And then we just found—like, we found goats that were just loose, and their pens burned down, so they were loose. We caught them, and we employed our emergency goat-roping skills, which was kind of funny, and not all the goats were as willing participants as the horses were. But one of them— her poor face was so swollen from being burned that just putting a rope around her face was hard, and she was actually really sweet and friendly, but you could tell it hurt. We finally just picked her up, and then she was kind of like too big to pick up, so it's a good thing my friend does cross-fit. I held part of the goat, and she held the rest of the goat. That's how we—we just do stuff like that when you have to. And then we just kind of—I mean that's the first day we worked until we thought it was going to get dark, and then we left and tucked our way back in the second day, and we did the same thing over.

Similarly, another evacuee mentioned that having the right social contacts facilitated the family's ability to have a place to stay during the fire. For example, this respondent after the Camp Fire in California told us:

We were fortunate in that we had contacts for animal sheltering. We were able to take twenty or thirty animals and evacuated to a friend/client who operates a rescue ranch for temporary housing. This same friend also worked with [a rescue organization] and was able to rescue our goats and pigeons and house them. Had she not been a part of that group, I do not know if our goats would have had water provided in time to save them.

This reflects that even though it might seem that luck or serendipitous moments led to better outcomes for evacuees and their animals, many of the outcomes were connected to access to resources. In this way, even decision-making is associated with the depth of one's social network. The more contacts a person has, the more options the person has for engaging in an evacuation process that allows for a certain level of agency. This reflects findings in disaster research in which social capital can improve outcomes for communities affected by disasters (Aldrich and Meyer 2015).

Another factor in decision-making is evaluating the risk of the hazard (McCaffrey 2015; Huang, Lindell, and Prater 2016). In our data and observations, evacuees consider the potential outcomes of the hazard event. As this program coordinator described, sometimes people evacuating may not fully comprehend the severity of the hazard and may think that they can return home to retrieve animals in a few hours:

> Right, "We plan on coming back, and everything will be fine, and what's a little water?" Even though the house might be damaged, they're not thinking about the fact that the pets are going to be left a long time potentially. So there seems to be—I'm guessing there's variable psychology in terms of whether they take their animals or not, based on the likelihood of damage expected.

This is related to "the myth of invincibility," a term in social psychology meaning that people believe that bad things are more likely to happen to other people than to themselves (Miedema, Hamilton, and Easley 2007). This goes beyond natural-hazard scenarios. For example, in a recent study of the Hawaii false alarm—the famous incident in which emergency management staff accidentally sent out a false alarm warning of a nuclear missile—Sarah DeYoung and colleagues (2019) found that respondents who received the text message perceived that it was more possible for others to die than it was for them. Essentially, it is possible that when faced with evacuation, people feel a certain level of denial about the experience. Thomas Drabek describes in *The Human Side of Disaster* (2018) that people may go through a period of sense making and denial in response to warnings. Amanda Ripley (2009) also describes this in her book about the World Trade Center evacuation; some people believed at first that the planes unintentionally crashed into the Twin Towers. Therefore, the denial phase of evacuation preparation could make it more likely that people may not leave with their pets because they believe that they can return soon to retrieve their pets. In other words, their perception of risk was inaccurate.

The concept of risk occurs in many theoretical models of disaster research. For example, in the Protective Action Decision Model (Lindell and Perry 2012) threat perceptions influence one stage of the decision-making process. If residents believe that they will be away from home for a only short period of time, it seems logical to assume that it will be relatively easy to come back and retrieve pets. Unfortunately, in a hurricane the water can get so high so fast that some companion animals do not survive.

This was the case for a family that we interviewed in Dickinson, Texas, after Hurricane Harvey. The mother of the respondent that we interviewed had gone to the boxing match between Conor McGregor and Floyd Mayweather that Saturday evening. She kept her dogs in a kennel enclosure in the backyard, facing the bayou. In all the years that she had been living next to the bayou, it had never risen into the yard, and there had been no warnings at that time. After she returned home that evening, floodwaters prevented her from getting back into her neighborhood. Her dogs drowned in their kennel enclosure. The son that we interviewed described his mother experiencing severe depression and feelings of guilt over her dogs' deaths. This case was not an instance of evacuation refusal but terrible circumstances.

Another common theme we saw throughout our fieldwork is that people must make difficult decisions during the disaster. One program coordinator in Florida after Hurricane Irma described her experience to us:

> I know I have so many animals. In like six minutes, I have to make choices. Do I—obviously, my family first, but we only have a one-story house. So where do you go? You go on the roof. It's only six feet; what if it's not enough? So it's like, "What if? What if? What if?" And it was very, very, very stressful. I live in a little town villa. Again, no garage. I only have two bedrooms. But that's the thing. If you want to make things work, you want to make things work. We stack up cages, so the huge cage is on the bottom, medium cages, and then small cages. Big dogs on the bottom, medium dogs here, cats right here. I mean, it was crazy, but we made it, luckily. There was no major damage. I got flooded a little bit just because the drainage system in Miami is not very good.

Not only do rapid-onset disasters cause stress, but the speed of onset makes it harder to plan the evacuation. One evacuee from Hurricane Harvey indicated that his cat carrier was already underwater on the first floor of his home by the time he thought about searching for it. Therefore, again, timing is important because the rapid onset of the hazard limits the choices that people have.

Even when there was time to evaluate and consider evacuation, many families lost their pets en route to their destination. During the Tubbs Fire, one family lost their cat at the fairgrounds where many evacuees stopped to reunite with one another. The gray-striped tabby jumped out of the family car, and for months after the fire volunteers engaged in trapping and camera spotting tried to find the cat. A cat did show up on the trail cam who looked like the missing cat but belonged to a family that lived contiguous to the fairground, and it was enjoying meals at the feeding stations set up for rogue fire cats. Volunteers who waited for weeks to trap the cat spotted on the trail cam were disappointed and frustrated that it was not the missing cat.

People also make long-term decisions about finding housing for their pets. One of the shortcomings of the PETS Act is that it supports evacuation operations in the acute phase of the disaster, so its provisions support the immediate transport, sheltering, and movement of companion animals before and during a disaster. However, displaced people and their animals face complexities after the disaster, as a Hurricane Harvey respondent mentioned:

> We stayed on the second floor of our home through the flood. We have torn out everything below four feet in our house. We now live in a fifth-floor apartment with our dog. He misses his backyard! We are waiting on insurance and SBA to make decisions about elevating our house and returning.

The long-term care of displaced animals also becomes a burden for organizations that lack capacity for expanding their physical space when there is a new influx of both owned and unowned displaced animals.

One volunteer after the Camp Fire described the fatigue and burnout related to the stress of deciding how to manage displaced animals. She said it was impossible to "save them all" and that many evacuees and volunteers face "tough decisions" about whether to euthanize an animal injured during the disaster or to manage the expenses associated with medical bills. These expenses include medical upkeep of pets, such as spaying and neutering, and injuries as a direct result of the fire, such as burns and internal lung damage.

This makes a sustainable foster system even more important. It may be difficult to find a central physical location for disaster animals because local shelters are already at capacity. A well-managed and organized database of a foster network can lead to an effective solution for relocating animals. Spaying and neutering can be a form of disaster mitigation since shelter numbers will be reduced in areas where pet overpopulation is not severe.

Managing foster animals is a part of pet evacuation logistics. A common theme throughout our fieldwork is the need for streamlining processes and information relating to evacuating animals. One volunteer we interviewed expressed frustration over the lack of an organized system for people to look for their animals:

> It was extremely frustrating in that sense. Like, I think everybody's hearts were in the right place, which meant a lot of people have irrational and emotional responses, but it was also really hard to see. The real failures were the ones that didn't get the most attention. So the real failure is that people needed to go to seven websites to go and look everyday because it was all gonna change every day, or you had to go stand in line in the smoke to have somebody look at a picture of your cat. That to me was the biggest failure, I think.

Even though foster systems and matching systems were in place, many organizations were undertaking those tasks and in some cases had not streamlined the tracking or matching processes. In other words, some dogs and cats that were adopted, fostered, or listed as missing did not have records that followed the animal through the sheltering and relocation process. In one example of best practices that we observed, a cat found in the burn zone would get an ID code, such as CF451, with a corresponding description of the cat (e.g., black-and-white cat with tipped ear, fluffy tail) and where it was found, and that number stayed with the cat even when it was spayed and then placed for adoption. The records were also stored electronically. This would increase the likelihood of reuniting the cat with the original family. Unorganized groups did not have similar tracking systems and relied only on hard-copy information tracking. Some volunteers considered quitting. In some cases, volunteers created new organizations because of poor database management. In the next section, we provide more details about how organizational management or processes were driven by volunteers who created new systems to run more efficiently.

Impromptu Animal Sheltering and On-the-Ground Decision-Making

Impromptu decisions can be beneficial for people in disasters (Kendra and Wachtendorf 2016). From our observations, new animal shelters also emerged after disasters and provided places for people to take lost and found pets. In Houston, an organization that existed prior to Hurricane Harvey changed strategies to manage pets during the disaster. While its focus before the disaster was on fostering without a brick-and-mortar shelter, it started an on-the-ground operation and temporary shelter after the hurricane. Located in a strip mall, it set up business inside a former grocery store. Ashley and one of our students visited the facility to observe the layout of the shelter and the system for managing hurricane animals.

Volunteers were at the front, directing people where to go. Crates were lined up in multiple rows, each with a dog inside, some covered with blankets to ease the dog's anxiety. On a clipboard on top of each crate, volunteers checked off and signed details about the dog's medication, food, walk, and time of completion. Dogs and cats were in separate buildings.

We discussed this impromptu setup with one of the shelter leaders, who indicated that the organization's primary goal was to address the pet overpopulation in the Houston area and to end the need for euthanasia. At least three organizers who worked with the shelter visited other local shelters to check euthanasia lists and then adopt the dogs out of the city shelters to get them adopted through their organization. Many breeds were the commonly surrendered pit bull mixes. Not all the dogs in the location were there because of the hurricane itself, but the organization was using the hurricane as a way to bolster their mission. Volunteers did not turn away any surrendered pet, so many animals were either picked up from other shelters or were owner surrenders.

Although the shelter had just opened and was in a temporary location, it still had numerous volunteers. Buses from Austin with more than fifty people on board traveled to Houston, and volunteers created a to-do list and assigned everyone a task. For example, many of the crates donated needed assembly. With a handful of volunteers this would have taken at least a week, but with the vast number of people volunteering, they were assembled within a day. Volunteers can be long term or short term, so even if someone wanted to help for just one day, the person would be given something to do.

Volunteers managed physical donations to prevent the inundation of unneeded supplies. The organization created a registry wish list of needed items. For example, the shelter leader told us about someone who went to PetSmart and bought ten dog crates to donate. Because he was buying them for the organization, he got a 50 percent discount. There was a medical supplies area, where a vet would also come in once a week. Veterinarians volunteered from all over the country, which was crucial to the success of the shelter, as so many of the animals needed some type of medical care. Medical supplies were also the type of supplies most needed but least often donated. We found this to be the case also when we visited animal shelters in the Carolinas after Hurricane Florence.

Impromptu sheltering emerged in other ways as well, one of the most common being on fairgrounds. These larger open areas provided the space necessary for pet crates and managing the influx of supplies, animals, and volunteers. This was true in Houston after Hurricane Harvey, in California after the Tubbs Fire, and in North Carolina after Hurricane Florence. One coordinator we spoke with managed the fairgrounds area in North Carolina, which became a staging area for animals. When a different rescue organization began evacuating a shelter and arranging for transport for the animals, by the time they loaded all of the pets into the trucks, they encountered flooding and had to turn back. They had nowhere else to go. The state fairgrounds emerged as a viable option. Initially, many of the pets coming in were coastal owner-surrendered dogs. Volunteers would get involved based on their expertise. For example, they could do animal care and organize donations and parking. This was a temporary solution, because an upcoming event limited the amount of time they had to use the fairgrounds. The coordinator discussed how the organizing took place:

> I was out front, and the veterinarian took care of the whole staging area. She had a system where they had all paperwork stay with the dog, and then each person of the team did the microchip, the vetting, making sure there were no injuries. I did not go there because my [preventive] rabies vaccination had run out. So I just stayed out of the way when the dogs first came in.

The management of volunteers to oversee pets during disasters can be time-consuming. One national organization that works with animals during disasters has built a structure of specialized volunteers to set up shelters. The leader of this organization told us:

> We really focused on just the volunteers and just getting them to specialize in the hands-on animal care, or at least actually setting up a shelter. They couldn't always have the interaction with the animals but [were] really focusing on [a] kind of expertise in setting up the shelter and really understanding how to care for animals in high-stress situations. So [we focused on] recognizing the behavior and having enough people there for the volunteers to feel really good that the animals are getting the best quality care—tender loving care—as possible, given the situation that they're in.

This organization assists with pet management during disasters only at the request of the community. Its model for volunteers has endured, and the group is very confident about the structure in place, which includes cross-training volunteers for multiple roles. While this organization existed before the disaster, it does come into communities to deal with impromptu situations in helping set up facilities and support the infrastructure already in place. However, even this organization has learned from disasters. The organizer told us:

> We've opened that up now to some other programs where the community can kind of strategize how they want to solve the problem for themselves, because we—same thing, large animals, like, what are you going to do with horses if someone is trying to leave, and they've got horses on their property, and the person's saying, "If you leave, I'm not going to feed your horses," what do you do? You don't leave; that's what happens. You don't leave. So finding alternate solutions for animals like horses, we're kind of opening up to allow for those kinds of solutions.

While the focus during disasters might typically be on household pets, this organization realized that when volunteers come into communities to help with pet sheltering, there are additional hurdles to overcome. However, this also emphasizes that evacuees, shelter coordinators, and others who manage animals are all involved in decision-making during disasters. This organization's short-term decision-making paid off by finding available space and supplies to take on lost and surrendered pets.

Colocating Shelters

One strategy in household pet evacuation and sheltering that affects decision-making is colocating shelters. Some shelter managers indicated that there are issues with bringing pets into shelters because some evacuees may have allergies or fear of animals. Colocation shelters, such as some of the ones in Texas after Hurricane Harvey, can keep animals and people close together but not in exactly the same place. One animal coordinator pointed out:

> I think the whole year, one of the things that showcased pretty nicely from my perspective is how much we just have this down. And also the importance of colocating shelters. It is just—it's almost as if there's just no excuse for it anymore. I mean, clearly, if the animals are safe. . . . So you could see why that was so great. I mean, it just

makes the people feel better; the animals feel better. There's less anxiety—I mean, it's already such a stressful situation, so to just have them close by, it just makes so much sense. And we really felt like it was an even bigger benefit to the disaster response, to be able to do that. Like, we had visiting hours scheduled; we had a nice area where the people could come and hang out with their pets.

As this coordinator mentions, colocating shelters can ease so much anxiety for pet owners and animals. Knowing that their pet is safe helps evacuees with this anxiety. This also alleviates concerns about pet allergies, dander, and dislike or fear of animals. The buildings are simply close enough together that pet owners can walk over to check on their pet. As another shelter coordinator mentioned, "I felt we were very successful in the way the center was set up. The evacuees with pets were separate from the evacuees without pets. All the pets were separate from the pet owners with twenty-four-hour access available to them." Evacuees who know their pet will be nearby and safe might also have fewer decisions to make about whether to leave a pet behind or how to manage the logistics of bringing the pet along.

Long-Term Solutions for Pets in Disasters: Centralized Information

If a pet becomes lost or runs away during an evacuation, where would you turn for information? This is one of the most frequent questions we encountered in conversations with program coordinators and evacuees. The sheer volume of information and various locations where lost pets can turn up can be overwhelming. After Hurricane Harvey, a variety of "Lost and Found Pets" pages emerged on social media, where people could post photos or descriptions of animals they had lost or picked up. A pet owner might check a local animal shelter as well, but with the number of organizations converging in an area after a disaster, there are numerous locations where a lost pet might end up. Therefore, one of the most frequent suggestions for improving long-term planning for pest in disasters is having a centralized location for information seeking. One program coordinator explained:

So we were trying to find a central place to post them all. We put them on adoptapet.com. But that was one of the biggest challenges, to have one site where people could look for their lost pets. It was different after Hurricane Ike. This hurricane was much, much different—the animal part of it. I was anticipating a lot more animals coming in than we actually got. I think the reason for that is because the human shelters allowed the pets to stay with their people. In Hurricane Ike, that didn't happen. We got a lot more animals in.

The number of evacuees still searching for their pets after disasters is staggering. In some cases, the pet had run off because it was scared. In others, the owner unintentionally left the pet behind because the evacuation happened so fast. In all cases there was uncertainty about the outcome and well-being of the pets. Creating a centralized location where everyone knows to check for their pets could decrease confusion about lost and found animals. Some shelters and program coordinators did what they could to centralize information during Hurricane Harvey. One coordinator described the organization's decision to find fosters for the animals that had been in its shelter: "[We cleared] the shelters to other states ahead of time so that we could use them for the incoming pets and aftermath. Our shelters stepped up wonderfully to create centralized areas for people to bring found and evacuated animals for others to come find their pets." This attempt to create a centralized area for lost and found pets is based on their experiences in knowing how difficult it can be to sift through vast amounts of information, photographs, and online social-media groups to find lost animals.

The Evacuation Process

Another hurdle in long-term planning and decision-making for pets in disasters is the planning for the evacuation process itself. As a shelter coordinator in Florida indicated, many were unprepared for going to a shelter and even less prepared for entering a shelter with their pets:

> I think people need to be informed. I think a lot of people would be able to keep their dogs if they knew before that if you want to go to a county shelter and keep your animal, you have to have your rabies done. The hurricane coming, you still have a week, go right now, check your records, [and] make sure you have everything because if you get hit, the power is out, you're not going to be able to do that. You're going to have no place to go. So nobody knew where to go.

In Florida during Hurricane Irma, shelters required vaccination and rabies records—something many people did not plan for. Even if an evacuation happens at the last minute, there may not be time to search for and find vaccination records for a pet. These types of documents might be lost during the evacuation, or the owner might not know where they are. It is not hard to see how this complicates matters for pet owners in making decisions about evacuating to public shelters. While such documents are necessary to ensure the safety of all the animals brought into the shelter, many were unaware of this. Planning for an evacuation, even if it seems unlikely, is important. One Florida shelter coordinator we spoke with ended up with fourteen fosters at her home. Those fostering pets for her shelter were calling for her to keep them at her house. She described her feelings about managing so many animals:

> So by the time they call about dog number fourteen, I panicked because I'm like, "What am I going to do?" What if something is critical that you have to make the decision, like, you have to go on the roof or something? And who do you get first? Like yesterday, I was getting panicky.

She points out the importance of planning ahead for these situations. If water were to rise in her location, how would she make it out with fourteen animals? Fortunately, everyone, human and animal, in her home was okay after Hurricane Irma. However, as she points out, people either did not know where to go or they encountered obstacles in evacuating, such as missing paperwork, and then they were unsure of how to comply. Another coordinator pointed out:

> Many people had no time to get all their pets for the evacuation, so better planning and letting people know sooner about possible evacuation is better. What I think is needed are more shelters where people can bring their pets or at least better planning on having rooms available for animals in need and ensuring larger crates so that animals are not in tiny crates for a week or more.

Many evacuees and volunteers from hurricanes and wildfires were concerned about issues of space and well-being for cats and dogs. This was particularly true for those who evacuated and planned on staying in hotels farther from home. Several respondents after Hurricane Irma mentioned their experiences with trying to find a hotel. One evacuee explained, "Every hotel was packed; somehow I was able to get one of the last rooms. Next time when I decide to evacuate, I will immediately call for reservations. When I moved to Florida, I knew hurricanes were possible, but I did not think it would happen for years." Another evacuee had a similar experience: "The number of hotels that turned me down because of my pet was terrible; this was one of the most difficult situations we had to deal with."

Another evacuee noted:

> I wish hotels and businesses would be more open and understanding to taking in pets during emergency situations. We had difficulty lo-

cating hotels, and hardly any would accept more than one or two animals. We were sometimes forced to lie and risked being fined or kicked out because we had nowhere else to go with our pets.

One of the most persistent rumors concerning the PETS Act was that hotels and motels are required to accept pets during disasters. This is not true, but long-term planning may include agreements with area hotels/motels to take in pets even if they normally do not and to waive pet fees and other requirements. This could potentially reduce some of the barriers evacuees faced when attempting to escape the floodwaters of Hurricane Irma. Evacuees made suggestions about shelters, given their experiences in Florida:

> There were only three shelters in the area that accepted animals, and they were all full. There need to be laws for pet owners to be able to protect their pets when any disaster like this happens. I was literally turned away at the door when I went to the shelter. One of my co-workers called to check on me, and it turned out they were staying at a hotel and invited me to stay with them. I don't know what I would have done otherwise.

For many Florida shelters during Hurricane Irma, evacuees had to register their pets for the shelter space ahead of time. While this promotes and encourages planning and early evacuation, it also means that someone who made a last-minute decision to evacuate or was forced to evacuate encountered shelters that were no longer accepting animals because they were at capacity.

Of course, emergency management officials and city managers advocate for early evacuation decisions. This can become complicated depending on the hazard. One coordinator of a national organization pointed this out:

> This psychology seems to be different for different kinds of disasters. So in areas that are prone to a lot of hurricanes, they tend to have a lot of evacuations—again, this is all a guess, but I think some of the hurricanes—Katrina, either pre- or post–Hurricane Katrina research showed this as well—but that psychology of evacuating all the time and then nothing happening. So you tend to leave your pets behind if it's the kind of disaster or the kind of area where you're getting a lot of evacuations, but nothing happens. It seems like with the fire, if it's in the moment, there's much more likelihood of, "We're out of here, and we're taking everybody," because it's a fire versus a flood or a tornado or a hurricane. You know, there seems, like, "Oh, the house will be fine. We'll just leave everybody here and just leave in case."

What is also important in this context is trust in information from official and nonofficial channels. For those who have evacuated many times in the past only to find that the storm did not cause as much damage as predicted, these false alarms might lead to less evacuation compliance. These decision-making factors can also lead to some people staying behind because of their pets. For instance, some evacuees told us they simply could not manage an evacuation with the number of pets they had (in some cases, more than eight dogs or various other animals). Because they refused to leave any pets behind, they simply did not leave. This proved true for other pet owners as well: "Our Yorkie is part of our family. We left our one-story house with our dog and went to a neighbor's two-story house. We decided not to evacuate, in part, for fear of being separated from our dog."

Therefore, even with shelters opening their doors to pets, some people refuse evacuation. The importance of disseminating information widely could potentially help, including all available pet shelters and a list of requirements for pets to be admitted to those shelters. However, it seems that if someone does not know what to expect when evacuating with a pet, the person may be hesitant. Reentry considerations for pets left behind become an important issue as well, as this evacuee from the Camp Fire mentioned:

> I have been evacuated before due to fire threat. While packing, there was always the thought in the back of my head, "Well, we'll be back in a couple of days." I mean, I knew by the smoke plume that this was real bad, but it wasn't until we got close to the fire itself that I realized how bad it really was, and even that didn't prepare me for the outcome. What is amazing is how many cats survived the fire and for so long afterward through terrible weather. It is now four months past the fire, and they are still finding cats. What is sad is how many cats are not being claimed. There have been many fantastic reunions but, sadly, not enough. I think too many people are either in too dire straits themselves or they assumed that their cat couldn't possibly have survived. There are cats who were locked up inside houses that survived the inferno.

This evacuee had expectations that she would be able to return home very soon after the wildfire. These expectations often do not match reality because the burn zone continues to be off limits for many weeks after the evacuation. However, her comment also highlights concerns about missing pets: the number of unclaimed and lost cats that were found even months after the fire. This further illuminates a need for centralized information to find owners as well as continuation of work on evacuation expectations, including providing information about pet-friendly shelters and required documentation and helping communities plan ahead for evacuation with their pets. One respondent we interviewed after Hurricane Irma commented:

> You can replace valuables and possessions, and it's better to be safe than sorry. Our deciding factor on leaving was seeing all the damage that Irma had done in the Caribbean Islands. When we went to get supplies, people were in such a panic; it was like seeing something out of the movies. Preparation and awareness are the most important thing.

Seeing the physical damage in news and other media prompted this evacuee to make the decision to evacuate. Of course, without adequate access to resources to evacuate, this decision cannot be followed by actual evacuation. Again, decision-making becomes more complex based on people's perception of the urgency of a need (e.g., "I can probably come back shortly to retrieve my pet," or "The storm doesn't look too severe"). They then decide what kind of action they will take, and then they must locate the resources to follow through with those actions.

Conclusion

People with pets have to make difficult decisions about how, when, and whether to evacuate. If evacuees perceive that a disaster will not be serious, they may not take precautions to prepare for an evacuation. If people are considering evacuating because they do consider the risk to be serious, they may still choose not to evacuate because there are not viable accommodations for pets. In some cases, there are pet-friendly shelters, but the evacuees feel that the experience will be too stressful for their animals. In some cases, in which hotels and other private companies accept pets during disasters, the pet fee may not be affordable. In addition to decision-making by household and individuals during and after disasters, organizations and people volunteering to manage animals in disasters engage in decision-making about staffing, time management, donations management, scale of operations, and the ways to partner with other organizations and agencies. Often these decisions are based on social networks and access to resources, as discussed throughout this book.

Harvey to Florence

Group Coordination, Event Leveraging,
and Key Organizational Strategies

Emergency managers (EMs) and animal welfare groups work toward the same outcome: to reduce loss of life. But there is often a lot of tension and conflict about how to arrive at that outcome. It would be too simplistic to say that the tension results because the animal welfare workers are pro-animal while EM's are pro-human. Many emergency management and local responders are animal lovers and proponents of animal welfare. Many people working in animal welfare also work in emergency management or have first-responder backgrounds, and many are aware of incident command system (ICS) protocols and structures. The goal of many EMs is to reduce loss of life of both humans and animals, as the goals set by animal welfare groups include improving the lives of people. For example, some animal rescue agencies specialize in providing exit support for people with companion animals escaping violent interpersonal relationships. Therefore, the groups have overlapping goals, even in nondisaster settings.

However, tensions that do occur between groups are not easy to overcome, especially in the intense phases of a disaster in which cooperation is essential for communication, organization, and delivery of services. Other factors that can make collaboration more complex include the characteristics of the various groups working to save animals in disasters. Consider the efforts and partnerships formed during the Hawaii lava flows to save animals and move supplies (Matheny, DeYoung, and Farmer 2020).

One volunteer described the efforts by the community to trap and relocate cats out of the path of the lava: "Most of cats were free roaming on ten acres of farmland. The major challenge was trapping these cats for evacuating. We trapped almost every night for two weeks when it was clear that the lava was coming in our direction. Then securing land and kennels to shelter the cats until there was a permanent relocation space was the second challenge." Another program coordinator during Hurricane Harvey described the organization's experiences: "Our biggest challenge was that owners were forced to leave their pets behind with the promise that 'another boat' would be back for the animals. . . . Often that didn't happen, so [a volunteer] started the Zello channel for us to work animal and agri [livestock] rescue from. Had owners been allowed to pull animals with them, we feel that the toll for the pets and livestock would have been far less."

How groups manage companion animals in disasters varies, depending on factors such as the scope of the disaster, the size of the organization, the type of organization, and the resources available to the organization. Other factors that influence organizational strategies in disasters include leadership, communication, and partnerships and collaborations (with other organizations). Ongoing tensions between animal welfare workers and emergency management often affect the organizations and their outcomes in managing pets in disasters. In this chapter we delve into some of the complexities and potential solutions at the organizational level. We also describe organizational best practices as well as case studies of organizational failures. The animal rescue and emergency management communities both have relatively tight-knit social networks. As we interviewed respondents, many people repeated that the "community is small"—everyone knows everyone in animal rescue. It is our hope that this chapter improves planning, practice, and coordination for all groups managing animals in future disasters.

Organizational Strategies: Innovative Tactics

Social Innovation

We found that groups, including animal welfare groups, employed a variety of innovative strategies during disasters. Social innovation is integrating a new process or way of doing something into a system to improve outcomes or enhance a process (Manzini 2014). Often social innovation means combining preexisting systems with other processes to meet a need. We found instances of innovation in the social landscape of managing pets and animals in disasters. Specifically, the convergence of volunteers can be difficult for organizations to manage. Some volunteers at animal shelters we spoke with provided insight into how they utilized existing social networks of volunteers to help or how they solved various problems encountered during the disaster response phase.

In Miami after Hurricane Irma, one nonprofit shelter coordinator described how its volunteer system worked with high schools in the area. Most students needed community hours to complete assignments or to graduate. The coordinator promoted the shelter and its program of fostering a dog or cat for a week for community-service hours. Students shared photos of taking care of the pet and posted images on the social-media pages when seeking adopters. Students could earn up to 170 community hours for fostering animals at the shelter to help with school requirements. Many students choose to volunteer more than once, accumulating thousands of hours by volunteering week after week. This permits them to earn money for financial aid toward tuition and helps the organization in finding fosters and promoting adoptions. As the program coordinator who managed this student volunteer system described:

> The word is spreading so much. Before, we were struggling to find fosters. Right now, people call me during the week enough that I have overbooked fosters for every week, and there's a waiting list for it. Because everybody wants to take a puppy home even though they don't know what it comes with. They're like, "I can't sleep; the puppy is howling all night long." "Yes, that's what they do because the mommy was there, and siblings were there, and now nobody's there. He's alone. You've got to cuddle." They will say, "I want to put him in the crate." "No, he doesn't crate. He's too small. You've got to sleep with him and comfort him because he's going to . . ." "He pooped all over the house." "Yes, you wanted a puppy? That's what puppies do." So next week, like, "You got older dogs?" So it's a learning experience for them. Some of them [went on to] veterinary schools.

The fostering system is providing teens and young adults with the chance to learn to care for animals. Additionally, having networks in place for fostering is important because it allows organizations to clear their shelters prior to an impending disaster to create space for any lost, found, or stray pets. They are also able to keep track of where the foster pets are located. Having an available foster network also means that those who could not take pets when evacuating could potentially use the network as a resource, if someone is able to care for their pet temporarily.

Some organizations encountered obstacles with volunteers and figured out along the way what worked best. One coordinator who asked for volunteers via a Facebook page had 250 volunteers arrive in one day. She encountered issues with sign-up sheets for various tasks and no-shows:

Probably the biggest challenge was I would say our sign-up sheet was not a good thing. So we had my computer person, who was fabulous, put out a sign-up sheet—it was genius. It would fill up so much, and then you couldn't fill up [anymore]. So then we had people that were like, "I want to volunteer. There are no more spots." I came in an hour early to get ready for a two o'clock shift. And less than fifty percent of the people that were signed up showed up. Two hours before that, we were turning away volunteers. We could have asked them to come back.

The idea was that having a sign-up online would help with the management of volunteers. This is not a new idea in disaster volunteering (Schmidt et al. 2018), but some animal rescue organizations doing ad hoc disaster work have been less nimble in adopting this practice. The volunteer manager we spoke with also mentioned that human resource management could have been more efficient where she was working for Hurricane Florence staging. She suggested that in the future she would have sign-ups for each hour, instead of shifts, to better ensure volunteers would show up or to anticipate that not everyone who signs up will come. This coordinator also found herself facing the question of how to feed the volunteers who were managing dogs and how useful some donations were in that regard:

Even little things—people were like, "I would have never thought to donate food for the volunteers." People brought tons of snacks. They got stored behind the back, and I didn't notice them. So later on that evening—it was like ten o'clock at night—I said, "Oh, there are snacks there." I walked over there, and one of vet people came, and I said, "Do you want a snack?" She goes, "Oh, my gosh, I'm starving." I felt so bad. . . . "We had these snacks for hours, and these people have probably all been starving." So little things like that, and then after that, somebody—a Golden Retriever rescue—ordered pizza the first night. I thought, "That's so nice." Then I saw a food-service provider. So I asked them if they would do a lunch. They ended up doing lunch and dinner for us the rest of time except for when I asked [them not to] because I didn't want to take too much away from one company. So, again, having one person—we ended up having double lunches because somebody didn't realize I had all these set up for lunch.

Various social innovations were necessary along the way during disaster response phases, but the shelter coordinator said she would know better next time. She indicated that identifying the little things she did not think of (such as donations of food for volunteers) was extremely useful for developing improved planning.

Technological Innovations

Certainly, various technologies have brought significant changes to disaster response, and this is true for animal shelters and managing pets in disasters. After one of the California wildfires, an organization focused on rescuing cats made use of trail cameras set up in various places to see if lost cats were still in the area. The wildlife cameras had infrared technology that took pictures of cats at various feeding stations. It was interesting how complicated it could be to identify a lost cat, especially for those unfamiliar with how this technology works. For example, the coordinator described this scenario:

> The infrared camera on the cat's fur—say, if you're missing a black cat, and you're going to describe the cat as a black cat, the infrared camera will sometimes show patterns or stripes or spots on a black cat, on their skin. So it looks like a tabby cat on the infrared, but in real life it could be a solid black cat. So maybe there was a lag in understanding that, so that led to some delay in reunification.

Approximately four months after the 2017 Tubbs Fire, about one hundred cats were reunited from the efforts of this organization and others they were working with to help with reunification. Trapping cats can be quite an endeavor, full of innovative strategies. This was the case in the story of Gus the cat, or "legend of Gus," as the cat shelter coordinators told us.

The organization described that its efforts to reunite cats with their owners started with the trapping process, beginning with documenting the location from which the cat went missing. This is known as placeholding and should happen immediately after a disaster. Food and water are set out in the area so you can trap the cat close to home. Gus's owner had evacuated to a city farther south, and this is where the cat had escaped. Because the cat was no longer near his home, they set up infrared cameras to see if they could spot him. Gus was a gray tabby cat, and they thought they had caught a glimpse of a tabby on the cameras. Others in the area had said, "Oh yeah, I've seen a gray cat around here." At about 2:00 A.M., the volunteers watching the camera saw the cat go into the trap. They used a remote trigger to drop the trap and catch him. But they realized that this was not Gus after all but a neighborhood cat. This was an unfortunate and disappointing ending for Gus's owner, because he had been hopeful. However, this was a long ordeal for the shelter coordinators, as they spent a lot of time searching for Gus, utilizing any resources they could think of, including cameras and remote-controlled traps.

The wildlife photography of the cats at the various feeding stations was a new concept to this organization. The founder of the group mentioned that they came up with the system of reuniting cats after Hurricane Katrina, but this simply involved taking pictures and sharing them. Not until after the Tubbs Fire in Sonoma County and surrounding areas were they able to purchase several brand-new cameras for this specific purpose. In a way, the disaster itself changed some of the decision-making of this organization. Paradise, California—the town destroyed by the 2018 Camp Fire—experienced a high rate of missing cats after the fire. Volunteers transferred the lessons they learned from trail cams after the 2017 Tubbs Fire and set up cams around Paradise, Concow, and surrounding areas.

Other innovations were apparent after the Sonoma County fires. In the early spring of 2018, we entered a neighborhood subdivision that had burned completely to the ground in the 2017 fires. There were remnants of burned-out cars left in the street, and many trees had black scars from the fire. In one neighborhood, Coffey Park, only a handful of houses survived of hundreds. Yet in the middle of this desolate and ash-covered neighborhood were feeding and shelter stations for lost cats: large plastic bins with lids and a hole cut out in the side. Inside the makeshift fire cat shelters was soft bedding so cats could hide away from the harsh elements. Contact information was taped to the front on a card that read, "If you see a cat here, contact this organization." It also noted, "Do not remove this. This is a cat feeding station," to make people aware of its purpose.

Technology has also made the use of social media more prominent, and recently volunteers with pet rescue organizations have developed a new app for smartphones that was tested in the Kincade Fire of 2019. The free application is Evac-U-Pet, and the app makers are based in Los Angeles County, California. A description from the website notes, "Evac-U-Pet is a network of like-minded animal lovers working to make emergency animal evacuations efficient and safe. Evac-U-Pet offers a social media platform that connects volunteers with those in need during emergencies [and] assistance with animal retrieval following emergency rescues."[1] Within the app, one can sign up as a volunteer to pick up animals or register a pet. The web page also includes links to checklists for evacuees and volunteers, including for small animals and equines. We spoke with the creators of the app, who said this about their decision to develop it after working with a wildfire evacuation in 2016:

Signs of reunited animals posted on the side of an elementary school in Paradise, California.

I was working with the barn owner who was looking to deploy a group of boarders at her facility to help evacuate animals. [She] had been contacted by her exotic-animal friends to help evacuate, and while we were doing it, I was driving the truck and trailer, and [she] was navigating. We had a kind of team of fellow boarders doing the same thing, and we were dealing with social media, the phone trees, local organizations, and it was all, for lack of better words, a hot mess. I mean, we were being deployed to places that had already been evacuated, and then we would go to the next place, and we could see flames, you know, and it just was not efficient. [She] walked up to me and said, "There's gotta be a better way to do this; we should make an app for this." I had a friend who owned a software company. I told him the idea, ran it by him. He said, "That's a great idea; I want to be a part of it."

As of January 2020, the app had approximately fifteen hundred registered users, with sixteen hundred registered animals. The app facilitated the rescue of sixty-six animals in the 2019 fire season in California. Despite this initial success, the app developers mentioned a desire to coordinate with local emergency management in the future. They discussed the idea of having a list of where animals are and how much help this could be in emergency response. Although they previously ran into issues of people involved with other county fire departments being confused about what it was people were doing and how they were coming in through the app, they have thought about how to make the process easier for all involved, especially when coordinating between volunteers listed in the app and rescue groups or emergency management at the local level. A member of the app development team described their ongoing efforts to improve animal evacuation by being integrated into the local emergency management system:

> That's kind of what we have already within the admin page [on our website], to grant access to other agencies so they have access on a read-only basis to mapping, a list, selection. Anything we can provide to any county agency that will get more animals out we will provide that to them. . . . We have been attempting to work with fire agencies and animal control, and a lot of city and county methods are paper trail and outdated and really slow. . . . Moving forward [there are] opportunities for training and certification of volunteers through the app, which would be stored in the app. So when they [emergency managers] need to get through somewhere, it's right there for them to see.

The creators' combined experience not only recognizes the problem of having an efficient central location for information and tracking, which was a resounding sentiment among many responders and animal shelter coordinators, but is also an example of an up-and-coming solution (at least in Los Angeles County). As one of the creators mentioned, "The only person who died during the Sand Fire in 2016 was going back to get his dog, and that really struck a chord with us at the time."

An app such as this could also be scaled up and applied in other disasters. As we found in the case of the Puna lava flows, many groups were informally linking up through online communication with lists of who had supplies and space for fostering and who needed fostering and supplies. The Evac-U-Pet app and other similarly designed tools would be useful in linking people in need with the people and organizations who can provide those resources.

Building Trust and the Power of "Local"

Just as stated in the broader organizational literature, if organizations, including those that manage animals, do not work together before a disaster, they are less likely to work well together and trust one another during the disaster (Ritchie and Gill 2007). Groups already well-known by community members and volunteers are more likely to create successful outcomes for people and animals. However, this is not to say that large established groups are the only ones that can and do manage animals well in disasters. The Hawaii Lava Flow Animal Rescue Network (HLFARN) is an example of an emergent group, one that arose specifically to meet the needs of pets in the disaster, run by ordinary citizens (Matheny, DeYoung, and Farmer 2020). HLFARN worked with local shelters and sanctuaries to coordinate efforts in finding placements and foster homes for displaced animals. These partnerships were essential because in many cases the local animal groups had contacts for technical expertise such as mobile spay clinics, a base of volunteers, and access to equipment for building animal enclosures. In social capital research, Daniel Aldrich calls these "horizontal ties" (2016, 408), and they can be essential in bolstering resilience. Based on our findings and observations in the social landscape of animals in disasters, horizontal ties are critical.

Knowing who has access to which resources and the ability to quickly mobilize those resources require coordination. Many respondents we interviewed described working with local emergency management and first responders and coordinating with nongovernmental organizations (NGOs) as a critical aspect of managing the sheltering of animals, such as this example from Hurricane Harvey:

> So, actually, one of the things that went very well was coordination with local jurisdictions. Once they know that we're here and know to call us, they—DPS, Texas Department of Public Safety, you know, the state trooper; we had a couple of their officers contact us and give us timely reports on what was needed and where it was needed. And we were able to respond to that quickly. They were very good about working with us to facilitate deliveries, either telling us what roads were open or providing police escorts. They did a great job in providing local help to unload the truck and manage the inventory. We had similarly good luck with the Texas AgriLife Extension Service, which is the Texas—it's the county agents—county agriculture agents. It's a system that's actually coordinated by or run by Texas A&M.

Similarly, during the Camp Fire, NGOs, emergent groups, and local government collaborated to organize shelter operations. Despite instances of tension and conflict between groups, coordination across agencies often works well in crisis scenarios. These cross-agency collaborations were also necessary because of the scope of the disaster and different types of animals that needed care during and after the disaster, as illustrated by this respondent's description of group collaboration after the Camp Fire:

So primarily what I did was look at and organize the shelter in place. So we had—when I was there, it was kind of right before—there was a lot of jurisdiction and [Organization 1]. Basically, [Organization 2] was moving toward paid positions and discontinuing the use of volunteers outside of the shelters. So what I was doing was looking at the shelter-in-place orders. We had—I wanna think—five hundred, just in Paradise, and so those are people who were calling, saying, . . . "My animal is up there," or people who were emergency responders in the field or animal rescuers spotting an animal and setting up a feeding station for that animal. Generally speaking, they were trying to evaluate animals if they were in unsafe situations, but they had a really large Barrow cow population. There were a lot of cats and few dogs that were still there and a lot of chickens. Chickens were left without adequate protection against predators.

This system of partnership and locally driven efforts mirrored the success that we saw in League City, Texas, where local animal shelters mobilized their volunteer base to set up a foster network for displaced animals during Hurricane Harvey. The network of people working together to provide stabling and hay for horses during Hurricane Florence was also dependent on social networks, trust, and an efficient system for logging, tracking, and communication. Of course, social media powered many of these partnerships and efforts. It would be a mistake to assume, however, that social media is the answer to how to improve systems in evacuations. Many evacuees and program coordinators described the need for a central location to check for missing or lost cats and dogs and, similarly, one location to post animals found after the disaster. Even people who managed animal sanctuaries for pigs and larger animals lamented that there was no central information repository or even a primary toolkit of information that people could use for key questions about evacuating their animals. There are many pages, groups, and efforts that focus on animals in disasters, but the information is not always specific to the location or disaster in which the evacuees are situated.

Group collaborations can facilitate successful evacuations and relocation of animals, such as these groups working together in the Hawaii lava flows in the summer of 2018. One of the animal rescue volunteers in Hawaii described their efforts:

I received a grant from Alley Cat Allies for evacuation expenses. I purchased fifteen walk-in dog kennels and modified them for cats. I was able to borrow sixty traps to do the trapping. A friend loaned me space on her property to set up the kennels. Hawaii Lava Flow

Animal Rescue Network got donations of food and litter for us for two months.

Some people living in Hawaii called this the "Coconut Wireless," an informal channel of information sharing among residents and community members. Many of the families in Hawaii have lived on the island for generations, and everyone knows whom to call to "pull a favor" or request support. This happened in many ways through different disasters. One respondent from the Camp Fire told us that the only way she was able to mobilize supplies for evacuating animals during the Camp Fire was through her contacts who already worked in animal rescue and sheltering before the disaster.

When outside organizations such as Red Rover arrive at a disaster site to support efforts, they recognize the power of local communities. In fact, Red Rover will not deploy unless the local jurisdiction managing the influx of evacuees specifically reaches out to the group for assistance. This avoids duplication of efforts by other groups, but also the response system in disasters in the United States allows local leadership to convey urgent needs to the state and outside agencies. This aligns well with the provisions of the Stafford Act, which outline that local emergency management is the primary leader in response and that agencies at the state and federal levels supplement resources and services at the request of local emergency management (Sylves 2019). Managing animals in disasters works well in this way, but in the following sections we also describe how leadership, flexibility of emergent groups, and organization of information are also important for meeting the needs of animals and people during and after a disaster.

Leadership in Organizations

Leadership is important for building trust among volunteers, the community, and everyone stationed at key points during a disaster (Trainor and Velotti 2013). Among the people we interviewed, if volunteers felt that leadership was unorganized, lacked compassion, or lacked technical expertise, the volunteers became resentful. They also expressed feelings of fatigue, anger, and disappointment. One respondent perceived failure in leadership as one of the main barriers to supporting people and animals in some of the key staging areas:

I saw this firsthand. There was too much ego involved in a situation that should not have ego. That's what I saw. If you didn't have the right shirt on, you weren't acknowledged as a worker, and it got really bad. Several of my co-volunteers quit. It was really hard to work

under those circumstances. Really hard, 'cause you were already—
we were already stressed, and to have to navigate that was really
hard. And then I felt like the person in charge of the group was not
a person who should be in charge. I don't feel like they were capable
of handling what needed to be handled. You need a really quick-
thinking, fast-moving, or, you know, future thinker [to] navigate
this. And that just wasn't there.

As we describe in Chapter 3, a local animal shelter coordinator managed
the shelter in deplorable and inhumane conditions during nondisaster times
and then engaged in corruption during the disaster by refusing to return
horses to people who were the owners. There were also concerns that the
shelter manager facilitated the adoption of animals for nefarious purposes.
This is not unlike other concerns we observed across social media in various
animal groups about the potential risk of having cats and dogs adopted at
no or low cost, because there is a risk that the animals would be used as bait
in dogfighting or other activities. Here we examine how and why people
who engaged in behaviors such as this maintained positions of power and
leadership. Low wages and a lax system of accountability may support conditions for cruelty (Lovell 2016). More research should examine leadership
and cruelty, especially because people in positions of power can take advantage of disaster scenarios to continue to exploit animals.

In many cases, people in leadership facilitated positive outcomes, and
many times people with expertise and leadership used their social connections to improve the well-being of people and animals. For example, we
interviewed program coordinators in California, Texas, and the Carolinas
who used their local contacts to mobilize resources and leverage staging
space for the animals in their shelters and networks after disasters in their
states. In other words, having good people skills is essential to be a good
manager of animals in disasters. The traits of "good" leadership that we saw
were present in a variety of groups: emergent groups, large-scale formal
organizations, and small local groups. The common traits that these leaders
shared were respect for volunteers, smart use of space and supplies, and
passion and enthusiasm about animal welfare. To creatively set up a space
in an abandoned grocery store as a staging area for hurricane pets also takes
social capital. The leaders and key decision makers in these processes also
had to have access to people who were working with someone in a position
that would give them access to these vital resources. Another kind of connection besides horizontal ties that is important in disasters is what Aldrich
calls "vertical ties," or ties to organizations, in his research on social capital
and disasters (2016, 408). This refers to someone with ties to people in higher

leadership who can move important resources to the community. A program coordinator working at one of the key field sites for cat rescue after the Camp Fire illustrates this connection:

> These are the people that would probably have some idea how to go about goal number one, because I don't know how to say enough good about what those groups are doing. If you can get to them and get a personal contact with them, it's just like pow, pow, pow, done. Horse pulled out, rescued, fed, triaged, treated—they are doing phenomenally well. I think their social-media links are weak; normally they want them that way for the same reasons, but they have the setups for sure.

This respondent is suggesting that there are some key people with financial resources and organizational power that can be leveraged to meet the needs of groups managing animals in disasters. The respondent is also suggesting that some of these people in power are not necessarily visible or active on social media. This returns to our earlier point that social media is not necessarily the ultimate solution because the real power of the network—either in the virtual world or otherwise—is the people. The following sections discuss in more detail how things can go badly in disasters; just as people can mobilize social networks, they can also make mistakes, and organizations can make poor decisions.

How Things Can Go Badly

Throughout our interviews, several themes emerge that illustrate how organizations can fail in managing animals during disasters. These include being overly territorial in managing a crisis, being overly rigid in adherence to protocol or top-down command, taking on too many animals beyond capacity or expertise, and failing to use resources creatively. A specific example of rigid adherence to the command-and-control structure is prohibiting people to reenter communities to do wellness checks on animals. While there is certainly a need to secure the scene and make sure that people do not reenter an unsafe community, evidence from our interviews suggests that the time line for prohibiting reentry was (at least in some cases) based on an arbitrary date rather than actual safety. Moreover, communication with community members about which tasks are carried out to ensure the safety of animals behind a barricade would minimize some of the stress, uncertainty, and anxiety about animal well-being.

A common thread in these failures is not incorporating the principles of harm reduction known as the Five Freedoms (Sawyer and Huertas 2018).

Tensions between broader emergency management and animal welfare groups can be complex and unfold in different ways. For example, during the 2018 lava flows in Hawaii tensions arose between community members and government workers, as explained by a volunteer with a rescue group:

> [Organization 1] also failed miserably and did very little to help until a huge public outcry happened over a month into the lava flows. [Organization 2] then came and sent two men from the mainland, but they were very secretive and not much help either. There was a huge lack of communication between all government entities, and all they cared about was blocking access so we could not save more animals.

Additionally, in the Camp Fire, many respondents indicated that local government officials had chosen to partner with only a select few organizations and did not use the power of local people and expertise of other organizations. In the case of the Camp Fire, many volunteers, coordinators, and evacuees described some issues they observed:

> You know, everything was about not welfare and well-being but . . . basically keeping the animals alive, without any kind of concern for behavior or wellness. So, run on fear. Secondly, they never stopped and said, let's bring in our external resources to help with this. Like [Person 1] is a resource. [Person 2] is a resource. Who in our community is a resource? And when they did, it failed because they're so in their box. The third thing is—and this is why I wish you could talk with [Person 3]—there has been no acknowledgment in all of this. There was no acknowledgment of the investment of the volunteers, like those airport volunteers. I can tell you. And the hotline volunteers, they are suffering serious PTSD. It was traumatic. It is traumatic. To have to deal with this with no leadership, no answers, no one listening to what the people who were actually doing the animal care.

While it is difficult to determine exactly what went wrong in disasters such as the Camp Fire, the frustration and fatigue of the volunteers were palpable. This related to their sense of helplessness and perceived ineptitude of the organizations managing the animals. One evacuee talked about her frustration in looking for her lost cat and having to go stand in line at multiple locations because there was no central location for posting all lost animals:

> Yeah, and then they're like, but if you want, you can go stand in line and see. I'm just like in tears at this point. And this very nice lady,

she was volunteering there, and she actually—she normally was an EMS [technician], and she had been going in—she had been taking pictures of the cats because all their [the organization's] pictures sucked. Some of them you couldn't even see the cat's faces. Just awful. And so she had the other pictures of the cat, and it had been cleaned up, and we could see it wasn't [my cat], but she was the only person there who had any compassion, who took the time to really look at my pictures and really listen to me. And I understand there's a lot going on, but it was literally only one person, and she actually saved [my cat's] picture, and she texts me later because she kept looking just in case, and that was the one person who treated me like a person.

In this case, the evacuee described how important it was that someone was interacting with evacuees with compassion and concern for their lost animals. She also described her perceptions about the failings at the organizational level and the inadequate response, which reflects sentiments from other volunteers and evacuees who felt that the scope of the Camp Fire was far too large for the county and one or two NGOs to handle:

But the other thing is [one agency] refused to accept help from outside, like respected outside groups. For a little bit, they were accepting help from [Organization 1], which is, like, a nationwide group that just helps out people, basically. . . . And there also was a bunch of groups who actually in the Tubbs Fire came up to help, and they were constantly met with roadblocks. They weren't allowing people up there to go search. . . . Cats and dogs were locked in people's houses that didn't burn, and these people [were] saying someone needs to go up and rescue them, and someone needs to go up and feed them. And nobody was, and so there [were] these animals that have been sitting in standing houses for over a week. There were people who went home to find their animals dead in their houses because they weren't allowing anybody to go up. They're like, well, people can go through our training, and if you're from out of Butte County, then it's three hundred dollars, and if you're in Butte County, it's like one hundred to one hundred twenty-five dollars but not until January. . . . They weren't escorting; they weren't letting anybody go up without escorts until November 27 or 28, at which point the fire was completely out, but it had been out in Paradise for weeks at that point. . . . There were so many things they could have done, but it's very frustrating when private groups are doing a better job than them—the county and other agencies. And the agencies are getting territorial about who's doing what and when. It's like, people are missing their pets; these people are hurting. They've lost everything; that is all that matters. These poor animals survived in literal hell, and your actions are keeping them from going home to safety and to people who care about them. The other major thing that could have been done better is [one organization] put out a statement a little while back saying that all animals have been rescued; there are no other animals up on the ridge. And that part is a huge, huge dent in our efforts because that made a lot of people lose hope.

When we asked about recommendations for improvements in future evacuations, she described many of the issues we discuss in Chapter 6 regarding decision-making. Again, she alludes to the extent of the disaster as too great for organizations to manage because the scope of the disaster was greater than the available resources:

The cars [blocking evacuation lanes] could be moved, and [the freed-up lanes] could be used as traffic lanes. Those are I think the two biggest things that could have improved the evacuation process. And then the understanding that this disaster was so huge that no one agency could have managed the entire thing. For as far as the pets and then in the future, other groups [should] be willing to accept outside help in understanding that extra resources in extraordinary situations require extraordinary measures. I think those are the three biggest things.

Many of these organizational issues and failures centered on the system for finding and tracking lost pets during the disasters. Again, in the case of the fires in Paradise a different evacuee talked about her family's experience in trying to find one of their cats after the fire. The cat was found by neighbors who had stayed behind to defend their land and house against the fire. The family we interviewed had successfully evacuated with some of their dogs and cats but were unable to find their oldest cat. They also lost goats and honeybees in the fire:

One of our other cats, Willie, [is] an ancient old cat. . . . So a few weeks after the fire people wanted to help. There was a family up there, and they had stayed and defended their property, and they have a big defensible area. And a lot of people sheltered there, but their son Ryan and his friend Colton were going around looking for people's pets, putting out pet food and stuff. And so I had texted him and said, "Can you go to [my house] and go see if you can see any cat, you know, our cat?" And they went there, and they found Willie, our old cat. I can show you a really cute picture of her. But they found Willie; they brought her—well, . . . they just took her to their friend's house, and we went and picked her up there. And she survived. Her ears are burned, and her whiskers were all scrunched. And the interesting thing about Willie—I was looking at her back; it looked like [it] was embedded with glitter. And I was like, "What the heck? What did she—why, how'd that happen?" And then Harry said, "Molly, it's iron pyrite from the creek." She went and rolled in the creek where it was wet, and that sand was all embedded in her back forever. She went and stayed with [another friend] afterward, and she was just brushing and brushing her; her hair is all singed on her back. There were iron pyrite flakes in her back then; it was like gold glitter.

The cat had found her way to the creek during the fires, and this is possibly how she survived. This also highlights that many of the fire cats looked different because of burn injuries or dirt and ash, which also made identification more difficult. Throughout our interviews and the social-media posts after the Camp Fire, organizers emphasized the message of "Your cat may look different!" so that people did not dismiss photos of cats that could be their missing pet.

Another issue that volunteers, coordinators, and evacuees brought up frequently was how frustrating it was that there was no organized process for tracking lost and found animals. When groups did set up systems for tracking animals or documenting tasks (such as trips to feeding stations in burn zones), the organizations had different systems or protocols, as one volunteer described:

They were feeding all sorts of animals, and it was a combination of [Organization 1], [Organization 2], and different animal control agencies that were called in through mutual agreements, and it was very interesting because all three of those main groups were running their own system. . . . That meant that there was literally just a different system for each group. There was no centralized data management; it was all one hundred percent on paper for the shelter.

This volunteer explained that there was no way of consistently categorizing which animals remained in the burn zone, which animals were rescued outside the burn zone, which animals had been fed and on what schedule, and other critical information about tracking lost or found animals after the fires. This highlights the need for organizations to work together to communicate the systems in place to maximize efficiency. In organizational studies of disaster management, the complexity of multiple groups can complicate response efforts. Again, the groups decide the scope of their response efforts based on urgent needs during the early phases of the crisis (Albala-Bertrand 2000). Although multiple groups responded to the Camp Fire, some engaged in infighting, had territorial issues of managing the disaster, or strictly adhered to top-down management and decision-making. All these factors, combined with the size and onset of the fire, led to catastrophic circumstances. Thus, it seems that the scope of the disaster may have been a core issue in the case of the Camp Fire. Another evacuee described her experience of searching for her missing cat after the fire. When asked, "Have you been searching the online groups that found cats?," she responded:

> Man, they were spread out everywhere. Like so many, uh, Facebook groups. In fact, the North Valley Animal Disaster Group—they're no longer [active]—as of, like, March 4, they don't have their database anymore. They have links to all of the other places. . . . It was really frustrating because you had to wait for the groups on Facebook—you had to wait to get accepted into the group, and then you had to post your data. Then it was just like a lot of people obviously trying to help, so that was kind of frustrating. It was also frustrating that they wouldn't post where the cat was found because then you can just search. . . . And we'd see a cat, and we'd say like, "Oh, that looks like it could be," but then we'd go look at every place that there were animals that we could go search. . . . We'd go there, but then sometimes they didn't know where they were: Were they found in Magalia? Were they found in Paradise? Were they found in Concow? You didn't know. So you'd go look at a cat that was found in Magalia or Del Oro. Well, that wasn't going to be your cat, but you didn't know that, you know, at the time, and countless times we went out to the airport to the place in Orville where there were cats; they didn't want people [to] just walk [into the shelter]. I mean, they were trying to be organized, you know, and I think in the 2008 fire it seemed more organized, but it wasn't the magnitude. That's the thing; the magnitude of this disaster, I think it was just so much, you know.

This also highlights that the definition of the event in terms of scope remains important for disaster research. From our observations, the Camp Fire was catastrophic (Quarantelli 2005). This affects the analysis of group response. This is not to say that the organizational response is "blameless" but that in catastrophic events, intergroup coordination may become even more important. In large and complex disasters, systems of information and tracking will operate more smoothly if information is streamlined so that evacuees and the affected community do not face an added burden when attempting to locate their missing pets.

A volunteer assisting with logistics expressed her frustration at the lack of systematic storage of information and tracking animals, including injured animals. Some severely injured animals were treated at veterinary hospitals farther away from the fires, so it was difficult for the owners to locate their animals. This volunteer mirrored the perceptions of evacuees concerning no organized system for tracking animals:

> Mostly they were injured, but people were just dropping animals off because they didn't know what to do, and that was right next to where first responders get housed at the fairground between the burn zone and the fairground. But there was no central database or information about the animals that had been evacuated, so even now people are still having to go and look on ten different websites. . . . An organization did a video montage . . . of the animals that they had—I mean, they fixed it, but that is the level of, like—those poor people who were looking for animals, the frustration. . . . The level of disorganization was horrific. So every time I went to the shelter, they were like, "Oh no, you have to fill out a lost form; where are they?" They just had boxes and boxes of loose paper forms, but they never have done anything with them. . . . There was no point to it. I do not doubt in any way, shape, or form that if animals were spotted in the burn zone, they were being fed. Like, because I went through, and I reorganized some. We discovered that for almost every single location, there were maybe six reports, right? But if you're not managing the information—how much it's just people fighting and arguing with each other. But from my point of view, from what I saw from both looking for animals and just viewing what their system was for the thousands of animals they were caring for, it was [just infighting]. Because prior to anything happening, they didn't have a system in place and a basic inventory control system to make sure they were not losing animals, because they did, and they lost the animals in the shuffle, which they admitted to. That to me was very clear that the whole effort was inefficient. And it's frustrating on every side.

Another respondent indicated frustration over the logistics for managing animals rescued from the burn zone. Again, the volunteers expressed concern about the welfare of the animals and the unorganized system that made reuniting pets with owners difficult. If it is time-consuming to look through too many online locations or to visit multiple physical locations (that may be far away), the odds are lower that people will be reunited with their pets:

> People dropped off dogs and cats at [the shelter location] and had to give their names and telephone number. Once [the shelter location] was full, people dropped off animals at [a different shelter location], which was a nonprofit animal rescue organization. This organization gave a number to pet owners and put a number also on the pet's crate to assist in finding the pet. Pets were put in small crates, and crate numbers were not consecutive so that it was hard for owners picking up pets to find their cat from three hundred cats. Too many animals, and one room was just for storage of donations, which could have been better used for offering the overcrowded animals more space. Crates were stacked on top of each other to house all cats. Some cats were in small crates for five days.

To find solutions for problems such as shelter overcrowding, volunteers came up with a foster system to move animals into homes as quickly as possible. A foster network was used during hurricanes and the Hawaii lava flow as well as during multiple wildfires in California. A woman and her friends started a grassroots foster network for dogs after the Camp Fire. She told us:

> We were both kind of disappointed that both the county and [Organization 1] are going to have nothing to do with this because of the liability. They said, "We don't want our names associated with this; if you guys want to do that, that would be awesome. We will send people your way. But that's just too much liability for us." I mean, all of us who were in the shelters helping the animals were like, "This sucks. This is not fun for the animals." These animals have got to get out of here, and there are so many people in the community who would like to help. There's got to be a way to get them out of here and get them there. . . . It's like, can you start calling these people and seeing if we can get them into foster and arrange them fosters? A week before, you have no time to do anything but go into panic mode. So most of the animals ended up getting picked up and put into foster homes one way or another without any kind of thoughtfulness about the process. And they allow basically for animals to go on a phone call directly out of the shelter into foster homes that

nobody had ever even met—just somebody who was a name who said, "I can foster." And then the unclaimed animals all went to local shelters. Paradise had reopened just the weekend before, and they took back their animals. Many of their animals pre-fire had been housed in [a] Chico animal shelter; they took them back from Chico Animal Shelter.

Here the respondent expresses possible feelings of conflict about wanting to get animals out of kennels and cages and into foster homes but maintaining some system for checking to see who is fostering the animals. The issue of foster accountability also came up with respondents in Hawaii and other states. There seems to be an optimal balance in allowing people to foster without giving animals away freely to people who might be harmful to the animals. We also heard secondhand accounts of people adopting low- or no-cost cats for gun target practice or baits for dogfighting and adopting dogs for dogfighting, as described in Chapter 3. However, it seems that being overly cautious in preventing animals from moving out of sheltering space and into foster homes could prevent people from fostering. Adoption rates did increase in association with foster programs—such as during Hurricane Florence in North Carolina—because a sudden influx of animals into people's homes statistically increases their exposure to shelter animals. Additionally, people like to share that they have adopted a "hurricane dog" or "fire cat" to boost social status.

Large Animals and Livestock: Preparation, Evacuation, and Rescue

While narratives of pets in disasters frequently focus on common household pets such as cats and dogs, many people keep farm animals as pets. Furthermore, there are other considerations for livestock affected by disasters, especially in relation to a farmer's livelihood. There are many more technicalities in rescuing large animals and livestock as well. Equine rescue can be particularly difficult, especially when emergency planning excludes large animals. Most of the interviews we conducted regarding large animals in disasters were from people working in the equine community. The national network of people working in large-animal rescue, including equine rescue—similar to observations of other animal welfare groups—is also a tight-knit community.

Horses became the focus of large-animal rescue among the respondents we interviewed, but other rescue shelters experienced challenges with other animals. In Texas, floodwaters destroyed a rabbit shelter. The volunteers there moved the bunnies early during the storm, but as the shelter coordinator described the situation:

> Hurricane Harvey gave us fifty-six inches of constant rain for thirty-six hours. . . . After the rain ended, the dams had to be opened, causing us to remain flooded for five weeks. End result, the only thing left of the rabbit rescue is the rabbits/bunnies. Our building collapsed in week three of flooding. All our feed and hay were lost in the first week.

Therefore, people working in planning and response should consider other animals not traditionally included in disaster planning. Often, evacuating, sheltering, and, if necessary, rescuing these animals become more cumbersome and difficult than it is for household pets. One person we interviewed in Miami had a hedgehog. Throughout our research, people mentioned having birds, snakes, fish, and many other animals. Smaller exotic animals are overlooked in disaster planning, and larger animals such as goats, horses, and pigs can be especially problematic because they are difficult to transport and shelter.

Planning and Preparation for Disaster

Disaster preparation for large animals often requires more in-depth planning and expertise. While all animal planning, evacuation, and sheltering are the responsibility of individual households, horses and other such animals can be more cumbersome. Large animals are not easy to transport, and there are not many evacuation locations that would accept pets such as horses, so the owner must find alternative ways to keep their large animals safe in the evacuation zone or ways to get their animals to safety. One respondent who helped with equine rescue after Hurricane Florence said:

> A big chunk of the issue is that there isn't much in the way of emergency planning for livestock. You know, I've had a conversation with the emergency management department of probably nearly every affected county in the last few weeks, and most of them will just tell you it's under control; go away. I mean, not in exactly those words, but they all know we don't have that many problems or whatever. I can show you twenty posts on Facebook in the last hour that are screaming for help [for their horses].

Tagging large animals such as horses is one common method to ensure that if the horse becomes lost, people can identify the owner. Many people do not know that microchipping is possible for horses or just do not do it. As one equine rescue respondent told us, "There is a protocol for it, but hardly anybody knows how to correctly check for it." While all her horses are microchipped, she recognizes this is not a routine practice for every person who owns horses. A microchip on a horse should be on the right side of the neck, halfway down, between the poll and the withers. However, this does not seem to be common knowledge, especially among people working with horses temporarily for purposes of disaster rescue and response.

Other methods for tagging horses are to paint a phone number across their body, write a tag that is tied into their mane or tail, or write information on their hooves. Writing on the side of a horse with a cattle marker ensures that someone can see the information from a distance. As another horse-rescue respondent mentioned, she tagged her horses by writing her name, phone number, and address with a Sharpie marker, then braided it into their manes, using a piece of coated wire so the tag would hold even tighter. Additionally, people should avoid putting halters or leads on horses unless they are breakaway because they can catch easily and result in horses becoming caught or stuck as they attempt to flee the hazard.

Equine Evacuation and Sheltering

Sheltering horses for an evacuee can get complicated, especially because of the possibility of abandonment. Who will care for an abandoned horse, and where should it go? One respondent told us that she approaches boarding horses for others with extreme caution, since she is usually dealing with complete strangers and does not have the insurance protection that rescue groups might have. While she has not had problems in the past herself, she described a neighbor who dealt with a horse that was left behind and abandoned:

> My neighbors have a huge boarding facility, and someone came and left at least five or six horses with them and just left them. You know, huge vet bills, and the neighbors were, unfortunately, not well prepared with consent forms and things like that. I watched all that unfold, and I thought, oh, that's an ordeal right there. So I think people need, at least, a limited power of attorney if they're gonna take people's animals in. And to be fair, so many people that have however many horses and just lost their house and their job and their livelihood and everything else—they don't have any idea what to predict or what's going to happen over the next two or three months.

As indicated here, there are numerous reasons for someone to leave a horse behind. Burdened with various troubles, someone simply may be unable to retain possession and take care of them. The implications are further complicated in areas where there is an overpopulation of horses. While this is a more limited problem than cat and dog overpopulation, neutering/spaying a horse is an expensive surgery. It is easy for someone to become overwhelmed with the financial cost of feeding and providing veterinary care for a horse, especially during times of disaster. People who are new horse owners may not be prepared for a disaster and have no means to move their animals out of the storm. We emphasize that additional education and outreach about horse care will be helpful in reducing impulsive horse adoptions. However, another critical aspect of supporting horses is for organizations to provide resources (in coordination with government response and relief) for horse owners who are experiencing a crisis or disaster (such as hay, boarding, and transport during a hurricane evacuation).

Fire evacuations for large animals bring about their own hurdles and problems. Jade, a horse owner in California, experienced a harrowing series of events in attempting to evacuate and then rescue her horse. She described the various obstacles she faced in her attempts to get to her horse:

> I left, but my horse lives less than ten minutes away, so I was like, well, I am going to get my horse the heck out of here. I just had a bad feeling about it, and I was like, I am going to go sit there. Well, by the time I got out, it took me forty-five minutes to make what should have been an eight-minute drive because I exited on the same road that people were evacuating out of Paradise on. So they were driving both lanes, you know; people going down the wrong way of the road because they were just trying to get people out. And then my horse happens to live off that same street. That particular place [where the horse was boarded] happens to be an evacuation zone for livestock. Well, the problem was you couldn't get in or out of the evacuation. Like it was supposed to be the place you take your horse if you get evacuated. The first problem was you couldn't get in or out, because once you got there, if you left, you weren't going to come out because we were inside the roadblocks.

While she was not attempting to leave the area, evacuation still proved to be problematic as traffic was so gridlocked. Furthermore, she was aware that the area where her horse was boarded was also the evacuation zone for any livestock; however, the fire was quickly approaching. This highlights the need for alternative plans. As she finally reached the area where her horse and approximately thirty others were located, she and a friend began talking about evacuating the horses from that location because the flames were visible and, in her words, "it just felt different." She had a trailer to evacuate her horse but no vehicle for the trailer. The next problem encountered was that she was in a red zone, and no one was allowed in to help rescue horses:

> I had three different people try to come with a truck and get in past the roadblock, and they wouldn't let anybody in. And one of them is a vet, and they would not let the vet inside. I had a trailer on the property, so if I could have gotten the truck, I could have hitched up, which was kind of what I was trying to do. Eventually somebody who is an EMT [emergency medical technician] was able to evacuate their horse, and I just gave her another horse to evacuate. It was her friend's horse, and her friend was in Texas at the time. And I was like, just take them home, because they were worrying about them. She took her trailer, but we couldn't get ahold of the other horse's owner, and I was like, just take [the horse] with you, because who knows what tonight is going to look like. Luckily, the lady was okay, because we stole her horse, and we gave her back. They wouldn't let anyone in, so this girl only got past the roadblock because she is an EMT. That is the only way she got in, and somebody else was able to pick up a couple horses because they were already behind the first line when we all got evacuated. Other than that, nobody could get in. Now the local rescue group had used that piece of property as their evacuation point, and, well, they left. They were like, this place is getting burnt; we need to get out of here. So they took their horses and all the panels that they normally use to set up temporary pens for the horses, and they left. They left all the boarding horses there— thirty horses. They took the ones that had been evacuated, and they left all the other ones.

Jade refused to leave her horse behind, even though she was unable to find help during the evacuation. As she noted, rescue groups that had helped other large animals to this location decided to evacuate for safety, but time ran out for Jade to evacuate with her horses. There was no alternative plan or ICS in place to support the remaining horses. A rescue group told Jade that they were going to come back, but they never did. She explained her frustration throughout this event:

> They did tell us they were going to come back for us, and they did not. In fact, they showed up with trailers and took panels [for the

horse pens], and I was like, "You won't even take the horses?" Yeah, I had to walk away [because] it was so frustrating. I know she was just doing what she was told by her superior, but I was like, "You could have taken two of them. Don't even take mine because my horse is difficult; leave him here, [and] take somebody else's." But they were so overwhelmed that they couldn't even think straight. So then we evacuated some of the horses on our own, four or five of them, and the rest of them, twenty-five or so, had to stay.

The inability to get the other horses out of that area left Jade and the others who stayed behind to help with limited options. They could have left with the rescue group and hoped that the horses would be okay. Or they could stay and do what they could to ensure the horses would be safe. They chose to stay behind:

We realized at two o'clock that we're alone; they're not coming back for us. There were twenty-four horses there and five of us left to take care of them, and none of us are firefighters. So it was like, well, go gas up the water truck—we have a really big water truck—and we filled it up and set up some temporary pens to be able to move horses into. We set up the pens in the arena because there was nothing to catch on fire. That was the whole reason we put them in the arena, you know; it's just sand, and there is nothing to fall on them. We were literally triaging at that point. . . . If that catches on fire, what's going to happen? So we moved horses around, and then we just waited. You could see it [the fire] coming off the hill just creeping toward us, and it ended up coming down the hill. . . . We just watched it glow in the distance. You could see it before it got dark, a few miles away, and then it just got closer and closer.

That evening, the California Department of Forestry and Fire Protection arrived with one truck available to water down the fire, after which the fire moved away from the horses. Jade was thankful that the arena was there because it created a fire break. She said, "I think we learned some things about creating our own fire breaks, because we got lucky as the fire jumped the road." She had to decide whether to leave the horses behind and evacuate or stay. The choice to stay meant that she and her colleagues did what they could to get the horses in safe positions. However, Jade also knew that she and the others who stayed behind were behind the fire evacuation road-blocks and would not be allowed back in if they went beyond them. When she knew her horse was safe, she left to help her parents evacuate. While the evacuation of the few horses and triaging of the evacuation zone for live-stock was an impromptu decision, afterward, Jade and other volunteers con-tinued to help with the evacuation of horses in the area:

> We had a couple people who had asked if we could go pick up their horses, and we picked those animals up. There were two that we knew and were hoping to find them alive. I don't know how those horses lived through the fire, but they did. If you saw where they were, it was so hot that their fence melted, and their rubber water bucket melted, which is just crazy to think about. I don't even know why they were still in their pens, but they were still there together. I was shellshocked.

Sometimes evacuating with animals, especially large animals, can prove difficult because of logistics. While Jade and her friend had a trailer, loading horses and other livestock into a trailer can be difficult. When asked if she had trouble coaxing the horses into the trailer, Jade told us:

> We didn't have a single horse that didn't want to load onto the trailer. And we talked about that later. Like this is so weird, because some-times horses don't want to get into a trailer, and all of them were like, "Let's get out of here." Some of them, I think, were so in shock from what they had been through that they just didn't have any fight or anything in them. Or they'd probably been so scared since the day before that they blew through any adrenaline they had.

Their experiences illuminate the importance of planning and including large animals in evacuation preparation. As noted, the boarding facility where her horse was located was also an evacuation destination for live-stock, but there was not an alternative plan in place in the eventuality that the boarding facility itself was in the line of the fire. However, Jade stayed behind for her horse until she knew it was safe. The other horses boarded at the facility would have been left as well, since the other owners would have been unable to get through the roadblocks or did not live in the area at all. Presumably, the boarding facility is responsible for the horses, but the ques-tion remains of how owners can oversee the evacuation and safety of ani-mals they cannot get to.

Rescue Operations for Large Animals

Once a disaster happens, many people volunteer or work with rescue groups, including those for animals. In South Carolina after Hurricane Florence, one woman involved in rescue operations as a volunteer described her rescue efforts in just trying to save one horse:

> What started [it] was a horse; somebody said their horse needed out. When we finally found the horse, seeing it standing in water covering his back for two days, he was in a locked chain-link fence. You couldn't even see him. When I finally got the national guard in to find him, he literally had his nose on the top of the chain-link fence, breathing water. I looked at them, and I said, "What are you all going to do?" And I jump in, and they just kind of looked at each other. I put the horse's head on my shoulder to hold it up out of the water, and it took us about four hours to break the fence to get him out and . . . he didn't make it.

With tears in her eyes, she described that it took her another four days to find out if the horse survived. While another organization arrived to help with the rescue, they focused primarily on bringing out dogs and cats. The volunteer was waiting for them to let her in and help the horse, because only she knew where it was located. One could sense her frustration at not being able to help more, even though she understood it was unlikely the horse could have lived through it anyway:

> The water had been covering his back for at least two days. Like I said, he probably wouldn't have made it anyway. Standing in water like that, he would have got river rot,[2] and all of his skin sloughed off. But people need to know you don't leave your animals in locked fences. He was in a locked chain-link fence. If you're gonna get a hurricane, you tag your horses, and you don't lock them up. . . . You lock them out of your barn . . . because if they get [in the barn], they're not gonna leave because it's a safe place. I tag all my horses, so if a tree falls, they still could get out and run, and I'll find them later. You take pictures of them so you know they're yours and so you have evidence they're yours and just let them go. Turn your horses loose.

Her frustration was not only with being unable to save the horse. She also saw so many problems concerning evacuation and planning for large animals. For example, owners unaware of the hazards might believe that keeping their horses in the barn is keeping them safe. However, if the barn or a pen floods, the horse will have no way out.

Another problem with evacuation and rescue is lack of technical expertise and official training for large-animal rescue. This is important, as pointed out by the volunteer, because those without technical training can injure animals if they are not careful. Many rescue groups that come into a disaster zone can hinder rescue operations because they do not know how to properly evacuate or rescue a large animal. The volunteer in South Carolina explained what would be most necessary in helping with large-animal evacuations:

> I would like to get a TL [stabilizer] [and] a taller rescue area that has the actual lift that you can lift the animals by air, by helicopter. But they're like six grand. When we've loaded the horse out, we got two of these blue barrels, and we put a tarp under [the horse] and put something around the chest so he didn't nose-dive in, and floated him out that way. It worked really well, but it's time-consuming to do—sling the hook to blue barrels to float a horse out could save more horses. Even cows [because] once they turn sideways, they freak out.

Eventually, she advocated that large-animal rescue in disasters should be carried out by private individuals trained and knowledgeable about horses and other livestock. Many rescue organizations that come to help are prepared to assist only with smaller animals such as cats and dogs. They do not have the equipment to evacuate bigger animals. Rescue operations for large animals can be dangerous not only for the animals but for people as well. As she summarily pointed out, "If they don't know how to handle a horse—you have to know what you're doing. If you don't, you're gonna get hurt."

Solutions and Moving Forward

As mentioned earlier, the Five Freedoms list (Sawyer and Huertas 2018) can inform future planning for managing animals in disasters. While this "do-no-harm list" centers the well-being of animals, we also suggest that the "do-no-harm" principles are important for volunteers, emergency responders, and community members. In other words, if certain bureaucratic barriers cause undue animal suffering during and after the disaster, then those policies should be revisited and revised. The lack of central locations and streamlined processes for animal tracking resulted in suboptimal chances for reuniting pets with their owners, and the messy process left volunteers feeling disillusioned, frustrated, and, in some cases, depressed.

In some cases local-level organizations did not get the resources requested from state agencies. During the Camp Fire, according to one co-leader of an animal response team, Butte County requested trained response teams to assist in evacuating animals from the fires but got only six. This respondent talked at length about the entire disaster being depressing and frustrating and the MOU system failing because of the scope of the fires. While this leader perceived that the problems with the response were caused by failure of state support, other volunteers we interviewed perceived the NGOs in partnerships with Butte County to be the cause of the response failure. One volunteer explained:

Mutual aid should have been utilized immediately per [the] California disaster plan, but [the rescue organization volunteers] instead chose to try to manage it all themselves and were completely unable to manage the demand of this fire. Animal rescue was an embarrassment to the many of us who were qualified to assist and turned away solely because [the organization] hadn't assigned us the appropriate credentials. As an owner of many animals myself, had I been in this disaster, I would be furious that my animals were not rescued due to politics, as has been the case in this fire.

What is clear is what worked well across all the disasters were flexibility, social innovation, partnerships, and working with local communities. We list the observations and themes from our data here as a core guide for organizations to enhance disaster planning, response, and recovery:

- Foster animals by using temporary homes to prevent shelter surge (such as Saving Grace did, moving dogs into foster homes so that rescued coastal dogs can be transported to an inland sanctuary).
- Use social media to get volunteers engaged and to organize information in one central location.
- Use resources smartly (trail cams, thermal scopes, volunteers).
- Harness the power of experts from past disasters (such as the Tubbs Fire cat trappers assisting with Camp Fire cats in Paradise).
- Have a purposeful system of volunteers, tasks, and support in staging areas, such as fairgrounds.
  - Set up hourly shifts for volunteers, and ask the "first surge" of volunteers to commit to response days after the early phase of the disaster.
  - Use a system of detailed notes on each animal (medical, feeding, transport, behavior).
  - Use electronic records and cloud storage.

- Identify volunteers with special skills and training.
- Consider Craig Fugate's (2011) advice on "whole community response": for animal systems this would be to focus on preventing a surge of animals; preventing euthanasia; reuniting pets with owners. Use all local resources and partnerships.
- Use the power of social networks. Calling in reinforcements to help, especially those who might have space to take in animals, or ability to transport or check on animals, can make a difference.
- Make sure that shelters accept evacuees with animals. Animal-friendly human shelters will increase compliance with evacuation orders. Colocating shelters are a feasible option so that people and animals are separate but evacuees can check on their pets when they like.
- Ensure that local decision makers for sheltering operations work with local animal sheltering services to develop updated ordinances that are more inclusive for breeds historically deemed as unsafe.
- Identify key strategies for communication with evacuees about their pets and animals.
  - Consider using an app for evacuees and responders managing animals to have continuous and relevant information about animal sheltering, boarding, and hubs for relief.
  - Use social media and activate a rumor-control team (official emergency management operations centers do this during activation; NGOs can adopt a similar system and/or work with the local office of emergency management).
- Avoid unnecessary systems of command and control. Securing a scene and protecting people from dangerous areas are important, but people should have access to trained escorts to reenter the burn and flood zones to check on their animals as soon as it is reasonably safe to do so. People will attempt to reenter the communities through illegal and unsafe means, regardless of the "rules," because they view their animals as family members. Setting up systems that allow people to retrieve animals early and engage in wellness checks as soon as it is safe to do so prevents emotional distress and long-term trauma.

Conclusion

Social innovation, group trust, and local partnerships all led to perceptions of better outcomes across the disasters for which we gathered data. One potential solution for the problem of tension between emergency management officials and animal welfare groups might be to employ certain strategies from social psychology. For example, the common in-group identity model highlights the similarities between groups to increase coordination (Gaertner and Dovidio 2005). Another related concept is the contact hypothesis, in which increased contacts with other people can increase coordination, but the groups need to view one another as essential in meeting some common goal (Paluck, Green, and Green 2019). In this case, EM groups and animal welfare groups could integrate into training sessions how to best communicate and partner with external agencies. For example, counties and townships in fire-prone or flood-prone areas should have training and drills that integrate animal shelters, veterinarians, and local trappers. The local trapping population (people who typically do TNR) know where all of the feral cat colonies are; they know who in the community is a skilled trapper (even beyond social media); and they have skills and equipment for humanely trapping animals before, during, and after disasters. While it would be ideal to have someone like Shannon Jay in every disaster—someone who is both a trained law enforcement officer and a skilled cat trapper—what communities may need is a system that empowers more people to operate with skill sets similar to Shannon's: a cadre of people trained in basic law enforcement and incident command who also practice detailed protocols for reuniting animals with their families.

Getting Ready

What Pet Owners Can Do to Be Prepared for a Disaster

*No matter how prepared you think you might be, you are not. I
really don't know how I could have been any more prepared—
this fire was just so fast moving. I realized that my home was
probably gone before I was even out of town.*

—Camp Fire evacuee (2019)

The respondent who shared her thoughts about the Camp Fire in this
chapter's epigraph highlights several core themes of our findings.
People engage in acts of kindness before and after disasters: this
woman, who lost her own home and pets in the fire, offered her property as
a feeding station and trail-camera site for volunteers who were tracking
other lost fire cats. Because a fire or other hazard event can move rapidly,
preparedness for evacuation is an important way to minimize loss of life of
both people and animals.

Throughout our fieldwork we observed instances of things going badly
and things going well from an organizational perspective. In this chapter
we focus on information pertinent to households and individuals and the
ways in which they can prepare to evacuate with their companion animals.
While not every household will experience a mandatory evacuation from a
hurricane or wildfire, nearly every household is at risk for household fires
or other emergencies. Some of the findings from our data are relevant for
preparing for such small-scale emergencies as well. We discuss ways that
households can bolster preparedness before a hazard event, ways to improve
the evacuation process, tips for reuniting with pets after the hazard event,
and grief and loss. While our book explores the broader social systems,
networks, and organizational issues related to animals in disasters, this
chapter discusses more practical applications and recommendations based
on the knowledge and experience that evacuees from previous disasters
shared with us. Program coordinators, volunteers, and other individuals

also offered solutions for minimizing harm in future disasters based on their experiences.

We also revisit some stories and lessons learned from previous chapters but include tangible ways in which the stories can be more than just cautionary tales and offer a basis for improving planning at the household level. We acknowledge that preparedness is, in many ways, connected with privilege (Blake, Marlowe, and Johnston 2017). It takes money to buy a battery-powered radio, to stock food and water for three days, and to stockpile other essential supplies. It also requires money to be able to evacuate to a hotel. It is difficult for people who rely on public transportation to navigate the evacuation process, and with their animals the process becomes even more challenging. Some families and individuals had emergency plans and kits, yet some of their animals still perished in the disasters. Therefore, we also acknowledge that evacuees indicated that sometimes planning for disasters seems futile, as one evacuee after the Camp Fire indicated. While preparedness is important, many evacuees emphasize that they did have a plan, but the scope of the hazard was simply too vast, and the onset of the hazard was too fast. This evacuee stresses that because the wildfires approached so quickly, there seemed to be little opportunity to enact the evacuation plans prepared before the fire:

> It's amazing to me that, you know, that we got our cat back or the ducks; I don't know how the ducks made it. It's crazy how—you know, but they had that little water right there. I guess, somehow. I think that the thing is that we just—there was no time to, you know, [try] all our kind of evacuation plans. There was no time to execute that at all. And you know, just lucky we were home and were able to get the dogs out.

This also illustrates that a disaster can unfold in minutes or even seconds. In nearly every disaster for which we gathered data, there were instances of evacuees not receiving a warning or alert, even as their home was on fire or underwater. In other words, it is important to be vigilant of the environment and surroundings during an emergency. One respondent in Paradise evacuated from her home because she heard rain on the roof of her mobile home, and that sound was not rain but ash falling from the approaching wildfire.

Similarly, the evacuee in Texas who lived near a reservoir was surprised that the water in the parking lot of her townhome was climbing the interior stairs of her home within mere hours. Neither of these evacuees received formal evacuation notices; rather, they saw that the hazard was quickly worsening around them, and they had to take action to protect themselves and their families, including their pets. Being ready to evacuate very quickly can often mean a difference in successfully bringing pets along during the hazard or pets unintentionally left behind. If a cat carrier, dog leash, and other supplies are in an easy-to-remember place (and share this plan with all family members), it is easier to ensure a safe evacuation. Of course, this becomes more difficult in households with multiple pets or households with family members that have medical and functional access needs. In many cases rapid-onset events have rendered successful evacuations of pets, as during the bushfires of Australia in January 2020. Approximately 250 pets and 1,100 evacuees were rescued from Mallacoota via a navy ship. The pets included cats, dogs, a rabbit, and a bird (Smith 2020).

Another reason to be prepared to manage animals in disasters is, as we know from the broader disaster literature on community response (Levine and Thompson 2004), that people may end up managing not just their own animals but animals of neighbors and in the community. That is what happened to these volunteers, who used a three-horse trailer to safely shelter horses during the Camp Fire:

> Yeah, so that's how we ended up. I am not even sure when the decision was made; the two of us were going to play first responder, but it was just a reaction to just there was clearly a need. And we managed to talk our way back up there, and then we went out—I think the first day we found nine horses, and I don't know how many goats, but that was the first day.

Again, while we realize that residents and volunteers "playing first responder" is a point of contention, data from this research project suggest that overall, grassroots and community efforts are often the primary force behind managing animal evacuations. Preparedness and technical skills for managing the evacuation can be different across species. Such was the case of Bandit, the horse described earlier, who unfortunately died during flooding associated with Hurricane Florence because she was stuck behind a chain-link fence. Horses, dogs, and other animals such as goats and donkeys do not fare well in flooding events if contained or tethered. In response to our survey, a program coordinator after Hurricane Harvey emphasized:

> For equine owners: Set them loose! They can swim huge distances over the floodwaters and survive. Those that didn't make it most often were on porches, left in pens/enclosures, left tied, or in barns/stalls. We had one lady find her horses two miles away safe and sound. Dog owners: *Never ever chain your dog!* We lost lives trying to rescue dogs off chains, and so many animals died this way too.

We are changing Texas laws to make this a crime. Business owners: *Please* suspend your rules during a disaster. This is *not the time* to be a jerk over a dog. First responders: *Please* allow people to bring their pets with them when at all possible the *first time*. We had too many lost pets due to those being forced to leave them behind and then being unable to find them.

This also emphasizes that there are ongoing tensions rooted in situations in which people are not allowed to bring pets on rescue boats or helicopters or in cases in which they are told that there are not pet-friendly shelters available.

Preparedness for Pets in Disasters

Preparing for a disaster can be daunting. It is also a task that many often put off because having to evacuate in an emergency seems far-fetched. This is especially true if one has experienced a false alarm in the past—when officials mandated an evacuation order and then nothing happened. However, while the PETS Act requires that states seeking federal assistance must include accommodation of pets and service animals in their emergency evacuation plans, many of these plans outline that it is the responsibility of owners to plan and care for their own household animals. Because the individual owners may not have immediate resources from outside groups or emergency officials during or after the disaster, following are some general guidelines about preparing pets for disasters.

Save a recent photo. It is extremely helpful to have a recently taken photograph to share with animal shelters and on social media in case a pet runs off and gets lost. Some shelter coordinators we talked to mentioned that this came up especially as a hindrance in finding lost cats, because many had photos of the pet only when it was a kitten or puppy. This is true for any pet, however, not just cats and dogs. Saving a recent photo that is backed up on the internet (for example, in a shared Dropbox or Google Drive file) means being able to show everyone what your pet currently looks like and having proof the pet belongs to you, if necessary. This increases the chance of matching found pets with lost pet posts.

Have a plan in case of separation from your pet. The vast majority of survey respondents who were evacuees of Hurricanes Harvey and Irma, in response to what they would do if they were separated from their pet, said it simply would not happen. As one respondent wrote, "I WAS NOT GOING TO BE SEPARATED FROM MY PET." This is, of course, a common sentiment;

however, experience shows that animals can get scared and run off. Cats, for example, can be skittish and hide. Therefore, there should be a plan in place in case separation happens during the evacuation process. Have the pet microchipped (which is easier for dogs and cats). Most important, the information attached to the microchip should be current. In the case of the Camp Fire, some owners of found cats were unable to be located because information was outdated or because the chip was not registered. If microchipping is not an option, having tags on the pet is also helpful, using breakaway collars for cats (in case they get stuck or caught). For instance, people tagged horses during Hurricane Florence in various ways: by writing on them with cow markers, braiding tags into their manes, or writing information on hooves.

Check pet-friendly options in advance. When looking for pet-friendly shelters and hotels/motels for future evacuations, check beyond the usual daily driving distance, as unexpected occurrences may mean driving farther than planned, and be amenable to backup plans. Unfortunately, during the disasters covered in this book, hotels that were pet-friendly quickly became fully booked, and for those attempting to leave the area, traffic was difficult. This meant searching for other options online while driving or attempting to come up with a plan during the evacuation process. Many encountered issues of finding out only once they reached a shelter that it would not accept pets (or in some cases, would not accept certain restricted breeds or required preregistration for pets with vaccination records). For example, one respondent noted that the reason she did not evacuate before Hurricane Irma was that her dogs were pit bulls, which are illegal to own Miami-Dade County. These restrictions mean that public shelters may not be an option. Another respondent told us that during Hurricane Irma, only three of the local shelters allowed pets. She was only able to find accommodations because a friend of hers was staying at a pet-friendly hotel and invited her to shelter with her at the hotel.

Sentiments about the law surrounding evacuation and animals in public shelters aside, the plan in place to evacuate to a public shelter fell through. Having backup plans could include other pet-friendly shelters outside the area where one lives, contacting friends and family on social networks to create a backup plan, or having plans to leave the area (if viable with transportation and resources).

Public Shelters, Hotels, and Traveling with Pets

One prominent issue from our findings is the difficulties evacuees faced when leaving with their pets. This was particularly true concerning hotels.

One respondent described every hotel being completely full, until her family was finally able to find one of the last rooms available. She said the next time her family decided to evacuate, she would immediately call for reservations. Another mentioned the "impossibility" of finding hotels with open rooms. She drove more than one hundred miles before finding a room in Valdosta, Georgia. Others described having to sneak around hotel rules for their pets:

> We had to leave Georgia on that Friday before the storm because the hotel had no more room after that. We did see dogs in crates in the back of a pickup truck in the parking lot of the hotel, as it had a two-pet max per room. We had three, but our one cat was always hiding. It seemed the owner would rotate his dogs so that each one could have time inside. The weather, however, was extremely hot, and it was a shame that the dogs had to be outside for any amount of time, especially in crates.

This was not the only evacuee who described having to hide pets from hotel employees. As another respondent from Hurricane Irma said, "We struggled to find accommodations during evacuation. We sneaked our animals into the first hotel in Orlando because we didn't originally plan on stopping there, and everything was booked." Finding accommodating hotels within driving distance and not completely booked proved a hurdle. Another respondent, born and raised in Florida but having never been so close to a hurricane, was a new pet owner. She said, "The number of hotels that turned me down because of my pet was terrible; this was one of the most difficult situations we had to deal with."

Others encountered problems with public shelters. Some shelters were full and could no longer accept pets and evacuees. Many respondents knew they were lucky if they found a place that took in their pets. As one evacuee noted, "We saw people coming in that had been sent away by shelters after they took them and their pets in. It was a sad situation for those owners who had to find other means during the flooding." A different evacuee from Hurricane Harvey in Houston described issues with finding shelter:

> The city was not prepared for the evacuees. We waited out in the pouring rain for hours while they decided what to open for a shelter. Then we had to wait for a Good Samaritan to give us a ride there. Once we made it to the George R. Brown Convention Center, we were turned away because of our dogs. Only by sweet angels and the grace of God did we make it a few blocks over to the Hampton Inn, where we stayed with our dogs.

While the convention center in Houston did eventually accept pets, this was not originally the case. As one news story reported, "Initially at least some pets were turned away, causing families to wait outside in the rain with their animals, but as of Sunday night that policy had changed" (Greenwood 2017). Evacuees expressed frustration with hotels and other evacuation destinations not being pet-friendly:

> I wish hotels and businesses would be more open and understanding to taking in pets during emergency situations. We had difficulty locating hotels, and hardly any would accept more than one or two animals. We were sometimes forced to lie and risk being fined or kicked out because we had nowhere else to go with our pets.

We emphasize that hotels and motels temporarily changing their policies in the event of disasters might help with the evacuation and sheltering process for people and their pets. While this is a decision for private businesses and corporations who typically operate under strict policies, perhaps suggesting that hotels accommodate pets (even if they typically do not) could incentivize decisions to help in this process during evacuations. This decision may even boost the public relations for the hotel chain or corporation.

While traveling with pets can bring about various unexpected problems, the issue of being able to travel is itself important. For instance, a few respondents mentioned that there was no gas available to leave, even if they chose to. For others, it was a matter that affected their planning for their pets, as one evacuee indicated:

> After the storm hit, we had a very hard time getting gas. Then when we found gas, they would only let us fill up our vehicles and not our gas cans. We needed to fill our cans to run our generator for the pets and ourselves to have AC and run our fridge and microwave in the RV. We were without power for ten days, as we lost our power pole in the storm. My fur babies are my kids, and where I go, they go.

In this case, being unable to run a generator affected this person's plans for keeping her pets safe and comfortable. However, for this family, evacuating without them was never an option. She reiterates a preparedness tip for general emergencies: always have at least half a tank of gas in your car. Again, while we acknowledge that this can be difficult for many families because of economic resources, people should consider this in planning, especially during hurricane and wildfire seasons. Having an adequate number of pet carriers, leashes, small transport kennels, and other supplies can make the evacuation process much easier and more feasible. Unfortunately, many pet-supply stores may sell out of carriers in the days leading up to a hurricane.[1]

Evacuating with Pets in Disasters

Whether prepared for evacuation or not, leaving with pets can bring about some challenges, such as sheltering. The first choice one must make is whether to evacuate at all. Even in voluntary evacuation zones, many may choose to stay behind. This also occurs during mandatory evacuations. For the respondents from Hurricanes Harvey and Irma, pets seem to be one prominent reason that one might not evacuate. For example, one respondent said, "People were being separated from their pets, and I won't leave my cats." Thus, it is a reasonable conclusion that some stayed behind because bringing their pets along did not seem feasible, and they would not leave them alone. As a respondent affected by Hurricane Irma mentioned, "We also had a foster dog with us, and I couldn't leave my dogs alone in the storm. I looked for shelters, but two of my dogs are over one hundred pounds, and I have a bad back. I couldn't take them with me to shelter, so I stayed in the house with them to protect them." This family's pets influenced the decision to stay home. Others declined to evacuate because they knew the logistics of having pets would be too complicated. One respondent told us that declining to evacuate was an easier option:

> It would have done more harm than good. We have too many animals; it would have been impossible to evacuate anywhere without leaving someone behind. The dogs were our primary concern, because the horses could get to higher ground, but transporting eight dogs and sheltering would've been impossible. But [evacuation] wasn't even thought of—no man left behind.

For households with multiple pets, the logistics and planning for evacuation become even more complicated. The family is faced with the possibility of leaving some pets behind if there is not enough room for transport, or several trips may be necessary to evacuate all of the pets. Some did do this. Many who left pets behind made provisions, such as leaving extra food and water, having a neighbor who was staying behind check on the pets, or setting pets loose so they could reach a safer location if needed. Throughout our work, people often state that they leave outside cats behind during evacuation. In some cases, people search for the cat before evacuation, but they cannot locate the cat quickly enough. This respondent took one cat with her but could not find the other as she was evacuating from the 2018 Camp Fire:

I left extra food and water. I did leave the bedroom window open a few inches, but I did not leave the door or cat door open because I felt she would be safer inside (if that's where she was hiding), and I thought (like so many others) I would be back home in a couple hours. That decision haunts me every single day.

This evacuee experienced intense grief and is still searching for her cat months later. She even hired someone with a cadaver dog to search for the remains so that she could have confirmation and closure. She still maintained hope that the cat may have escaped the fire.

Sometimes people must evacuate, but there is no possibility for bringing pets along. This is especially true in an emergency or one in which they are being rescued—where saving human lives is the most important goal for first responders. However, hurricanes may give some warning to allow time for evacuations. In the case of the wildfires in California, the evacuation process was very different, and some never received any warning at all. Many respondents indicated that nothing could have convinced them to evacuate sooner because "sooner" was not a relevant concept in the situation. There was no time between learning of the fire and the decision-making because the fire was too fast. One evacuee woke up when a neighbor notified her during the Camp Fire, and only then did they evacuate. Another evacuee said, "If I had known sooner—I got no notification until my daughter called to tell me she was leaving. I went out and took one look at the sky and came back in and told my husband and roommate that we needed to leave." There was no evacuation notice in some cases for the wildfires and no time to prepare for evacuation with pets. Camp Fire evacuees described some of the direst circumstances because of the scope and rapid onset of the fire. As we describe throughout the book, many people felt a sense of doom, and some evacuees were certain that they and their pets were going to perish in the disaster. Despite these grave circumstances, many evacuees also still believed that they might be able to return to their home shortly after the danger had passed—only to discover that they were prohibited from reentering the community for weeks. This caused a lot of confusion and anger among the people who lived in Paradise and wanted to return to check on the status of their animals.

There were also feelings of regret and deep sadness when evacuees imagined the ways in which their pets might have perished. Cats locked inside houses, based on information from other interview data, seemed to be cases of accidentally leaving cats in the house because the family was away at work for the day or because they evacuated very quickly and could not locate the cat quickly. For instance, one evacuee in Sonoma County told us she simply did not have time to find the family's cats. Firefighters were knocking on their door in the middle of the night telling them they had to leave immediately. These differences in types of hazards are important in understanding the evacuation decisions made by pet owners. As another wildfire evacuee noted, "Pets are family. When we realized there was fire in close proximity, we started gathering animals and their supplies. We did not have time to think about other items. Our primary focus was getting ourselves and pets out to safety."

Other factors that affect decisions to leave are resources and money. One respondent, when asked why she did not evacuate said, "We didn't have enough money to travel," while another mentioned not having a car. Being able to safely get out of an evacuation zone, with pets that evacuees refuse to leave behind, is an important consideration. As we describe throughout this book, for some who do not evacuate, it is not a matter of choice but of circumstance. However, small steps toward preparedness can improve chances of companion animals and humans surviving the hazard event and evacuating safely.

Planning Ahead

Disaster kits are often mentioned as part of preparedness planning, but what should a disaster kit for pets include? Some of the basic necessities are a three-day supply of food and water, medications, leash/crate, and vet records. As one evacuee from the Carr Fire in California described:

> Worked in emergency preparedness before retiring and had been through several evacuations and warnings in the past couple years. Packed and repacked many times. I had the guest room set up since the previous Carr Fire with emergency-preparedness items, including lists taped on the wall of what to take if I only had x amount of time. I had two portable file cases with number-one important stuff—animal records, passport, copies of credit cards, et cetera. Only had time for the number-one file. My meds, all cat stuff, including a large folded dog crate and small litter box, food, et cetera— that proved invaluable, since the first two nights were housed in a roommate situation with two dogs and three other cats. Also had a briefcase with every single paper, including insurance policy for the house. . . . That all helped but did not work perfect because I spent my fifteen minutes mostly looking for my cat.

Those who did evacuate for Hurricanes Harvey and Irma noted things they wished they had brought with them. Some of the frequently mentioned items were blankets, a cat box, and litter. Bringing leashes and extra water was also important. Some evacuees did have "go kits" ready, especially for areas affected by wildfires. As one respondent said, "We took the kits and pets. That's all." Having supplies prepared beforehand can make evacuating during an emergency easier. At the very least, having a prepared list is useful. Cats often need crates. Some people during the Hurricane Harvey evacuations improvised by using Styrofoam coolers with air holes poked in them. While these are not adequate for the long term, if crates are unavailable, other possible options can work. People who sheltered in place and evacuated to the second floor of their townhomes or houses often mentioned that they wished they had had pee pads for their dogs, because when the first floor was flooded, they could not take the dog out and the only option was to have the dog pee in the tub, which seemed too stressful and confusing for the dog.

Evacuees also offer advice on what to do and what not to do. For example, if people are unable to evacuate their horses in hurricanes, they should *not* lock the horses behind fences or in barns. The horses should be released from enclosures so they can get to safety. People can tag their horses for identification if they have to leave the area because of flooding, but the horses should be turned loose. This is *not* the case for horses in wildfires. During a fire, horses can run back into barns out of fear and confusion. In wildfires, horses, goats, and other large animals should not be loose in an area where they are able to return to the barn, so they must be placed in a safe location with a defensible fire-protection area. In other words, fire preparedness and flood preparedness for horses are different. Of course, in both instances, prior evacuation out of the hazard zone is ideal. Our advice is based on the unfortunate scenarios we have learned about from our respondents who were unable to evacuate with their horses.

Dogs left chained to porches or in crates were a notable problem in multiple hurricanes for which we gathered data. Many believed that it would keep the animals out of harm's way and away from the floodwater. One evacuee of Hurricane Irma in Florida described her past experiences with this:

> After the 2015 flood we could not find anyone to keep our other dog for us, so we ended up tying her up in the backyard and visiting her every day. The fence was pushed down from floodwaters. She ended getting tangled up and unable to get out of the sun or to water and died. She had underlying medical issues. We were devastated.

This highlights the importance of accurate and reliable information. While many people might question why someone would tie up a pet during or after a disaster, as this evacuee mentioned, the fence was broken and she had no other way to keep the dog on the property, so she thought it was the safest choice. Sometimes residents do not realize what options they have for keeping their pets safe. Education and outreach are critical to explain to people what will harm their animals in disasters.

Many interviewees mentioned issues with first responders and business owners. As others who experienced disasters have noted many times over, businesses (especially hotels/motels) should temporarily suspend no-pet policies to help people who are trying to evacuate with their animals. For first responders, this is a more difficult conundrum because their focus is to save human lives. Many responders and shelter managers adhere to narratives about saving space for people in emergencies. This means that solving issues such as space limitations should be included in drills for large-scale hazards. Planning exercises should include pets and the space that they need for evacuation and sheltering. Again, colocation worked well in past disasters, as well as MOUs with sites for evacuated animals (fairgrounds, universities with agricultural space, sports arenas, and even unoccupied grocery and retail store space).

Most important, preparedness can be enhanced with access to information on how to evacuate pets and when. There are tools to successfully get pets out of harm's way, even in incredibly stressful circumstances. Residents should sign up for weather alerts, follow local news and other sources on social media to find updated sheltering information, and have a list of contacts to call for boarding or other sheltering options in case of a hazard event.

Grief and Coping

In all our fieldwork observations, evacuees, volunteers, and program coordinators described the psychological impact that disasters have on people, such as problems sleeping and stress when there were reminders of the disaster (being stuck in traffic triggered memories of the evacuation; the sound of rain caused hurricane survivors to recall flooding). This volunteer lived in Chico, California, and was aiding families who evacuated from the Camp Fire in Paradise:

> I worked directly with those evacuees and medically for a little bit but mostly when they were coming in; they were coming in shell-shocked, and you had ninety-year-old people who had lost their homes, and they were devastated. [I have] seen tons of PTSD [post-traumatic stress disorder], and back then it [was] more grateful to be alive, and now it's sleeplessness, nightmares, depression. If they get stuck in traffic here, they panic because they were stuck on that road

coming out of Paradise, and it was flames everywhere. So I've seen a lot of that. And the two men that I'm talking about have PTSD.

When evacuees have lost their homes, their neighborhood, and their sense of safety, it is often their animals to which they turn for comfort and a sense of normalcy. Just as another evacuee described her feeling that "hope dies last" in referring to the hope she had in finding the family animals, many evacuees hold on to hope that their animals will be found alive and that they will be reunited. This was also evident in the recent bushfires in Australia, when viral images, stories, and videos of people whose family cat or dog survived the fires made their way around the world. The tone of those news stories and mini-documentaries is that "the family pet survived, so there is a silver lining to this entire horrible event." In one case, a cat hid in an outdoor pizza woodstove and survived the fire (Radio New Zealand 2020). In another case, a fluffy white cat returned to her family, her fur singed and gray from ash (Winter 2020).

Future research efforts should include examinations of the effect of pet loss on postdisaster coping and recovery. It is also important to understand the mechanisms that bolster resilience situated in the human-animal bond. For example, some people who fostered animals had a bond with their animal during the disaster and later adopted the dog or cat. We hypothesize that people who go through a disaster with animals have a different level of coping than people without animals or people who lose animals. Of course, some people do lose animals during the disasters, but some pets survived from the same household. We saw evidence of depression and grief among not only people who lost their own pets but also volunteers who managed animals during and after the disaster. Volunteers need specific training and resources for mental health in disasters in which there may have been animal fatalities or injuries.

There should be documentation and research on outcomes of long-term psychological adjustment and coping of people who lost some or all their animals. Additionally, little is known about ranchers, farmers, and people who lose large animals or livestock to natural disasters. A sense of identity and purpose can be linked with animals, such as the "self-object" companion animal (Schaffer 2011). Additional research is needed in broader areas of pet loss in disasters, including agricultural animals, wildlife, feral and stray animals, zoo animals, and other animals that are vulnerable to disasters.

The bushfires from 2019 into 2020 in Australia drew significant attention because of the koala bears whose lives and habitats were destroyed. A video of a woman saving a koala bear, wrapping her own shirt around the burned animal, went viral on social media. Sadly, the koala known as Lewis later died (Berlinger and Yeung 2019). While videos and stories such as these are important in highlighting the impacts of extreme weather associated with climate change, the people and animals in these disasters experience psychological trauma long after the media attention associated with the disaster has waned.

Pet loss during Hurricane Katrina was associated with significantly high postdisaster distress (Lowe et al. 2009). Other studies explore the relationship between disaster coping and pet loss after Hurricane Katrina (Hunt, Al-Awadi, and Johnson 2008; Zottarelli 2010), but fewer studies focus on pet loss from wildfires, earthquakes, lava and volcanic events (e.g., Goto et al. 2006), and more recent disasters. It is important to emphasize that there can be guilt, depression, and trauma associated with managing pets and animals during and after the evacuation. Many people had the dual role of being both an evacuee and a volunteer for animal management. People who are exposed to the hazard event, especially if they managed injured or dead animals, should be debriefed and assessed. Psychosocial first aid can be used by nonprofit organizations after disasters and should continue to be used for responders, volunteers, and community members affected by the disaster. Loss of animals should not be minimized or dismissed. While animals are, of course, not people, they are family members, and the level of attachment that people have to their animals cannot be ignored. As one Hurricane Harvey evacuee said, the loss of his dog was worse than his divorce. This suggests that pet loss can have long-term and serious effects on emotional well-being and mental health. It is also important to note that many volunteers who engage in animal rescue during and after disasters are also exposed to human death and dying. As one respondent shared with us after the Camp Fire, two teenage volunteers working with an animal rescue group found bodies of people in cars (who had likely died attempting to evacuate). These experiences exacerbate the outcomes associated with volunteer PTSD.

One of the other volunteers we spoke with after the Camp Fire described how she managed the donation hotline for phone calls that came in across the country. She said that someone in a faraway state would talk about their cat dying and how they felt connected to the victims of the fire because of that loss. There might be something to this worth exploring. As frustrating as it may be for the hotline operators to hear about a cat that someone in a faraway state lost years ago, it is fascinating that this seems to be the underlying connection or cause for the prolonged and focused media attention on the animals of every disaster. During the flooding in New Bern, North Carolina, after Hurricane Florence, when people saw the kitten climbing on the shoulders of rain-soaked Robert Simmons Jr. while evacuating, the photo became a viral sensation. People felt compassion for Simmons and his community (Carter 2018). Animals are powerful because their presence can mobilize the importance of certain issues, which can in turn mobilize physical and financial resources for the communities affected by disasters.

Spaying and Neutering as Preparedness

Day-to-day preparedness includes storing supplies and making plans for companion animals (and other large animals). However, it is also important to think about broader long-term solutions to reducing animal suffering in disasters. In the emergency management world, mitigation involves steps and actions taken to reduce future losses (Sylves 2019). For this reason, we categorize spaying and neutering efforts as animal disaster mitigation. One program coordinator describes how pet overpopulation relates to disasters:

> But, wow, it totally makes sense for us to go into Texas, which has got this very vulnerable population. Disasters often really bring out the animal welfare issues. So in the Houston area, the spay/neuter issues there and overpopulation—when a community already has pet overpopulation issues and then a disaster happens, it becomes even more apparent, the kinds of issues when you see the animals coming in. There may be heartworm—and Katrina was a huge heartworm issue. It's like, "Oh, my gosh, every single dog has heartworm." Clearly no one is doing heartworm preventative in this area. With Houston, it was like, "Okay, spay/neuter is an issue." None of them were spayed or neutered.

Pet overpopulation also means that more resources and efforts need to be allocated for disaster preparation. For example, in Hurricane Maria in 2017, volunteers flew animals from the shelters in Puerto Rico to the northwestern United States. The same program coordinator who highlighted pet overpopulation in Texas described this further:

> Then, of course, Hurricane Maria was a totally different situation, because those were animals that were just swept—actually, I think they came from the shelters. So the same type of situation, where they were in shelters and got them out of the shelters to make room for others that were being rescued at the time.

While communities and organizations engage in creative ways to foster animals or move them out of disaster areas, one of the main causes of shelter overcrowding is pet overpopulation. We again emphasize this point because spaying and neutering may be among the most critical aspects of preparedness. From our observations, towns and communities with high pet overpopulation experience greater challenges managing animals during disasters, which may be related to a high number of households with multiple cats (and dogs), more free-roaming animals before the disaster (i.e., strays and feral animals), and physical animal shelters and sanctuaries being at or beyond capacity before the disaster. These factors combined mean a difference in the services available for owned and unowned animals during and after the disaster. While groups such as Red Rover can assist the community in sheltering operations during the acute phase of the emergency, there is still a limited amount of space to house animals that were found, surrendered, or boarded during the disaster.

And unfortunately, many of the areas with high pet overpopulation are prone to hurricanes and other hazards. We spoke with a program coordinator in Miami after Hurricane Irma who told us that pet overpopulation is a persistent problem and that surrendered animals are at risk for euthanasia:

> Once the owner surrenders, the dog gets three days, or they put him to sleep. Because they consider something is wrong with the dog—he's a biter; he's not adoptable. An owner surrender is kind of like a death sentence. So they always say, "Owner surrender, rescue needed immediately" or "Has time until tomorrow, six o'clock P.M."

Groups and organizations should provide year-round education about spaying and neutering to local communities, not just before or right after a disaster. Furthermore, organizations should make it easy for families and individuals to spay and neuter their pets by providing vouchers, waivers, and coupons. Mobile clinics can also increase rates of spaying and neutering because of the increased access to veterinary medical services.

There should also be education and resources to reduce postdisaster animal surrenders, specifically, concerning how animals experience and display trauma. Litterbox and toilet issues for cats and dogs after disasters can cause people to surrender pets. Pets need time to decompress and readjust after the disaster. As occurred in the case of the cat adopted as a "family secret" from another evacuee after the Tubbs Fire, the cat stopped urinating in inappropriate locations after several weeks of adjustment into a quiet and safe setting. If the cat or dog is still displaying signs of distress after several weeks have passed in the new location or after being relocated after the hazard, it is important to contact a veterinarian or other specialist who can recommend medicine or behavioral treatment.

To be better prepared for disasters, here is a list of recommendations for people who have companion animals:

- Check to see if the animal has a microchip when you adopt your pet from a shelter. Ask the shelter to provide you with the registration information associated with the microchip, and record this information with your important documents (such as animal medical records).
- Make sure that the microchip information is linked with your current cell-phone number. After disasters, many pets had microchips with phone numbers that were no longer in service.
- Have a recent photo of your dog or cat on your phone, and back up the file to "the cloud" (such as a Google file or folder).
- If you have a large animal, such as a horse, become familiar with resources and networks that can help with transport, boarding, and feeding (e.g., Fleet of Angels).
- Spay or neuter your companion animal, and talk to your peers and children about the importance of spaying and neutering animals to keep them healthy and to prevent pet overpopulation (which makes disasters worse). Many cities and town shelters offer vouchers or discount programs for low-cost spaying and neutering.[2]
- Do not assume that you will be able to return in any reasonable time frame if you are evacuating because of a wildfire, hurricane, or other event. Assume that you may be away for six weeks or more, and consider that your apartment or home may be flooded or destroyed.
- Make sure that your cat carrier, leashes, and other supplies are stored in a place that you can easily get to in case of a rapid evacuation.
- Do not assume that boarding for pets will be available locally during a disaster. If you live in a coastal community, talk to friends or relatives farther inland (before hurricane season starts) about their willingness and ability to accommodate you and your animal in an emergency.
- Make sure that you are enrolled in a warning or alert system. Consider getting a battery-operated weather radio so that you can continue to receive alerts if the power goes out.
- Seek mental health services if your animal is lost, injured, or dies in a disaster and your grief feels unbearable. There are virtual pet-loss support groups.[3]
- Make sure that you tell someone when and where you are going if you are trying to engage in early community reentry to check on your animal. Of course, you should try to coordinate with local officials to check on the well-being of your animal. Document

your requests. Consider sharing information with press and media if all requests are ignored and/or there is no information shared with community members about animal well-being.

- Make sure you contact someone about your pet if you live alone and suspect you are becoming ill with COVID-19.

Conclusion

Former FEMA director Craig Fugate said, "Plan for the whole community" when preparing for disasters (Fugate 2011; see also Edwards 2013). This means that even if one person in a position of power does not view pets as family members, the individual still must plan for the inevitable in which people will make decisions about evacuation based on the safety and well-being of their pets. Communities should enforce codes for animal welfare in nondisaster times and provide support services for animal care in nondisaster times. Laws preventing pets from being left in hot cars or being left outside during extreme cold should be enforced so that standards for animal care are in place and normalized before a disaster happens. As this volunteer described, many animals were left behind in her coastal town in South Carolina:

Sarah DeYoung and students at a pig sanctuary.

I live down the river, so—not Matthew but the storm before Matthew—we went in with [the] National Guard and pulled my pony out. . . . The second time I evacuated my horses was before the hurricane, so I already knew it was coming, but a lot of people left, and they left cats, their dogs. They left them in chains; they left them locked in their houses. So they can't get anywhere, so I went in with [my] county animal control, and we went in and started taking animals out.

We view this problem as a reflection of the resources that the community had before the disaster, the culture of animal care, and the conditions of the hazard. To strengthen the system of animal care, people need just and equitable communities, and vulnerability should be included in education and resource planning. While handing out animal carriers prior to a disaster is a helpful activity that will likely increase evacuation compliance, a long-term resilience planning model should enable animals and humans to thrive.

Appendix

Methods

We gathered the primary data for this book through research funding from the National Science Foundation (Decision, Risk, and Management Science program, award number 1760447). Throughout the course of the research funding period (October 2017– March 2019), we gathered primary mixed-methods data for seven major disaster events: Hurricane Harvey, Hurricane Irma, Hurricane Florence (North Carolina and South Carolina), the Tubbs Fire (Santa Rosa, California), the Hawaii lava flows of 2018, the Carr Fire (Shasta County, California), and the Camp Fire (Paradise, California). We collected face-to-face qualitative interviews of evacuees and program coordinators, as well as online surveys from evacuees and program coordinators.

Program coordinators worked with groups ranging from small ad hoc animal rescue groups to large national formal organizations. Program coordinators include law enforcement, animal control, city animal shelter staff, animal sanctuary coordinators, nonprofit volunteers, and other people involved in managing animals during the major disasters for which we gathered data. We include mixed-methods primary data from in-person and web-based surveys of 366 evacuees (205 from Hurricane Harvey, 110 from Hurricane Irma, 48 from the Camp Fire, and 3 from the Tubbs Fire) and 49 program coordinators from six states (includes volunteers, managers, first responders, and animal shelter coordinators), as shown in Table A.1.

The project provided funding and training for seven students from the University of Georgia to travel with the researchers for research deployment.

TABLE A.1 RESPONDENTS

Event	Locations	Time	Evacuees	Program coordinators
Hurricane Harvey	Texas: League City, Dickinson, Port Arthur, Houston	Fall 2017	205	5
Hurricane Irma	Florida: Miami	Fall 2017	110	3
Tubbs Fire/Santa Rosa	California: Santa Rosa	Fall 2017*	3	4
Hawaii lava flow	Puna District and Hilo	Summer 2018	N/A	12
Hurricane Florence	North and South Carolina: Wilmington, Myrtle Beach, Raleigh	Fall 2018	N/A	5
Camp Fire	California: Paradise, Chico	Fall 2018*	48	6
Carr Fire	California: Shasta County, Trinity County	Fall 2018	N/A	14
Total			366	49

*We collected face-to-face responses in the spring following the event—six months after the Tubbs Fire and four months after the Camp Fire.

We provided participants with informed consent statements. The research was approved by the IRB at the University of Georgia and Illinois State University. Some of our descriptions in the book include observations from visiting field sites, informal conversations in the field about event timing or other details, and news media accounts about the disaster. When reporting findings from primary data, we redact organization and individual names unless the information that is described is already available through public news or other sources. We use pseudonyms for animals and people in describing or quoting individual evacuee experiences.

Questions on the instruments for data collection for evacuees requested information about type of pet, timing of evacuation, supplies gathered for evacuation, evacuation destination, demographic information, and sheltering. Questions on the instrument for program coordinators requested information about organizational capacity, roles, decision-making, barriers to success, and facilitators of success in the evacuations.

There are approximately twenty-six hours of combined audio data from fieldwork interviews, debriefs, and observation and approximately 340 pages of written transcription from the aggregate audio data. Analyses for these data first underwent initial open-coding content analyses by the two lead researchers. We conducted the first round of open coding by each reading through the data responses to create labels and identify common properties that emerged from the data (Saldaña 2015; Strauss and Corbin 1990). This technique is aligned with grounded theory to create categories of responses that can then be used to develop the prominent themes that emerge through the data. We used these initial themes to inform the chapters included in this book. For the second round of coding, the researchers used a shared document of the compiled data to create a detailed list of categories and subthemes that emerge from the data and are described in detail throughout the book. These themes provided meaning and deeper understanding of what emerged in the data from in-depth interviews.

We analyzed quantitative data analyses from Texas, Florida, and California (survey responses) using the Statistical Package for the Social Sciences to produce descriptive data and analyses. Evacuation decision-making (yes/no) is the primary dependent variable, while number of pets, time to prepare, status of veterinary care, species of pet and status (cat, dog, or other; spayed/neutered/microchipped), and household demographics are the independent variables. These findings are highlighted in Chapter 6 on timing and evacuation decision-making and in Chapter 5 on privilege (demographic data). The survey data also include open-ended data that we coded for thematic information such as key concerns, barriers to evacuation, psychosocial information, and evacuation or recovery concerns unrelated to pets.

Notes

FOREWORD

1. The text of the Pets Evacuation and Transportation Standards Act (2006) is available at https://www.congress.gov/109/plaws/publ308/PLAW-109publ308.pdf.

INTRODUCTION

1. When we made the final edits for this book, COVID-19 (novel coronavirus) had changed the daily lives in almost every community in the United States and throughout the world. Companion animals provide comfort to humans in times of uncertainty, and success stories of record fostering and adoption during the pandemic made news headlines in the United States. However, animals suffer during COVID-19. Spay and neuter clinics have been halted or slowed because of social-distancing requirements. When owners die from COVID-19, the pets go to animal shelters. Increases in unemployment will likely lead to higher rates of animal surrender and pet overpopulation. Instances of stigma against animals as disease vectors have also occurred. We continue to study these important issues from a sociological perspective.

2. The text of the Pets Evacuation and Transportation Standards Act (2006) is available at https://www.congress.gov/109/plaws/publ308/PLAW-109publ308.pdf.

3. Impression management is the process of attempting to influence the way that others view a person or organization through social interactions or other mechanisms (see, e.g., Leary and Kowalski 1990).

CHAPTER 1

1. Sebastian E. Heath and Robert D. Linnabary (2015) address the issue of spaying and neutering as important to managing animals in disasters. However, this is rarely

articulated by emergency managers; nor is it found in the pet preparedness checklists commonly circulated during hurricane and wildfire season.

2. Ironically, Hawaii also has a progressive spay and neuter program in which cats and dogs can be sterilized at low or no cost.

3. For an example post of the comments, see Brisby 2018.

CHAPTER 2

1. It is also important to acknowledge that there are variations across the human social landscape about the ways in which animals are ascribed value. Animals may be kept as livestock for meat, or community animals may be viewed as "wild"; nonetheless, domestic companion animals in disasters, such as cats and dogs, are more often described as family members (although levels of care for these animals also vary because of access to resources and other issues).

2. For examples of the impact of comfort dogs during disasters, see Therapy Dogs International, n.d.

CHAPTER 3

1. Previously this varied by state, with some states imposing only misdemeanor penalties.

2. Here the respondent hints that the local officials took advantage of this man because of his age and race. We delve more into race and stereotypes in Chapter 4. There is a scarcity of research on racism and discrimination in companion animal reunification after disasters. This example highlights the need for more research and advocacy in this area.

CHAPTER 5

1. Predominantly Black portions of Port Arthur and many communities in Southeast Texas have experienced decades of exploitation and pollution by oil companies, gentrification, and redlining.

2. For an examination of diversity in emergency management, see Frank 2020.

3. Some additional Black-led animal rescue organizations include Miss Pat's Cats of New Jersey, Kolony Kats of Philadelphia, and Jennifer Barnes TNR Queen.

4. Wings of Rescue also indicated that its flights included both humanitarian and animal aid after Hurricane Dorian.

5. Wraparound care is a holistic model of care for individuals and families with severe mental illness or who are experiencing homelessness, addiction, or other major needs. See, e.g., Smelson et al. 2018.

CHAPTER 6

1. We, the authors, grew up in the southern region of the Appalachian mountains. Sarah is from North Carolina, and Ashley is from Kentucky. Throughout our lives we have heard comments about people from the South and Appalachia and how they treat animals.

CHAPTER 7

1. See the application's website, at https://evacu.pet.

2. The veterinary medical term for this is "dermatophilosis." It is a bacterial skin infection and is equivalent to a third-degree burn in a human. We warn our readers that online images of this condition can be disturbing.

CHAPTER 8

1. Sarah learned this right before Hurricane Irma. She was living in Georgia at the time and went to a pet store to purchase cat carriers. She had to go to three different stores before she found one with carriers in stock (and she ended up buying a small dog carrier that was suitable for a cat).

2. For example, in Delaware, residents can apply to obtain a voucher for spaying and neutering to reduce the cost to twenty dollars. To be eligible, the applicant must be a resident of the state and enrolled in the Special Supplemental Nutrition Program for Women, Infants, and Children (WIC), the Supplemental Nutrition Assistance Program (SNAP), or other services. See the Delaware Health and Social Services Fixed and Fabulous website, at https://fixedandfab.com.

3. For a list of pet-loss resources, see Best Friends Animal Society, n.d.

References

Albala-Bertrand, J. M. 2000. "Responses to Complex Humanitarian Emergencies and Natural Disasters: An Analytical Comparison." *Third World Quarterly* 21 (2): 215–227.

Aldrich, D. P. 2016. "It's Who You Know: Factors Driving Recovery from Japan's 11 March 2011 Disaster." *Public Administration* 94 (2): 399–413.

Aldrich, D. P., and M. A. Meyer. 2015. "Social Capital and Community Resilience." *American Behavioral Scientist* 59 (2): 254–269.

Alpert, B. 2015. "Katrina Brought Billions of Dollars—and Quite a Bit of Fraud." *NOLA. com*, August 21. https://www.nola.com/news/article_44e9c0fd-7a8c-51e3-ae07-02 b81abb47d1.html.

ASPCA. n.d. "Pet Statistics." Accessed December 15, 2020. https://www.aspca.org/ animal-homelessness/shelter-intake-and-surrender/pet-statistics.

Bastian, B., J. Jetten, and L. J. Ferris. 2014. "Pain as Social Glue: Shared Pain Increases Cooperation." *Psychological Science* 25 (11): 2079–2085.

Berlinger, J., and J. Yeung. 2019. "Lewis the Koala Dies One Week after Rescue from Australia Bush Fire." *CNN*, November 26. https://www.cnn.com/2019/11/26/ australia/lewis-koala-dead-intl-hnk-scli/index.html.

Best Friends Animal Society. n.d. "Pet Loss and Grief Resources." Accessed February 19, 2021. https://resources.bestfriends.org/article/pet-loss-and-grief-resources.

Birkland, T. A. 1997. *After Disaster: Agenda Setting, Public Policy, and Focusing Events.* Washington, DC: Georgetown University Press.

———. 2006. *Lessons of Disaster: Policy Change after Catastrophic Events.* Washington, DC: Georgetown University Press.

Birkland, T. A., and S. E. DeYoung. 2011. "Emergency Response, Doctrinal Confusion, and Federalism in the Deepwater Horizon Oil Spill." *Publius* 41 (3): 471–493.

Blake, D., J. Marlowe, and D. Johnston. 2017. "Get Prepared: Discourse for the Privileged?" *International Journal of Disaster Risk Reduction* 25:283–288.

Blakie, P., T. Cannon, I. Davis, and B. Wisner. 1994. *At Risk: Natural Hazards, People's Vulnerability, and Disasters*. London: Routledge.

Bolin, B., and L. C. Kurtz. 2018. "Race, Class, Ethnicity, and Disaster Vulnerability." In *Handbook of Disaster Research*, edited by H. Rodriguez, W. Donner, and J. E. Trainor, 181–203. Cham, Switzerland: Springer.

Brackenridge, S., L. K. Zottarelli, E. Rider, and B. Carlsen-Landy. 2012. "Dimensions of the Human-Animal Bond and Evacuation Decisions among Pet Owners during Hurricane Ike." *Anthrozoös* 25 (2): 229–238.

Brisby, K. 2018. Post to "Snopes Tips" Facebook page, September 15. https://ms-my.facebook.com/groups/441333919315986/permalink/1885896491526381/.

Brown, D. 2018. "Saving Pets without a Permit: Good Samaritan Arrested after Helping Animals Survive Florence." *USA Today*, September 22. https://www.usatoday.com/story/news/2018/09/22/florence-good-samaritan-arrested-after-helping-pets-during-storm/1397025002/.

Bulsara, M., L. Wood, B. Giles-Corti, and D. Bosch. 2007. "More than a Furry Companion: The Ripple Effect of Companion Animals on Neighborhood Interactions and Sense of Community." *Society and Animals* 15 (1): 43–56.

Carter, A. 2018. "Here's the Story behind the Viral Hurricane Florence Photo of Robert Simmons Jr. and Little 'Survivor.'" *News and Observer*, September 15. https://www.richmond.com/weather/ap/here-s-the-story-behind-the-viral-hurricane-florence-photo/article_a4fe0100-e58c-50d6-bcfe-58131de54a28.html.

Cattafi, A. 2008. "Breed Specific Legislation: The Gap in Emergency Preparedness Provisions for Household Pets." *Seton Hall Legislative Journal* 32:351–374.

Census Reporter. 2018a. "Paradise, CA." http://censusreporter.org/profiles/16000US0655528-paradise-ca/.

Census Reporter. 2018b. "Port Arthur, TX." http://censusreporter.org/profiles/16000US4858820-port-arthur-tx/.

Davies, I. P., R. D. Haugo, J. C. Robertson, and P. S. Levin. 2018. "The Unequal Vulnerability of Communities of Color to Wildfire." *PLOS ONE* 13 (11): e0205825. https://journals.plos.org/plosone/article?id=10.1371/journal.pone.0205825.

DeYoung, S. E., J. Sutton, A. K. Farmer, D. Neal, and A. K. Nichols. 2019. "'Death Was Not in the Agenda for the Day': Emotions, Behavioral Reactions, and Perceptions in Response to the 2018 Hawaii Wireless Emergency Alert." *International Journal of Disaster Risk Reduction* 36. https://www.sciencedirect.com/science/article/abs/pii/S2212420918305077.

Drabek, T. E. 2018. *The Human Side of Disaster*. Boca Raton, FL: CRC Press.

Dynes, R. R. 1970. *Organized Behavior in Disaster*. Lexington, MA: D.C. Heath.

Edwards, F. L. 2013. "All Hazards, Whole Community: Creating Resiliency." In *Disaster Resiliency*, edited by N. Kapucu, C. V. Hawkins, and F. I. Rivera, 43–69. New York: Routledge.

Enarson, E., A. Fothergill, and L. Peek. 2018. "Gender and Disaster: Foundations and New Directions for Research and Practice." In *Handbook of Disaster Research*, edited by H. Rodríguez, W. Donner, and J. E. Trainor, 205–223. Cham, Switzerland: Springer.

Evans, R. D., and C. J. Forsyth. 1997. "Entertainment to Outrage: A Social Historical View of Dogfighting." *International Review of Modern Sociology* 27 (2): 59–71.

Farmer, A. K., and S. E. DeYoung. 2019. "The Pets of Hurricane Matthew: Evacuation and Sheltering with Companion Animals." *Anthrozoös* 32 (3): 419–433.

Farmer, A. K., L. Zelewicz, T. Wachtendorf, and S. E. DeYoung. 2017. "Scared of the Shelter from the Storm: Fear of Crime and Hurricane Shelter Decision Making." *Sociological Inquiry* 88 (2): 193–215.

Federal Housing Administration. 2019. "FHA INFO #19-07." https://www.hud.gov/sites/dfiles/SFH/documents/SFH_FHA_INFO_19-07.pdf.

Fonseca, R. 2018. "Mountain Lion P-64, Famous for Frequent Freeway Crossings, Found Dead in Woolsey Fire Burn Zone." *LAist*, December 7. https://laist.com/2018/12/07/mountain_lion_p-64_found_dead.php.

Foster, M. 2005. "'I Would Rather Have Been in Jail': Superdome Evacuations Enter 2nd Day; Refugees Get Showers, Food in Houston." *Decatur Daily*, September 2. http://archive.decaturdaily.com/decaturdaily/news/050902/jail.shtml.

Frailing, K. 2012. "Fraud in the Wake of Disasters." In *Crime and Criminal Justice in Disaster*, 2nd ed., edited by D. W. Harper and K. Frailing, 157–176. Durham, NC: Carolina Academic Press.

Frailing, K., and D. W. Harper. 2017. "Fraud in Disaster." In *Toward a Criminology of Disaster*, edited by K. Frailing and D. W. Harper, 109–139. New York: Palgrave Macmillan.

Frank, T. 2020. "Disaster Management Is Too White, Official Tells Congress." *Scientific American*, July 29. https://www.scientificamerican.com/article/disaster-management-is-too-white-official-tells-congress.

Fritz Institute. 2006. *Hurricane Katrina: Perceptions of the Affected*. San Francisco: Fritz Institute.

Frommer, S. S., and A. Arluke. 1999. "Loving Them to Death: Blame-Displacing Strategies of Animal Shelter Workers and Surrenderers." *Society and Animals* 7 (1): 1–16.

Fugate, C. 2011. Testimony in *Improving the Nation's Response to Catastrophic Disasters: How to Minimize Costs and Streamline Our Emergency Management Programs; Hearing Before the Subcommittee on Economic Development, Public Buildings, and Emergency Management of the Committee on Transportation and Infrastructure, House of Representatives*. 112th Cong. 5. https://www.dhs.gov/news/2011/03/30/administrator-craig-fugate-federal-emergency-management-agency-transportation-and.

Fussell, E., and E. Harris. 2014. "Homeownership and Housing Displacement after Hurricane Katrina among Low-Income African-American Mothers in New Orleans." *Social Science Quarterly* 95 (4): 1086–1100.

Gaertner, S. L., and J. F. Dovidio. 2005. "Understanding and Addressing Contemporary Racism: From Aversive Racism to the Common Ingroup Identity Model." *Journal of Social Issues* 61 (3): 615–639.

Geldenhuys, K. 2018. "NSPCA-Linking Animal Cruelty to Other Crimes When Going to Court." *Servamus Community-Based Safety and Security Magazine* 111 (11): 56–59.

Gigerenzer, G., and W. Gaissmaier. 2011. "Heuristic Decision Making." *Annual Review of Psychology* 62:451–482.

Glassey, S. 2014. "Shooting Them Isn't the Answer: Why Pets Matter in Disasters." Paper presented at Australian and New Zealand Disaster Management Conference "Earth: Fire and Rain," Queensland, Australia, May 5–7.

———. 2018. "Did Harvey Learn from Katrina? Initial Observations of the Response to Companion Animals during Hurricane Harvey." *Animals* 8 (4). https://doi.org/10.3390/ani8040047.

Goto, T., J. P. Wilson, B. Kahana, and S. Slane. 2006. "The Miyake Island Volcano Disaster in Japan: Loss, Uncertainty, and Relocation as Predictors of PTSD and Depression." *Journal of Applied Social Psychology* 36 (8): 2001–2026.

Greenebaum, J. 2009. "'I'm Not an Activist!': Animal Rights vs. Animal Welfare in the Purebred Dog Rescue Movement." *Society and Animals* 17 (4): 289–304.

Greenwood, A. 2017. "Here's How You Can Help Animals Affected by Hurricane Harvey." *Today*, August 29. https://www.today.com/pets/hurricane-harvey-flooding-how-help-save-animals-pets-t115618.

Hamideh, S., and J. Rongerude. 2018. "Social Vulnerability and Participation in Disaster Recovery Decisions: Public Housing in Galveston after Hurricane Ike." *Natural Hazards* 93 (3): 1629–1648.

Heath, S. E. 1999. *Animal Management in Disasters*. St. Louis, MO: Mosby.

Heath, S. E., P. H. Kass, A. M. Beck, and L. T. Glickman. 2001. "Human and Pet-Related Risk Factors for Household Evacuation Failure during a Natural Disaster." *American Journal of Epidemiology* 153 (7): 659–665.

Heath, S. E., and R. D. Linnabary. 2015. "Challenges of Managing Animals in Disasters in the US." *Animals* 5 (2): 173–192.

Huang, S. K., M. K. Lindell, and C. S. Prater. 2016. "Who Leaves and Who Stays? A Review and Statistical Meta-analysis of Hurricane Evacuation Studies." *Environment and Behavior* 48 (8): 991–1029.

Huang, S. K., M. K. Lindell, C. S. Prater, H. C. Wu, and L. K. Siebeneck. 2012. "Household Evacuation Decision Making in Response to Hurricane Ike." *Natural Hazards Review* 13 (4): 283–296.

Hughes, T. 2018. "New Evacuations Ordered as Fast-Flowing Hawaii Lava Blocks Major Volcano Escape Route." *USA Today*, May 30. https://www.usatoday.com/story/news/2018/05/30/hawaii-volcano-lava-forces-new-evacuations-big-island/655332002/.

Hunt, M. G., H. Al-Awadi, and M. Johnson. 2008. "Psychological Sequelae of Pet Loss Following Hurricane Katrina." *Anthrozoös* 21 (2): 109–121.

Irvine, L. 2009. *Filling the Ark: Animal Welfare in Disasters*. Philadelphia, PA: Temple University Press.

Kalof, L., and C. Taylor. 2007. "The Discourse of Dog Fighting." *Humanity and Society* 31 (4): 319–333.

Kelman, I. 2020. *Disaster by Choice: How Our Actions Turn Natural Hazards into Catastrophes*. Oxford: Oxford University Press.

Kendra, J. M., and T. Wachtendorf. 2016. *American Dunkirk: The Waterborne Evacuation of Manhattan on 9/11*. Philadelphia, PA: Temple University Press.

Knowles, H. 2019. "Bahamas Shelter Staff Listened as Dogs Howled amid Dorian Floods—Then Went Silent." *Washington Post*, September 9. https://www.washingtonpost.com/science/2019/09/10/bahamas-shelter-staff-listened-dogs-howled-amid-dorian-floods-then-went-silent/.

Lambert, K. 2014. "Summarizing Reasons for Surrender and Stakeholder Perceptions within the Published Literature on Companion-Animal Relinquishment." Ph.D. diss., University of Guelph.

Leary, M. R., and R. M. Kowalski. 1990. "Impression Management: A Literature Review and Two-Component Model." *Psychological Bulletin* 107 (1): 34–47.

Lee, J. Y., and S. Van Zandt. 2019. "Housing Tenure and Social Vulnerability to Disasters: A Review of the Evidence." *Journal of Planning Literature* 34 (2): 156–170.

Levine, M., and K. Thompson. 2004. "Identity, Place, and Bystander Intervention: Social Categories and Helping after Natural Disasters." *Journal of Social Psychology* 144 (3): 229–245.

Lindell, M. K., and R. W. Perry. 2012. "The Protective Action Decision Model: Theoretical Modifications and Additional Evidence." *Risk Analysis: An International Journal* 32 (4): 616–632.

Lovell, J. S. 2016. "Understanding Farm Animal Abuse." In *The Routledge International Handbook of Rural Criminology*, edited by J. Donnermeyer, 137–146. London: Routledge.

Lowe, S. R., J. E. Rhodes, L. Zwiebach, and C. S. Chan. 2009. "The Impact of Pet Loss on the Perceived Social Support and Psychological Distress of Hurricane Survivors." *Journal of Traumatic Stress* 22 (3): 244–247.

Lynch, M. J., R. G. Burns, and P. B. Stretesky. 2010. "Global Warming and State-Corporate Crime: The Politicalization of Global Warming under the Bush Administration." *Crime, Law and Social Change* 54 (3): 213–239.

Manzini, E. 2014. "Making Things Happen: Social Innovation and Design." *Design Issues* 30 (1): 57–66.

Matheny, S., S. E. DeYoung, and A. K. Farmer. 2020. "Analysis of Material Convergence, Logistics, and Organizational Typology of Animal Supplies in the 2018 Puna Lava Flow." *Natural Hazards Review* 21 (3). https://ascelibrary.org/doi/10.1061/%28ASCE%29NH.1527-6996.0000383.

Maurantonio, N. 2017. "'Reason to Hope?' The White Savior Myth and Progress in 'Post-racial' America." *Journalism and Mass Communication Quarterly* 94 (4): 1130–1145.

McCaffrey, S. 2015. "Community Wildfire Preparedness: A Global State-of-the-Knowledge Summary of Social Science Research." *Current Forestry Reports* 1 (2): 81–90.

McDermott, S., K. Martin, and J. D. Gardner. 2016. "Disaster Response for People with Disability." *Disability and Health Journal* 9 (2): 183–185.

McIntyre, K. E., and R. Gibson. 2016. "Positive News Makes Readers Feel Good: A 'Silver-Lining' Approach to Negative News Can Attract Audiences." *Southern Communication Journal* 81 (5): 304–315.

Melanie. 2016. "So Many Pets Survived Hurricane Matthew Because Shelters Took in Their Whole Families." *Life with Dogs*, October. https://www.lifewithdogs.tv/2016/10/so-many-pets-survived-hurricane-matthew-because-shelters-took-in-their-whole-families/.

Melo, R.T.M. 2020. "We Didn't Start the Fire . . . Did We? Analyzing Why California Cannot Seem to Extinguish Its Worsening Wildfire Problem." *Villanova Environmental Law Journal* 31 (1): 165–192.

Mesa-Arango, R., S. Hasan, S. V. Ukkusuri, and P. Murray-Tuite. 2012. "Household-Level Model for Hurricane Evacuation Destination Type Choice Using Hurricane Ivan Data." *Natural Hazards Review* 14 (1): 11–20.

Mezeul, M. 2018. Facebook post, July 6. https://www.facebook.com/mike.mezeulii/posts/10100979799627437.

Miedema, B., R. Hamilton, and J. Easley. 2007. "From 'Invincibility' to 'Normalcy': Coping Strategies of Young Adults during the Cancer Journey." *Palliative and Supportive Care* 5 (1): 41–49.

Morrison, M. L. 2007. "Health Benefits of Animal-Assisted Interventions." *Complementary Health Practice Review* 12 (1): 51–62.

NASAAEP. n.d. "NASAAEP Best Practice Working Groups." Accessed February 18, 2021. https://www.thenasaaep.com/workshp-resources.

Neale, R. 2019. "Hurricane Dorian: Mandatory Evacuation Order Set for Brevard's Barrier Island." *Florida Today*, August 30. https://www.floridatoday.com/story/news/2019/08/30/hurricane-dorian-evacuation-melbourne/2169512001.

Nelan, M. M., S. Penta, and T. Wachtendorf. 2019. "Paved with Good Intentions: A Social Construction Approach to Alignment in Disaster Donations." *International Journal of Mass Emergencies and Disasters* 37 (2): 174–196.

Neumayer, E., and T. Plümper. 2007. "The Gendered Nature of Natural Disasters: The Impact of Catastrophic Events on the Gender Gap in Life Expectancy, 1981–2002." *Annals of the Association of American Geographers* 97 (3): 551–566.

Oelbaum, J. 2017. "Why Texans Dove into Harvey's Toxic Floodwaters to Rescue Bats Barehanded." *Good*, September 7. https://www.good.is/features/rescuing-bats-after-hurricane-harvey.

Paluck, E. L., S. A. Green, and D. P. Green. 2019. "The Contact Hypothesis Re-evaluated." *Behavioural Public Policy* 3 (2): 129–158.

Peacock, W. G., and C. Girard. 1997. "Ethnic and Racial Inequalities in Hurricane Damage and Insurance Settlements." In *Hurricane Andrew: Ethnicity, Gender and the Sociology of Disasters*, edited by W. G. Peacock, B. H. Morrow, and H. Gladwin, 171–190. London: Routledge.

Peacock, W. G., S. Van Zandt, Y. Zhang, and W. E. Highfield. 2014. "Inequities in Long-Term Housing Recovery after Disasters." *Journal of the American Planning Association* 80 (4): 356–371.

Quarantelli, E. L. 1988. "Disaster Crisis Management: A Summary of Research Findings." *Journal of Management Studies* 25 (4): 373–385.

———. 1994. "Looting and Antisocial Behavior in Disasters." University of Delaware Disaster Research Center Preliminary Paper #205. https://udspace.udel.edu/handle/19716/590.

———, ed. 2005. *What Is a Disaster? A Dozen Perspectives on the Question*. London: Routledge.

Radio New Zealand. 2020. "Australia Fires: Mega-fire Will Form When Huge Blaze in Victoria Joins Up with Fires over Border, Authorities Say." *RNZ*, January 6. https://www.rnz.co.nz/news/world/406747/australia-fires-mega-fire-will-form-when-huge-blaze-in-victoria-joins-up-with-fires-over-border-authorities-say.

Rauktis, M., and H. Lee. 2019. "Animal Ownership in Low-Income Households: Is There a Relationship between Human and Animal Food Insecurity?" http://d-scholarship.pitt.edu/35957/1/Progress%20Report%20for%20the%20Florence%20Stier%20Award_final_1.21.pdf.

Reed, A., S. E. DeYoung, and A. K. Farmer. 2020. "Companion Animals and Online Discourse: Rescue, Reunification, and Victim-Blaming and Evacuation Compliance in Wildfire and Hurricane Events." *Anthrozoös* 33 (6): 727–742.

Reid, J. A., R. A. Haskell, C. Dillahunt-Aspillaga, and J. A. Thor. 2013. "Contemporary Review of Empirical and Clinical Studies of Trauma Bonding in Violent or Exploitative Relationships." *International Journal of Psychology Research* 8 (1): 37–73.

Ripley, A. 2009. *The Unthinkable: Who Survives When Disaster Strikes—and Why*. New York: Harmony.

Ritchie, L. A., and D. A. Gill. 2007. "Social Capital Theory as an Integrating Theoretical Framework in Technological Disaster Research." *Sociological Spectrum* 27 (1): 103–129.

Roberts, S. O., and M. T. Rizzo. 2020. "The Psychology of American Racism." *American Psychologist*, June 25. https://doi.apa.org/fulltext/2020-45459-001.html.

Rodriguez, H., J. Trainor, and E. L. Quarantelli. 2006. "Rising to the Challenges of a Catastrophe: The Emergent and Prosocial Behavior following Hurricane Katrina." *Annals of the American Academy of Political and Social Science* 604 (1): 82–101.

Rossman, S. 2017. "Dozens of Dogs Abandoned, Left Unable to Escape as Irma Bears Down." *USA Today*, September 10. https://www.usatoday.com/story/news/nation -now/2017/09/10/dozens-dogs-abandoned-left-unable-escape-irma-bears-down/ 651030001/.

Saldaña, J. 2015. *The Coding Manual for Qualitative Researchers*. Thousand Oaks, CA: Sage.

Sawyer, J., and G. Huertas. 2018. *Animal Management and Welfare in Natural Disasters*. Abingdon, UK: Routledge.

Scarlett, J. M., M. D. Salman, J. G. New Jr., and P. H. Kass. 1999. "Reasons for Relinquishment of Companion Animals in US Animal Shelters: Selected Health and Personal Issues." *Journal of Applied Animal Welfare Science* 2 (1): 41–57.

Schaffer, C. B. 2011. "Human-Animal Bond Considerations during Disasters." https:// citeseerx.ist.psu.edu/viewdoc/download?doi=10.1.1.488.7004&rep=rep1&type=pdf.

Schmidt, A., J. Wolbers, J. Ferguson, and K. Boersma. 2018. "Are You Ready2Help? Conceptualizing the Management of Online and Onsite Volunteer Convergence." *Journal of Contingencies and Crisis Management* 26 (3): 338–349.

Schoenbaum, T. J. 2012. "Liability for Damages in Oil Spill Accidents: Evaluating the USA and International Law Regimes in the Light of Deepwater Horizon." *Journal of Environmental Law* 24 (3): 395–416.

Siebeneck, L. K., and T. J. Cova. 2012. "Spatial and Temporal Variation in Evacuee Risk Perception throughout the Evacuation and Return-Entry Process." *Risk Analysis: An International Journal* 32 (9): 1468–1480.

Siebeneck, L. K., M. K. Lindell, C. S. Prater, H. C. Wu, and S. K. Huang. 2013. "Evacuees' Reentry Concerns and Experiences in the Aftermath of Hurricane Ike." *Natural Hazards* 65 (3): 2267–2286.

Smelson, D. A., C. K. Perez, I. Farquhar, T. Byrne, and A. Colegrove. 2018. "Permanent Supportive Housing and Specialized Co-occurring Disorders Wraparound Services for Homeless Individuals." *Journal of Dual Diagnosis* 14 (4): 247–256.

Smith, T. 2020. "Safe at Last: 1,100 Bushfire Victims and 250 Pets Dock near Melbourne after Gruelling 20-Hour Journey on HMAS Choules in Navy Evacuation from Mallacoota." *Daily Mail Australia*, January 4. https://www.dailymail.co.uk/news/ article-7850909/1-100-bushfire-victims-250-pets-land-ashore-navy-evacuation -Mallacoota.html.

Stone, D. 2002. *Policy Paradox: The Art of Political Decision Making*. Rev. ed. New York: W. W. Norton.

Strauss, A., and J. Corbin. 1990. *Basics of Qualitative Research*. Thousand Oaks, CA: Sage.

Sutton, J., E. Spiro, C. Butts, S. Fitzhugh, B. Johnson, and M. Greczek. 2013. "Tweeting the Spill: Online Informal Communications, Social Networks, and Conversational

Microstructures during the Deepwater Horizon Oilspill." *International Journal of Information Systems for Crisis Response and Management* 5 (1): 58–76.

Sylves, R. T. 2019. *Disaster Policy and Politics: Emergency Management and Homeland Security.* Thousand Oaks, CA: CQ Press.

Therapy Dogs International. n.d. "DSRD (Disaster Stress Relief Dogs)." Accessed February 18, 2021. https://www.tdi-dog.org/OurPrograms.Aspx?Page=DSRD+(Disaster+Stress+Relief+Dogs).

Thompson, A. 2020. "Yes, Climate Change Did Influence Australia's Unprecedented Bushfires." *Scientific American*, March 4. https://www.scientificamerican.com/article/yes-climate-change-did-influence-australias-unprecedented-bushfires.

Thompson, K. 2015. "For Pets' Sake, Save Yourself! Motivating Emergency and Disaster Preparedness through Relations of Animal Guardianship." *Australian Journal of Emergency Management* 30 (2): 43–46.

Thompson, K., D. Every, S. Rainbird, V. Cornell, B. Smith, and J. Trigg. 2014. "No Pet or Their Person Left Behind: Increasing the Disaster Resilience of Vulnerable Groups through Animal Attachment, Activities and Networks." *Animals* 4 (2): 214–240.

Tierney, K., C. Bevc, and E. Kuligowski. 2006. "Metaphors Matter: Disaster Myths, Media Frames, and Their Consequences in Hurricane Katrina." *Annals of the American Academy of Political and Social Science* 604 (1): 57–81.

Tierney, K. J., M. K. Lindell, and R. W. Perry. 2001. *Facing the Unexpected: Disaster Preparedness and Response in the United States.* Washington, DC: Joseph Henry Press.

Trainor, J. E., and L. Velotti. 2013. "Leadership in Crises, Disasters, and Catastrophes." *Journal of Leadership Studies* 7 (3): 38–40.

TrapKing. n.d. "About Trap King." Accessed December 15, 2020. https://trapkinghumane.org/about.

Travis, H. J. 2014. "Children and the Human-Animal Bond: Minimizing Pet Loss during Disasters." In *Teaching Compassion: Humane Education in Early Childhood*, edited by M. R. Jalongo, 133–145. Dordrecht, Netherlands: Springer.

Vaughn, C. 2018. "Accomack Working on Pet Shelter for Hurricanes, Other Emergencies." *13 News Now*, November 2. https://www.13newsnow.com/article/news/local/virginia/eastern-shore/accomack-working-on-pet-shelter-for-hurricanes-other-emergencies/291-610699807.

Voigt, L., and W. E. Thornton. 2015. "Disaster-Related Human Rights Violations and Corruption: A 10-Year Review of Post–Hurricane Katrina New Orleans." *American Behavioral Scientist* 59 (10): 1292–1313.

Weaver, H. 2013. "'Becoming in Kind': Race, Class, Gender, and Nation in Cultures of Dog Rescue and Dogfighting." *American Quarterly* 65 (3): 689–709.

White, G. L., S. Fishbein, and J. Rutsein. 1981. "Passionate Love and the Misattribution of Arousal." *Journal of Personality and Social Psychology* 41 (1): 56–62.

Winter, V. 2020. "'It's Like the Apocalypse Lifted': Cat Returns Home after a Week Lost in Bushfires." *The Feed*, January 8. https://www.sbs.com.au/news/the-feed/it-s-like-the-apocalypse-lifted-cat-returns-home-after-a-week-lost-in-bushfires.

Wisch, R. F. 2020. "Overview of States That Prohibit Breed-Specific Legislation by State Law." Animal Legal and Historical Center. https://www.animallaw.info/article/overview-states-prohibit-bsl.

Wisch, R. F., and A. Dillingham. 2017. "Table of State Holding Laws." Animal Legal and Historical Center. https://www.animallaw.info/topic/state-holding-period-laws-im pounded-animals.

Young, R. L., and C. Y. Thompson. 2017. "Morality as a Discursive Accomplishment among Animal Rescue Workers." *Deviant Behavior* 38 (8): 879–894.

Zinda, E. S. 2017. "American Cerberus: Pit Bulls and Psyche in the United States." Ph.D. diss., Pacifica Graduate Institute.

Zottarelli, L. K. 2010. "Broken Bond: An Exploration of Human Factors Associated with Companion Animal Loss during Hurricane Katrina 1." *Sociological Forum* 25 (1): 110–122.

Index

Sarah E. DeYoung is an Assistant Professor at the University of Delaware as a Core Faculty member for the Disaster Research Center and the Department of Sociology and Criminal Justice and the Joseph R. Biden, Jr. School of Public Policy and Administration.

Ashley K. Farmer is an Assistant Professor of Criminal Justice Sciences at Illinois State University.